The Public Domain
in New Mexico
1854 - 1891

The Public Domain in New Mexico 1854 -1891

by Victor Westphall

ALBUQUERQUE
THE UNIVERSITY OF NEW MEXICO PRESS

The publication of this book is made possible
by a grant from the Ford Foundation

Manufactured in the United States of America
by the University of New Mexico Printing Plant

Library of Congress Catalog Card No. 64-17807
First Edition

To Frank D. Reeve

Contents

Maps

Acknowledgments

I WISH to express my thanks to Professor Frank D. Reeve, who directed this study in its original form as a doctoral dissertation, and whose interest and patience guided me through many vicissitudes to the completion of the project.

I have profited much from the help of members of the staffs of the Library of Congress, National Archives, Department of Interior Library, Denver Federal Records Center, Denver State Historical Museum, Denver Public Library, Bureaus of Land Management at Washington, Denver, and Santa Fe, University of New Mexico Library, University of New Mexico Law Library, and at Santa Fe, Library of the Museum of New Mexico, Federal Court House, Legislative Reference Council, Office of the Secretary of State, and State Land Office, besides numerous individuals acknowledged in the text.

I am greatly indebted to my wife, Jeanne, and sons, David and Douglas, who not only aided substantially but also gave constant encouragement; to Mrs. Josephine Burdette, who typed the manuscript and furnished many helpful suggestions; to Miss Josephine Adamson, Washington, D. C., who copied statistics in the National Archives for the material in the Appendixes beyond 1891; and to Mrs. Peggy Carter, who executed the maps.

Introduction

"CAPTAINS OF INDUSTRY are at best second lieutenants in New Mexico; the land's the thing!"[1]

This is the story of that land in the four decades following the American occupation of the Territory. The Treaty of Guadalupe Hidalgo of 1848 guaranteed the title rights of former Mexican citizens. The rest of the land was public domain and became subject to disposal under the various land laws of the United States.

When the first surveyor general arrived in New Mexico, in 1854, to initiate the survey and land disposal programs in the newly acquired Territory, he entered a domain known to Americans only through traders on the Santa Fe Trail, an occasional adventurer, or the few Government officials who preceded him.

The country was steeped in a tradition of sharp practices emanating from the conduct of former officials far removed from Spanish and Mexican authorities by distance and difficult terrain. Yet the majority of the people were simple, honest folk who had long lived under the domination of the native *ricos* and *politicos*.

A problem of the new Federal land officials was to acquire the confidence of the long subjugated populace and to curb the nefarious tendencies of top echelon natives. Likewise, it was necessary to guard against the tradition of sharp practices rubbing off on the gradual influx of Anglo migrants, many of whom brought their own proclivity toward exploitation. The evolution of this problem saw the exploitation by the Anglos of the large grants of land made by former Spanish and Mexican governments, as well as the small landed holdings of the masses, especially in areas away from the older settlements, and a common joining by elements of all classes,

---

1. Joseph Miller, *New Mexico: A Guide to the Colorful State*, VII. (In Preface by Charles E. Minton).

as well as certain Government land officials, in circumventing Federal laws and procedures in acquiring the newly created public domain.

Most of the population of the semiarid Territory was concentrated in the valley of the Rio Grande and its tributaries where irrigation made possible the growing of corn, beans, chili, and a few other vegetables and fruits. The average native kept sheep and a few goats that roamed the mesas above the water courses.

The population was concentrated in villages for mutual protection against marauding Indians. The Comanche dominated the regions to the northeast and east. The Utah and Jicarilla Apache pressed in from the north. The Navaho on the west and the Apache on the south completed a ring around the settlements. These Indians, while periodically friendly, comprised a continuing menace to the life of valley dwellers and, even more, to their flocks and other worldly possessions.

No surveyed boundary lines delineated this vast, sparsely populated area. The towns roughly outlined the area of habitation. Santa Fe was the heart of the land. Taos to the northward, nestled in the foothills of the western slope of the Sangre de Cristo Mountains, was the northern limit of the area. Anton Chico, in the southeastern reaches of the same range, constituted the eastern border. The southern boundary was Socorro, on the banks of the Rio Grande, flanked by the San Andres Mountains to the east and the Magdalena range to the west. Settlements approaching Mount Taylor delineated the western boundary.

Within this area, the principal settlements were along the Rio Grande. South from Santa Fe, they were Algodones, Albuquerque, and Belen. Other small settlements were scattered along the valley. Aside from these, the chief populated areas sprang up along the route of the Santa Fe Trail. They were Las Vegas and Tecolote as well as the more ancient San Miguel.

South of Socorro, the dreaded Jornada del Muerto had to be crossed before reaching another center of population in the El Paso area. In 1843, the long journey between these settlements was shortened somewhat by the successful establishment of a colony in the Mesilla Valley.

Beyond these areas, settlement was limited by lack of population pressures and the presence of hostile Indian tribes. Further expansion did not occur until after the American occupation and then it was heralded by the activities of Government surveyors. Areas of progression occurred in approximately the following order: north from the Mesilla Valley; along the Canadian River where it flows eastward; east from Tijeras Canyon in the region surrounding present Moriarty; along the entire length of the Hondo River to its confluence with the Pecos; in the area fanning out southward from Silver City; the Bluewater, San Mateo, Grants area; in the vicinity of Folsom and Springer in the northeast; and south from the bend of the Canadian to the Pecos Valley as far as the area surrounding Fort Sumner. Surveying in these areas was largely completed by 1876, and by the end of the next decade, most of the remaining territory was surveyed and thinly settled.

Abbreviations

(B.L.M.) Bureau of Land Management, Santa Fe, N.M.

(F.R.C.) Federal Records Center, Denver, Colo.

G.N.M. Annual Reports of the Governor of New Mexico Territory.

H.E.D. House Executive Document.

L.O.R. Annual Reports of the Commissioner of the General Land Office of the United States.

(N.A.) National Archives, Washington, D.C.

S.E.D. Senate Executive Document.

S.G.R. Annual Reports of the Surveyor General of New Mexico Territory.

S.I.R. Annual Reports of the Secretary of the Interior of the United States.

Stat. L. United States Statutes at Large.

(W.R.C.I.S.) Western Range Cattle Industry Study, State Museum, Denver, Colo.

1. Establishing the Surveying System

PROBABLY the only monuments that have been erected to the memory of Government land surveyors are those that these surveyors placed on the face of our land. These monuments are accurate answers to the question of land locations and are the basis of our system of orderly ownership and transference of land titles. They are fitting memorials to the courage and skill of our land surveyors and will remain as long as the Federal Government stands. Their work was not spectacular, yet it paved the way for our national expansion. Theoretically they went where settlement demanded their presence, but in practice they often preceded the boldest of pioneers.

When William Pelham, the first Surveyor General of New Mexico, arrived in Santa Fe on December 28, 1854,[1] he had already been in office nearly five months, having been appointed by President Franklin Pierce with tenure to start on August first of that year.[2] The office of Surveyor General had been created by an Act of Congress approved July 22, 1854.[3] The chain of command from President Pierce to Mr. Pelham consisted of Robert McClelland, the Secretary of the Interior, and John Wilson, the Commissioner of the General Land Office.

Pelham was in Washington City, as our national capital was then called, when he received his appointment. Shortly before his departure, near the end of August, he received his instructions and perceived that one of his first duties would be to examine the country in preparation for the execution of the public surveys. Information had reached him that it was infested with bands of roving hostile

---

1. *S.G.R.* 9/30/55, 34 Cong., 1 Sess., *H.E.D.* No. 1, 301 (840).
2. John Wilson, Commissioner of the General Land Office, to William Pelham, Surveyor General of New Mexico, 8/5/54 (B.L.M.).
3. *Stat. L.* Vol. X, 308-310.

Indians who "would render it unsafe to life and property, if not impossible for a small surveying party to pass."[4] With this observation in mind he requested authorization to call upon the commander of the nearest military post for an escort suitable for the protection of the party.[5]

The request was passed on to Secretary of the Interior McClelland, and the latter's reply did not reach him until he arrived in Austin, Texas.[6] McClelland denied the request by stating that there was no provision of law which authorized the employment of military forces for protection unless forcible opposition had been offered, or was likely to be offered, to surveying parties. If such a contingency should arise, an Act of May 29, 1830, was to direct his conduct.[7] This act made it lawful for the President to order the state or district marshal to protect surveyors from forcible opposition.[8] In faraway New Mexico it was somewhat like saying that if a surveyor was being scalped, he could request the President to order the marshal to give him protection.

Pelham traveled to New Orleans by way of Cincinnati and the Ohio and Mississippi rivers, and then by steamship to Port Lavaca, Texas, where he departed on the most perilous as well as time-consuming portion of his journey. His trek to San Antonio was uneventful;[9] but from here it was necessary to traverse the country of the dreaded Comanches. Fortunately for Pelham's safety he was able immediately upon arrival at San Antonio to make connections with Major Emory's Boundary Commission,[10] which was traveling to El Paso in the pursuance of its task of running and marking the line established between Mexico and the United States.[11]

The trip to El Paso took nearly six weeks, the party arriving at that location on December 4, 1854. Within a few days Pelham set

---

4. William Pelham to John Wilson, 8/17/54 (B.L.M.).

5. *Ibid.*

6. *Ibid.,* 1/26/55.

7. Robert McClelland, Secretary of the Interior, to John Wilson, 9/8/54 (B.L.M.).

8. *Stat. L.,* Vol. IV, 417.

9. Pelham to John Wilson, 12/31/54, 1/29/55, 4/28/55 (B.L.M.).

10. John Wilson to Pelham, 11/25/54 (B.L.M.).

11. P. M. Baldwin, "A Historical Note on the Boundaries of New Mexico," *New Mexico Historical Review,* 5:116-137. For the earlier history of this boundary survey see, *S.I.R.* 12/4/52, 32 Cong., 2 Sess., *H.E.D.* No. 1, 37-45 (673).

out on a reconnaissance of the Rio Grande Valley to select a suitable point for the intersection of the principal meridian and the base line.[12]

In his instructions to the surveyor general, Commissioner John Wilson was understandably lacking in detailed knowledge of the wild frontier of this new Territory, and thus he allowed the surveyor general considerable leeway in the execution of his duties. Wilson stated, as a desideratum, that the principal meridian should run near the suburbs of Santa Fe and that the base line should intersect it possibly as far south as a point fifty miles east of the junction of the Rio Grande and the Rio Puerco. An alternate suggestion allowed, if expedient, the fork of the Rio Grande and the Rio Puerco as the junction point.[13] This would place the principal meridian about fifty miles west of Santa Fe.

Surveyor General Pelham followed the second suggestion. "Agreeably to your instructions I selected a hill about six miles below the mouth of the Puerco river, which is two hundred feet high and of a rocky formation. This hill is nearly round, and is washed at its base by the Rio Grande. I have therefore established this hill as the initial point, and have caused a suitable monument to be erected on its summit."[14]

His choice was probably dictated by expediency. Since he made his approach from the south, it is assumed that he knew little about the terrain west of Santa Fe, where he placed the principal meridian, nor is it likely that he was acquainted with that fifty miles east of the junction of the Rio Grande and the Rio Puerco, where Commissioner Wilson's first proposal would have placed the principal meridian. It was simply convenient to place the initial point within the main traveled reaches of the Rio Grande Valley.

Pelham had little to do during the five months of his trip to Santa Fe, but this was quite changed when he reached his journey's end. His duties in connection with Spanish and Mexican land grants were of a minor but important character.[15] The procrastination of the United States Government in not giving proper authority or support for adequate settlement of land claims was distracting. Each

---

12. Pelham to John Wilson, 12/4/54 (B.L.M.); *L.O.R.* 11/30/54, 33 Cong., 2 Sess., *H.E.D.* No. 1, 97 (777).
13. *L.O.R. Ibid.*
14. *S.G.R.* 9/30/55, 34 Cong., 1 Sess., *H.E.D.* No. 1, 303 (840).
15. Pelham to John Wilson, 5/29/55 (B.L.M.).

surveyor general was plagued with this situation until 1891, when a Court of Private Land Claims was finally established to adjudicate the claims. Tasks dealing with the public domain constituted the major portion of the work. Pelham's instructions covered in detail the eight sections of the act creating the office of Surveyor General of New Mexico. Section 1 provided for the survey of the land in New Mexico. Sections 2, 3, and 4 made donations to actual settlers. Sections 5 and 6 reserved land for school and university purposes. Section 7 granted pre-emption rights. Section 8 gave authority to report on private land claims originating before the Treaty of Guadalupe Hidalgo of 1848.[16]

Even so simple a thing as renting a suitable office and purchasing furniture for it presented the surveyor general with complicated problems. The house finally selected was of typical adobe with a dirt floor. His consternation can be imagined at the thought of keeping up appearances such as were commonplace in the East.

A budget of $3,000 a year for office rent, fuel, books, stationery, and incidental expenses was meager by eastern standards of purchasing power, and in New Mexico its sparseness was aggravatingly apparent. This problem was made doubly complicated by his observation that the native population was governed in great measure by appearances and he felt bound to keep up these appearances, in order, as he explained, "to command the respect of the Mexican population. . . ."[17]

Some chairs, made of common pine plank, were finally found that cost two dollars and a half each. Six chairs with cane seats cost forty dollars and, as he regretted, "would have cost from twelve to fifteen dollars per dozen in the states. . . ."[18] He was relieved at

---

16. *L.O.R.* 11/30/54, 33 Cong., 2 Sess., *H.E.D.* No. 1, 97-103 (777). In the first years of the Territory's existence, Pelham was also charged with the duties of register and receiver. Thomas A. Hendricks, Commissioner of the General Land Office, to Jacob Thompson, Secretary of the Interior, 10/1/58 (N.A.). The first land office for New Mexico was established on May 24, 1858, and opened in Santa Fe on November 24. The first register was W. S. Davidson and the office of receiver was first filled by W. A. Street. Hendricks to Pelham, 10/1/58 (N.A.).

17. Pelham to John Wilson, 4/26/55, John Wilson to Pelham, 4/7/55 (B.L.M.). The register and receiver at Santa Fe had comparable problems when their office was established. Wm. A. Street, Receiver, to W. Medill, Comptroller, 8/5/59; Street to Medill, 9/16/59; and Street to Hendricks, 12/30/59 (F.R.C.).

18. Pelham to John Wilson, 4/26/55 (B.L.M.).

being able to purchase mahogany chairs, sofa, and table for the court room; however, for the rest he resigned himself to the native custom. Commissioner Wilson was informed that it was necessary to purchase carpets for the floors because even the poorer class of natives carpeted their floors.[19] Not added was the information that the carpet of the natives was "a coarse domestic fabric called gerga. . . ,"[20] which undoubtedly was quite inexpensive. Experience indicated the utility of covering the walls with canvas, in the commonly practiced manner, to protect the papers and documents from the dirt of the adobe walls.[21]

Having established an office as passably as was possible under the circumstances, the surveyor general set about the duties that he had traveled so long and wearily to commence. On March 9, 1855, he let his first contract (for the survey of the principal meridian from near the Jemez Mountains to the southern border, and base line for 24 miles on either side of the principal meridian).[22] Instructions required that the deputy surveyor selected for this task should be of well established skill and reputation because the base and meridian lines form the groundwork for all subsequent surveying operations. It was prescribed that the same deputy surveyor be used to run all these lines in order to insure uniformity, and it was strongly urged that, for the same reason, the same crew be used throughout the operation. As a prerequisite, the deputy selected needed to be familiar with the use of Burt's improved solar compass, and also the theodolite; the former for determining latitudes and ascertaining compass variations; the latter for taking long-course sights and bearings of mountain ranges where it might be necessary to take angles in order to establish distances of inaccessible objects.[23]

Pelham's choice of a deputy for this work was John W. Garretson, "a surveyor of acknowledged ability, energy and experience,

19. *Ibid.*

20. R. L. Duffus, *The Santa Fe Trail*, 161.

21. Pelham to John Wilson, 4/26/55 (B.L.M.).

22. *S.G.R.* 9/30/55, 34 Cong., 1 Sess., *H.E.D.* No. 1, 303 (840); Deputy Surveyor John W. Garretson, *Field Note Book*, No. 17, 16, 17; *L.O.R.* 11/30/54, 33 Cong., 2 Sess., *H.E.D.* No. 1, 100 (777), explains that the price for base lines, principal meridians, and standard parallels was not to exceed twenty dollars per mile and that township and subdivisional lines should be limited to twelve dollars per mile.

23. *L.O.R. Ibid.*, 98.

and . . . a gentleman of respectability and integrity."[24] Garretson
had previously worked for Pelham when the latter was surveyor
general of Arkansas.[25]

After signing the contract for surveying the base line and principal meridian, Garretson gathered together his materials and his
surveying crew.[26] He was required to furnish all supplies and materials with the exception of a standard chain with which to compare
his own from time to time.[27] This chain had not yet arrived, so Garretson delayed his departure for the initial point of survey until
March 26. Even then the standard chain was not at hand but he
hoped that it would be soon and could be forwarded to him. He
waited in vain and finally sent two of his men posthaste to El Paso
to get one of the chains awaiting shipment to the surveyor general.[28]

Meanwhile, Garretson and the rest of his crew were busy locating
and monumenting the initial point of survey, selected earlier by
Pelham, on the west bank of the Rio Grande[29] about six miles south
of the junction of the Rio Grande and the Rio Puerco[30] and about
120 chains northwest of Lajoya.[31]

On April 14, Garretson's messengers returned from El Paso with
the standard chain and the following day, surveying was started on
the principal meridian south from the initial point. After the surveying had progressed for 60 miles, operations had to be suspended
because there was no water on the Jornada del Muerto. By the 27th
of April the surveying party had returned to the initial point and
started the survey of the principal meridian northward.[32]

Meanwhile, Surveyor General Pelham had not sent his special
instructions to Deputy Surveyor Garretson.[33] As a consequence,

---

24. Pelham to John Wilson, 4/1/55 (B.L.M.).
25. *Ibid.,* 4/20/55. This letter states that Garretson did surveying in Arkansas; and personal interview, Land Office personnel, August 12, 1954, revealed
that Garretson had previously worked under Pelham in Arkansas.
26. Deputy Surveyor Garretson, *Field Note Book,* No. 18, Introduction
(B.L.M.).
27. Personal interview, Land Office personnel, August 12, 1954.
28. Pelham to John Wilson, 4/1/55, 6/30/55 (B.L.M.).
29. Deputy Surveyor Garretson, *Field Note Book,* No. 18, Introduction
(B.L.M.).
30. *S.G.R.* 9/30/55, 34 Cong., 1 Sess., *H.E.D.* No. 1, 303 (840).
31. Deputy Surveyor Garretson, *Field Note Book,* No 14, Introduction
(B.L.M.). A chain is 66 feet.
32. *Ibid.,* Nos. 14, 18.
33. Pelham to John Wilson, 4/1/55 (B.L.M.).

after he had surveyed 48 miles of the principal meridian north of the base line, Garretson learned of a serious error he had committed. He had surveyed 108 miles of the principal meridian while using the wrong length for the standard chain. Included in his measure were the handles of the chain, while only the space between the rivets on the handles was the proper measure. Thus 2,160 dollars' worth of work had to be re-done. Mr. Garretson can hardly be blamed for stating that "The remarkably foolish penchant for novelty has cost me the running of 108 miles twice."[34]

By May 15, Garretson was resurveying the principal meridian north from the initial point.[35] It was not only necessary to resurvey the work but, in addition, it was essential that the old monuments be destroyed.[36] It was almost August before the survey was corrected. Garretson had hoped to finish the entire principal meridian by that time.[37]

After the late summer and fall rains, Garretson was able to continue the survey of the principal meridian south from the initial point, as well as 45 miles and 40 chains of the base line.[38] He stopped two and one-half miles short of the 24 miles scheduled for survey to the west because of very rugged terrain, lack of settlements, and the improbability of the soil ever being cultivated.[39]

It is hard today to realize the difficulties faced in the early surveying of New Mexico. Man and nature joined in a conspiracy that only an iron will and steadfast determination could overcome; and always in the background was the entangling web of Government red tape that took slow cognizance of the onerous conditions to be encountered.

The most pressing difficulty was the ever present danger of attack by Indians. The problem of living in inhospitable and rough surroundings was annoying, no doubt, but could be taken more or less in stride by men inured to frontier conditions. Not as terrifying as the danger of Indian attack, but fully as worrisome in its way, was the nagging difficulty of securing funds and instructions from Wash-

---

34. Deputy Surveyor Garretson, *Field Note Books,* Nos. 14, 18, Introduction (B.L.M.).
35. *Ibid.,* No. 18.
36. Hendricks to Pelham, 9/7/55 (B.L.M.).
37. Pelham to John Wilson, 4/20/55, 6/30/55 (B.L.M.).
38. Pelham to Hendricks, 11/30/55 (B.L.M.).
39. Deputy Surveyor Garretson, *Field Note Book,* No. 17, 16, 17.

ington. It must have been trying indeed for these men to see their problems handled in the same routine manner as would perhaps suffice back East where communications were relatively good.

It was customary for the inhabitants of New Mexico to live in settlements to afford them mutual protection from Indian attack. Surveying crews, nevertheless, had to leave the settlements and could not even take advantage of favorable terrain to repel attack.[40]

In case of danger from Indian attack, the surveyor general could call on the President to order the marshal in the Territory to give him protection. This proved to be so unwieldy a procedure as to be highly impracticable, if not impossible. As a result, Pelham was forced to do exactly what he had been denied permission to do—to call on the commander of the nearest military post for protection for his surveying crews. In the spring of 1857, Garretson had his animals stolen by Indians. Although they were recovered, he lost several days and was under heavy expense during the whole period. Pelham recommended that deputy surveyors working at a distance from the larger settlements be furnished with a military escort sufficient to protect them from bands of hostile Indians. Unless this was done, he felt that the public surveys in the Territory would be greatly retarded, because no deputy surveyor would "be willing to risk his life and property for the remuneration allowed by the government for his services."[41]

In May 1858, hostile Indians were hovering around the camp of Deputy Surveyor A. P. Wilbar, who was surveying in the Conejos Valley, in present southern Colorado, and threatening to stop his work. Pelham requested "that a sufficient escort be furnished to Mr. Wilbar at the earliest practicable period if it can be done without injury to the public service."[42]

The following year he appealed to the Superintendent of Indian Affairs at Santa Fe, Colonel James L. Collins, who was planning a talk with the Comanche Indians in the vicinity of the Canadian River. Deputy Surveyor R. E. Clements was engaged in executing public surveys there and all his property and provisions had been taken from him by these Indians except his compass, chains, and

---

40. Pelham to John Wilson, 7/22/55 (B.L.M.).
41. *S.G.R.* 9/30/57, 35 Cong., 1 Sess., *H.E.D.* No. 11, 255 (919).
42. Pelham to General John Garland, 5/29/58 (B.L.M.).

animals. Pelham urged Collins to carry out his plans "at the earliest possible period, in order to quiet the Indians and allow the public surveys in that portion of the Territory now under contract to be completed."[43]

Collins informed Pelham that there was little he could do about the situation, that Clements had been informed of the need of a military escort before leaving for his survey location near the Texas line, and that the best thing to do was to call in the military for protection.[44]

In this case the surveying party was released by the Indians only on condition that they abandon their work on the Canadian fork of the Arkansas River.[45] They had already surveyed 163 miles, 42 chains, and 39 links of exterior and subdivision lines. There was no alternative but to give up this work and leave the country. Surveyor General Pelham felt that no further surveying could be done there without great risk to life and property; accordingly, he released Clements from his contract and assigned him elsewhere.[46]

Danger from Indian attack continued for several years. In 1861 surveys along the Canadian River, and in Navaho country, were possible only because of the availability of military escorts.[47] The following year much needed surveys were held up because of the bitter hostility of the Navaho and Apache Indians in the central and southern portion of the Territory. It was unsafe to operate outside of the settlements without a strong military escort and such protection could not be counted on as a regular arrangement.[48]

The abortive invasion of New Mexico by Confederate troops in 1861-62 had so occupied the armies that Indian tribes were emboldened to increase their depredations. By the fall of 1862 this danger was alleviated and the armed forces in New Mexico, under General James H. Carleton (with Colonel Kit Carson commanding in the field), were preparing to subdue the savages. In 1863, a vigorous war was waged on the Navaho and Apache Indians and no forces were available to escort deputy surveyors in the field; consequently,

43. Pelham to Colonel James L. Collins, 7/7/59 (B.L.M.).
44. Collins to Pelham, 7/7/59 (B.L.M.).
45. *L.O.R.* 11/30/59, 36 Cong., 1 Sess., *S.E.D.* No. 2, 188 (1023).
46. *S.G.R.* 9/1/59, 36 Cong., 1 Sess., *S.E.D.* No. 2, 296 (1023).
47. *S.G.R.* 8/29/61, 37 Cong., 2 Sess., *S.E.D.* No. 1, 574, 575 (1117).
48. *S.G.R.* 9/29/62, 37 Cong., 3 Sess., *H.E.D.* No. 1, 118 (1157).

no contracts were let for surveying the public lands during that year.[49]

Most of the Mescalero Apache and Navaho Indians were rounded up and herded to the Bosque Redondo to eke out a short but unhappy existence. In 1865 the Mescalero Apaches escaped to their native haunts and by July 20, 1868, the Navahos were again occupying their old lands, having been allowed to do so by treaty negotiations.[50]

Danger to surveying parties continued to the extent that in 1864[51] and 1865 no surveys were contracted for or executed.[52] During 1866 there were no surveys, but promise of military protection in the field, if it should be necessary, led to hopes of being able to resume surveying operations without too much further delay.[53] This hope materialized the following year[54] and by 1871 settlers and surveyors alike were sanguine of a brighter outlook for the future, and settlement was constantly extending as fear of the Indian diminished and population increased.[55] Intermittent depredations continued for another fifteen years but were confined largely to the southwestern part of the Territory,[56] where surveys were extended in spite of the danger.

The country itself was discouraging. While attempting to survey the principal meridian south of the base line during a dry season, Deputy Surveyor Garretson was forced to pay seventy-five cents a gallon for water for his men and mules.[57] It is small wonder that he delayed that portion of the survey until the rains came.

Funds and instructions from Washington were always a problem. About a week after receiving his first surveying contract, Garretson urged that Pelham make some arrangement with Washington for paying him for surveying other than by drafts. It was impossible to get money for drafts without submitting to great loss because of the

---

49. *S.G.R.* 9/30/63, 38 Cong., 1 Sess., *H.E.D.* No. 1, 89 (1182).
50. William A. Keleher, *Turmoil in New Mexico, 1846-1868*, 468.
51. *S.G.R.* 9/1/64, in *L.O.R.* 10/3/64, 85.
52. *S.G.R.* 8/7/65, 39 Cong., 1 Sess., *H.E.D.* No. 1, 110 (1248).
53. *S.G.R.* 8/16/66, 39 Cong., 2 Sess., *H.E.D.* No. 1, 470, 471 (1284).
54. *S.G.R.* 7/19/67, 40 Cong., 2 Sess., *H.E.D.* No. 1, 325, 326 (1326).
55. *S.G.R.* 9/19/71, 42 Cong., 2 Sess., *H.E.D.* No. 1, 178 (1505).
56. Charles F. Coan, *A History of New Mexico*, 399.
57. Pelham to Commissioner, General Land Office, 9/28/55 (B.L.M.).

scarcity of coin and the excessive number of drafts thrown on the market in the Territory.[58]

The Governor was spending $70,000 on a state house and penitentiary. Major Emory was expending $168,000 on the Boundary Commission. The Army officers and civil authorities also had drafts on the market and the aggregate was more than $1,000,000 per annum. Currency was principally in Mexican silver dollars, which bore a premium over gold of six per cent, and which in disbursements by public officials counted only at par; consequently, it was difficult to convert Government drafts into disbursable funds without loss. Indeed there was not money in the country sufficient to purchase the drafts.

Furthermore, an excessive amount of time was required to get the drafts in the first place, since a surveying contract might take twelve months to complete, and two additional months for examination of the notes, computation of the areas, and drawing of the maps for transmission to Washington. To return the draft for payment of the survey contract took no less than four months and even then drafts could not be used. Because of the difficulty of cashing the drafts locally, they had then to be sent to St. Louis or New Orleans to be cashed, which consumed another three months of time. Thus an aggregate of twenty-one months was not an unusual time for a deputy surveyor to realize a cent on his surveying contract.[59] It might be as much as two or three years. This condition also worked a hardship on the settlers, since they could not file on land until the plats were returned to the local land office, and this required as long as the delivery of the drafts.[60]

Because of the delay caused when Garretson misinterpreted the length of the standard chain, it was not until June 30, 1855, that Pelham was able to send the accounts for the initial survey to Washington. At the time he was unable to send maps to accompany the other papers because his stationery had not arrived from El Paso and he was unable to find suitable map paper in Santa Fe; nevertheless, he expressed the hope that the field notes would be sufficient

58. John W. Garretson to Pelham, 3/20/55 (B.L.M.).

59. Pelham to John Wilson, 3/30/55 (B.L.M.).

60. Lowell O. Stewart, *Public Land Surveys: History, Instructions, Methods,* 71. Slow payment to deputy surveyors was not much improved until the contract system was abolished in 1911.

evidence of the work being properly done and that remittance could be made on the strength of these notes. He promised to send the maps as soon as possible.[61]

By July 27, Pelham was able to send the plats; however, officials in Washington had no intention of sending any money until these plats arrived. On September 7, 1855, receipt of the plats (and the field notes by the previous mail) were acknowledged and Commissioner Hendricks promised that Garretson's account would be immediately adjusted and that remittance would be requested by drafts on New York.[62]

In this last letter another financial matter was cleared up that had been pending for several months. On May 4, 1855, Commissioner John Wilson called Pelham's attention to a regulation that, if completely enforced, would have added further to Garretson's financial discomfiture. Wilson reminded Pelham that in the blank forms of contract a certain percentage was stipulated to be retained from contracts to deputy surveyors for the purpose of having these surveys examined.[63]

When Wilson's letter arrived, Pelham realized that Garretson would be severely damaged by the enforcement of its content and wrote Wilson explaining why. He agreed that the idea of retaining part of the money from each contract, in order to have the work examined, was in general a good one; however, he did not see how it could apply to the base, meridian, and standard correction lines. These lines would be run through country infested with Indians, thus making their survey far more expensive than ordinarily would be the case. In addition, an examiner would be under the same kind of expense, which would make further inroads on the profits from the original survey. Pelham stated his intention of applying this principle to the survey of subdivision and of township lines; but, in the case of the lines in question, since to examine them would require nearly a fourth of the amount of the contract, he felt that to deduct anything from that amount would be highly unfair. What is more, in his contract with Garretson, he had not stipulated any deduction because he had considered it unthinkable that any would be required.[64]

---

61. Pelham to John Wilson, 6/30/55 (B.L.M.).
62. Hendricks to Pelham, 9/7/55 (B.L.M.).
63. John Wilson to Pelham, 5/4/55 (B.L.M.).
64. Pelham to John Wilson, 7/22/55 (B.L.M.).

In the meantime Wilson had left office as Commissioner of the General Land Office and was replaced by Thomas A. Hendricks, who finally agreed to waive examination of base and standard lines. At the same time he made it clear that the surveyor general was still responsible for the work of his deputy surveyor while the latter and his bondsmen were to be held legally responsible for the work.[65] Had Hendricks not yielded on this point, Garretson would have had to carry out his contract with probably no profit to himself. Conditions in New Mexico were hard at best, and Washington officialdom made them no easier.

Pelham capably established the public surveying system in frontier New Mexico; but, he was strong willed and confident of his own abilities and almost disdainful in his impatience of the restrictions imposed on him by his Washington superiors. As a consequence, he was not always tactful or diplomatic in his dealings with those superiors; therefore, early antagonisms arose that led ultimately to his resignation on August 29, 1860.[66] He had left Washington six years earlier with optimism and good humor. Now he was leaving office in a cloud of bitter feeling centered around a host of irritations that culminated in the disallowance of the purchase of some candles for a night watchman.

> As the Treasury Department deemed proper to place the funds appropriated by Congress for the construction of vaults for the preservation of the records of this office in the hands of the Superintendent of Public Buildings for this Territory, who construed them in such a manner as to render the appropriation useless and entirely thwart the action of Congress in the matter, it became necessary, for the safe keeping of the land titles of the country entrusted to my care to employ a watchman, and keep a dog upon the premises, and it is necessary that this watchman shall be provided with lights for use at night. This explanation I trust will be sufficient to enable you to approve the purchases made.[67]

When Pelham left office as surveyor general he served as deputy surveyor under the new head, A. P. Wilbar. His last contract for

65. Hendricks to Pelham, 9/7/55 (B.L.M.). George C. Whiting was Acting Commissioner for a short while before Hendricks took office.

66. *S.G.R.* 8/29/61, 37 Cong., 2 Sess., *S.E.D.* No. 1, 589 (1117).

67. Pelham to Joseph S. Wilson, Commissioner of the General Land Office, 7/14/60 (B.L.M.).

surveying was on November 15, 1860.[68] Oral tradition indicates that Pelham was sympathetic to the Southern cause in the Civil War.[69] Some time after this he moved to Texas, where he was still residing in 1874.[70]

When Pelham left office, there was owing him $463.35 for an incidental expense account. He had not been paid because the money was not available at the time.[71] In 1873, to secure this unpaid amount, he enlisted the aid of John Hancock, of the House of Representatives. Hancock was told that the only redress for Mr. Pelham was to apply to Congress for relief.[72] Fourteen years after his resignation, Pelham was informed that he was finally to be paid.[73]

---

68. Joseph S. Wilson to G. E. Burbank, Army paymaster at San Antonio, Texas, 7/9/68 (N.A.).

69. Personal interview, Land Office personnel, August 12, 1954.

70. Samuel S. Burdett, Commissioner of the General Land Office, to Rep. John Hancock, 8/22/74 (N.A.). Pelham was living at Onion Creek P. O., Travis County, Texas.

71. Joseph S. Wilson to Pelham, 8/7/60 (N.A.).

72. Willis Drummond, Commissioner of the General Land Office, to Rep. John Hancock, 12/15/73 (N.A.).

73. Burdett to Pelham, 8/26/74 (N.A.).

2. The Public Surveys

SURVEYOR GENERAL PELHAM was instructed to survey only in areas toward which settlement was tending and to survey only township exterior boundaries in areas unfit for cultivation. Standard parallels or correction lines were to be established at each fourth township or twenty-fourth mile north of the base line and at every fifth township or thirtieth mile south of the base line. No specific provision was made for following the usual practice of locating guide meridians at intervals of forty-eight miles east and west from the principal meridian; in fact, it was implied that circumstance should dictate their delineation, so an irregular pattern evolved (Map 1). His long experience in public surveying qualified Pelham to lay out the basic pattern in New Mexico, where initiative and individual judgment were required to a high degree.[1]

His superiors in Washington urged that he make a reconnaissance of the Territory as soon as possible after his arrival in New Mexico. The purposes were to determine the utility of the rectangular surveying system in New Mexico and to ascertain the localities most in need of survey.[2] Pelham had already traversed the valley of the Rio Grande and the Jornada del Muerto on his journey to Santa Fe. Now his duties were numerous and vexing and it was not until June 19, 1858, that he was able to make a further study, in the field, of the surveying needs of the Territory. At this time he visited the valley of the Canadian and its vicinity.[3] This is the only trip he was able to take for this purpose, even though on such visits all his necessary expenses were to be paid,[4] and for the rest he had to depend on the reports of his subordinates. During his last two years in

---

1. *L.O.R.* 11/30/54, 33 Cong., 2 Sess., *H.E.D.* No. 1, 97-100 (777).
2. *Ibid.*
3. Pelham to Hendricks, 6/30/58 (B.L.M.).
4. *L.O.R.* 11/30/54, 33 Cong., 2 Sess., *H.E.D.* No. 1, 99 (777).

office, he was repeatedly and unjustly charged with extravagance,[5] which reason, together with his pressing duties in Santa Fe, kept him from further examinations of the Territory. He was undoubtedly aided by the findings of a number of military expeditions before and during his stay in office. Between the opening of the Mexican and Civil wars, there were no less than fifteen Government explorations within or across the Territory of New Mexico.[6]

Commissioner John Wilson had informed Pelham that the great body of settlements would presumably be found in the valley of the Rio Grande.[7] This was in general true; nevertheless, the first requests for surveys by actual settlers came in 1855[8] from the region of Fort Stanton (established earlier that year)[9] and the confluence of the Rio Bonito and the Rio Ruidoso. Pelham decided against surveys here in favor of those on the Conchas and Canadian, where rapid settlement was expected[10] (Maps 2-3). His decision was based, in part, on the isolation of the Fort Stanton area, the dangers from Indian attack, and the difficulties of crossing the San Andres Mountains with the second standard parallel south. The last named line would be necessary to tie in this region with the public surveys in progress. No surveys were made in the Fort Stanton area until 1867.[11]

Pelham was given wide discretionary powers in the selection of areas to be surveyed. His suggestions in this matter were never questioned; however, in the fall of 1857 he asked for and received permission to make surveys without application to the General Land Office. He wanted to choose his own survey locations in order

---

5. Acting Commissioner Joseph S. Wilson to Pelham, 8/9/59 (B.L.M.). This is but one of several letters from Joseph S. Wilson unjustly charging Pelham with extravagance. During his tenure in office, he served under three other Commissioners of the General Land Office: John Wilson, Thomas Hendricks, and Samuel A. Smith. None of them were critical of his expenditures.

6. A. B. Bender, "Government Explorations in the Territory of New Mexico, 1846-1859," *New Mexico Historical Review*, 9:31. On this subject see also, Ralph P. Bieber, "Letters of William Carr Lane, 1852-1854," *New Mexico Historical Review*, 3:179-203; and, George Leslie Albright, *Official Explorations for the Pacific Railroads*, 1853-1855.

7. *L.O.R.* 11/30/54, 33 Cong., 2 Sess., *H.E.D.* No. 1, 97 (777).

8. Pelham to Commissioner of the General Land Office, 8/31/55 (B.L.M.).

9. General Garland to Pelham, 5/17/55 (B.L.M.).

10. Pelham to Hendricks, 5/24/56 (B.L.M.).

11. Map to accompany *S.G.R.* 7/19/67, 40 Cong., 2 Sess., *H.E.D.* No. 1, 325-334 (1326).

to avoid the long delay of having them selected in Washington.[12] The granting of this request is significant, because it shows great faith in Pelham's judgment and because it was not accorded to any of his successors. More important was Pelham's choice of survey locations under this permission.

The administration of the public lands in the United States was inaugurated at a time and place when and where all available land was, in varying degrees, suitable for agricultural purposes.[13] Later, in New Mexico, this was not true, yet the Government did not change the policy. From the beginning the policy in New Mexico was to survey only land that was agricultural in the sense that it was arable. The entire question of land arability was variously interpreted by different commissioners and surveyors general. Pelham started out with a strict interpretation; but, as he became acquainted with the land and the people, his definition broadened to include pasture lands.[14]

Having been forewarned that he would probably find the bulk of the settlements to be in the Rio Grande Valley,[15] in 1856, Pelham turned his attention to surveys there.[16] His interpretation of what constituted the Rio Grande Valley took in an area roughly thirty-six miles in width (Maps 2-3). Only a small portion of this land could be cultivated but, as he explains, there was the factor of coordinating the survey of private land claims and also future public surveys. There seems to be another reason why these townships were subdivided.

Much of this area was in the Jornada del Muerto and could grow no crops (Maps 2-3). Why then was there any excuse for subdividing the area? The answer lies in the fact that there was a strong possibility of artesian well development at the time. This was suggested, in 1855-56, by Brevet Captain John Pope, who was assigned by Secretary of War Jefferson Davis to explore the possibilities of artesian

---

12. Pelham to Hendricks, 10/11/57 (B.L.M.); Hendricks to Pelham, 11/17/57 (N.A.).

13. Public Lands Commission, *Preliminary Report,* 1879, 46 Cong., 2 Sess., *H.E.D.* No. 46, XIX (1923).

14. *L.O.R.* 11/30/54, 33 Cong., 2 Sess., *H.E.D.* No. 1, 98 (777); Garretson to Pelham, 4/2/56 (B.L.M.); *S.G.R.* 9/30/58, 35 Cong., 2 Sess., *H.E.D.* No. 2, 297 (997).

15. *L.O.R.* 11/30/54, 33 Cong., 2 Sess., *H.E.D.* No. 1, 97 (777).

16. Pelham to Hendricks, 8/30/56; Hendricks to Pelham, 10/14/56 (B.L.M.).

well development near the 32d parallel of latitude in connection with possible railroad development.[17]

Pelham believed that artesian well development would cause settlement of the regions involved, and in view of Pope's findings, had to consider both the lower Pecos and the Jornada areas.[18] The lower Pecos Valley was out of the question for surveys because of its inaccessibility and the danger from Indian attack. This left the Jornada—an area near the prosperous and productive Mesilla Valley.[19] An abundance of artesian well water would have caused an influx of population and would have justified the surveys there.

Important surveys under Pelham extended to other regions as well. In September of 1857 the surveyor general received a petition from a large number of persons requesting the survey of the territory known as the Valles about forty miles northwest of Santa Fe. This area was surveyed early the following year. On March 13, 1858, a contract was let with R. E. Clements for the survey of a large block of exterior township boundaries in the upper Pecos Valley. That same year surveys were made near Galisteo, where settlements by claimants under the Donation Laws had been disputed since 1855.[20]

Pelham was early aware of one problem for which neither he nor several of his successors could find a solution. The great majority of the 80,000 people who became citizens of the United States upon annexation of New Mexico were comparatively poor. Their chief claim to affluence was generally a small strip of irrigated land along some river or stream, which they held by right of possession, as it was handed down from father to son. The United States at all times recognized their right to title in this land; nevertheless, three circumstances prevented the granting of official title under the land legislation prior to 1891. The land was invariably in narrow strips that fronted on a winding watercourse and extended back from it

---

17. Secretary of War, *Annual Report*, 12/1/56, 34 Cong., 3 Sess., *H.E.D.* No. 1, 212-216 (894); Robert Hay, *Report of the Artesian and Underflow Investigation*, 52 Cong., 1 Sess., *S.E.D.* No. 41, Pt. 3, 144, 145 (2899).

18. Captain John Pope to Pelham, 2/25/56 (B.L.M.).

19. P. M. Baldwin, "A Short History of the Mesilla Valley," *New Mexico Historical Review*, 13:314, describes the Mesilla Valley as that part of the Rio Grande Valley lying between Elephant Butte Dam and Juarez, Mexico. It includes part of Sierra and Doña Ana counties in New Mexico and El Paso County in Texas.

20. Pelham to Hendricks, 3/29/58, 3/13/58, 4/29/58 (B.L.M.).

more or less at right angles to its frontage. This was not compatible
with the rectangular pattern that was the mode of United States
surveys. Then too, it was the custom of these people to live around
a plaza where they could rally in case of Indian attack. In contrast,
national land laws required actual residence upon the land. A third
deterrent was the common ownership of pasture and woodland in
back of irrigated areas.[21]

The situation was allowed to drift in the old manner of possessory
rights. This was poor policy because technically the land was public
domain and was so designated on official maps. An unprincipled
person could theoretically make entry on any of these more than
five thousand small-holding claims.[22] In theory, it was the policy of
officials to protect the owners of these lands. "The ownership of lots
in this country [was] well known, and universally acquiesced in,
with rare exceptions. Long continued occupation, with the consent
of the Government and all parties interested, constitute[d] as just
a claim as property [was] held by anywhere."[23]

In practice, this land was not always safe from exploitation; however, it was by another method that the native settlers were more
frequently dispossessed of their holdings. As the native population
increased and land became scarcer in the established settlements, it
was not uncommon for enterprising individuals to pioneer in new
areas, seeking out land which had a water supply. In these new
regions they could acquire land under the land laws of the United
States; nevertheless, they were often ignorant of their rights and
duties under these laws and unscrupulous persons filed the land
out from under them. This was especially true in the 1880's, when
cattle raising came into more prominence and land with water was
sought by graziers.[24]

Alexander P. Wilbar, Chief Clerk under Pelham, was appointed
to the office of surveyor general on August 29, 1860.[25] He was to
serve but little over a year and to be replaced because of the Repub-

21. *L.O.R.* 9/13/90, 27.

22. *G.N.M.* 9/15/90, 51 Cong., 2 Sess., *H.E.D.* No. 1, 590, 591 (2842).

23. *L.O.R.* 9/13/90, 29.

24. Personal interview, Celestino Padilla, April 18, 1960; *L.O.R.* 10/7/86,
49 Cong., 2 Sess., *H.E.D.* No. 1, 90, 91 (2468); Secretary of the Interior, *Fraudulent Acquisition of Titles to Land in New Mexico*, 1885, 48 Cong., 2 Sess., *S.E.D.*
No. 106, 29.

25. *S.G.R.* 8/29/61, 37 Cong., 2 Sess., *S.E.D.* No. 1, 589 (1117).

lican administration of Abraham Lincoln. His predecessor had resigned, and charges of extravagance were later used to ease Wilbar out.[26]

Requests for surveys in the San Juan Valley of northwest New Mexico were the most persistent of any submitted during his administration; however, the area was difficult to reach with surveys, so early in 1861 Wilbar asked Captain Charles Baker for a report on the region. Baker's report on the settlements and mines there was so favorable that Wilbar promised to report to the Government with a view to having surveys made in the vicinity.[27] The early promise of the region, however, was not permanent. It was soon almost wholly abandoned by miners as the difficulty of importing provisions became apparent, and as the mines failed to materialize as expected. Hostility of the Indians also proved to be a strong deterrent to permanent settlement.[28]

John A. Clark, of Freeport, Illinois, came into office with the new Republican administration. His commission, for the usual four-year term, bore the date of July 26, 1861,[29] and he took charge on October 9 of that year.[30]

Clark took office during the troubled times of the Civil War when the annual surveys dwindled until from 1863 through 1866 there were none at all (Appendix III). Thus the first years of Clark's administration were taken up largely with reconnoitering the Territory and making plans for surveys. Actual surveys in New Mexico under Clark were limited, by Indian hostilities and lack of military protection, to the vicinity of Fort Stanton, the Hondo River, and the Mimbres Valley[31] (Maps 2-3).

The chief characteristic of Clark's administration was a determined effort to abide by the governmental policy of surveying only truly arable land. Clark personally examined these areas to make

---

26. Alexander P. Wilbar to J. M. Edmunds, Commissioner of the General Land Office, 6/8/61, 10/9/61 (B.L.M.).

27. Wilbar to Captain Charles Baker, 1/31/61, 2/28/61 (B.L.M.).

28. *S.G.R.* 8/29/61, 37 Cong., 2 Sess., *S.E.D.* No. 1, 577 (1117). Frank D. Reeve, "A Navaho Struggle for Land," *New Mexico Historical Review*, 21:1-21, has information on the later settlement of the San Juan country.

29. Edmunds to John A. Clark, Surveyor General of New Mexico, *Clark's Commission*, 7/26/61 (N.A.).

30. Wilbar to Edmunds, 10/9/61 (B.L.M.).

31. Joseph S. Wilson to Clark, 4/20/67 (N.A.).

sure of selecting only land suitable for settlement and cultivation. He believed that, except for a few townships on the Canadian River, not *one per cent* of the land then surveyed in New Mexico could ever be cultivated.[32] This was undoubtedly a reflection on Pelham's surveys on the Jornada del Muerto.

Dr. T. Rush Spencer took charge of the surveyor general's office on May 15, 1869.[33] Surveys made under Spencer were not extensive. He proposed to make surveys on the San Juan, Cimarron, Canadian, Pecos and Gila rivers, and near Fort Wingate, and in southwest New Mexico.[34] Actually his surveys were confined to a region on the upper Pecos River, north of the Bosque Redondo Indian Reservation, and to southwest New Mexico (Maps 2-3). In the Pecos region he made some attempt to confine surveyed areas to the demands of actual settlers, while in southwest New Mexico his activities were governed by requests for surveys from settlers residing in the vicinity of newly discovered mines.[35]

Spencer was the first of three successive surveyors general to become aligned with the dominant Republican political element in the Territory for mutual gain. William Blackmore, an early English land grant speculator, while making notes on important land grants in Spencer's office in 1871, was introduced to Charles P. Clever, Santa Fe attorney. The two formed a profitable association. The following year Spencer, "with unprecedented dispatch," held the Cebolla Grant to be valid and recommended its confirmation by Congress. The attorney for the grant claimants was Thomas B. Catron. As early as 1870 Spencer himself was in the land grant business with Elkins and Catron, having secured a fifth interest in the Mora Grant.[36] That same year he was an official of the Maxwell Land Grant and Railroad Company with William A. Pile, Gover-

---

32. Clark to Edmunds, 12/20/62 (B.L.M.). Maps 2 and 3 of surveyed areas reveal that he came close to achieving his objective.

33. T. Rush Spencer, Surveyor General of New Mexico, to Joseph S. Wilson, 5/15/69 (B.L.M.). Benjamin C. Cutler became Surveyor General on August 26, 1868; Cutler to Joseph S. Wilson, 8/29/68 (B.L.M.). He died in office on October 18, the same year; David J. Miller, Chief Clerk, to Joseph S. Wilson, 10/18/68 (B.L.M.).

34. Spencer to Joseph S. Wilson, 7/16/69 (B.L.M.).

35. *L.O.R.* 10/27/70, 41 Cong., 3 Sess., *H.E.D.* No. 1, 109 (1449).

36. Herbert O. Brayer, *William Blackmore: The Spanish-Mexican Land Grants of New Mexico and Colorado, 1863-1878,* 150, 159, 167, 219.

nor of New Mexico Territory, John S. Watts, John Pratt, and Miguel A. Otero.[37]

James K. Proudfit, a native of Madison, Wisconsin, assumed the duties of surveyor general on September 30, 1872.[38] His administration is characterized by his struggle for constantly increased survey appropriations at a time when Congress was calling for retrenchment. In 1874 he asked for $125,000 for surveys, but Commissioner Drummond in his estimate to Congress requested only $40,000. Drummond pointed out that in New Mexico, from 1855 through 1873, upwards of $440,000 had been spent for surveying 4,860,410 acres of land, while the area disposed of by the Government, up to June 30, 1873, by homestead entry, cash sales, etc., was less than 150,000 acres.[39] Drummond was very liberal with his figure of the area disposed of since actually less than 30,000 acres was patented (and less than 63,000 acres entered) through 1873 (Appendixes IV and V). This would seem an ample backlog of surveyed land to take care of any reasonably sudden demand; nevertheless, Proudfit attempted to prove that it was not. He pointed out that there had not been a great demand for land but that the day was rapidly approaching when this would change. Indian depredations had largely ceased, permitting expansion into new areas. In time past, settlers had been able to purchase land from private grants, but now land was becoming more costly because of the approach of railroads and the expectation of mineral discoveries. Proudfit proposed that all the land in the Territory be surveyed as rapidly as practicable, as had been done in such states as Illinois and Wisconsin.[40]

What he overlooked, or perhaps chose not to see, was the great dissimilarity in the arability of the land in New Mexico and that

37. Harold H. Dunham, *Government Handout: A Study in the Administration of the Public Lands, 1875-1891*, 223.

38. Drummond to James K. Proudfit, Surveyor General of New Mexico, 9/9/72 (N.A.). Spencer was in ill health during much of his stay in office; Joseph S. Wilson to Spencer 11/30/70 (N.A.). He died 6/19/72; David J. Miller, Chief Clerk, to Drummond, 6/19/72 (B.L.M.).

39. Drummond to S. B. Elkins, House of Representatives, 2/16/74 (N.A.). His figure for the area surveyed is correct.

40. *S.G.R.* 10/7/72, 42 Cong., 3 Sess., *H.E.D.* No. 1, 123, 124 (1560). His arguments for increased appropriations were similar throughout his administration.

of the states that he used as examples. There had been no change
in the official Government policy requiring that land must be
capable of growing crops in order to be homesteaded or pre-empted.
There was, however, a growing tendency to overlook this requirement in actual practice. Whether this was good or bad depends on
certain points of view. On the one hand it did break the law; on the
other, it made for more rapid settlement of the land, with cattle
ranchers serving as a catalytic agent in the process.

By 1873 Proudfit was openly propagandizing for the cattle industry in New Mexico and striving to secure increased appropriations
to accommodate its needs for surveys.[41] In 1874 he enlisted the aid
of S. B. Elkins, Delegate to the House of Representatives, to secure
this increase. It was quite convenient for him to call upon Elkins
since both, together with Marsh Giddings, Thomas B. Catron, and
William W. Griffin, were incorporators of the Consolidated Land,
Cattle Raising and Wool Growing Company, incorporated October
19, 1872, three weeks after Proudfit took office. Home offices were at
Fort Bascom, Santa Fe, and Denver, and operations were planned
in San Miguel County and in Colorado.[42]

His survey locations (Maps 2-3) were particularly interesting in
the northeast part of the Territory and the Pecos Valley. Railroad
talk was in the air and probably had some influence on the surveys
in the northeast. Of more significance, the Prairie Cattle Company
came to control most of the area now embraced by Union County.[43]
This was a Scottish firm incorporated on September 15, 1883.[44] The
Pecos Valley "was solely and strictly a cattle country—there were no
other interests—and there were large herds."[45]

In 1876 Proudfit was asked to resign. Afterwards, he entered into
a contract with Lewis Kingman for more claims than one deputy
could survey in a single season (the time allowed). The contract

41. *S.G.R.* 8/15/73, 43 Cong., 1 Sess., *H.E.D.* No. 1, 99 (1601).

42. Western Range Cattle Industry Study, *New Mexico Cattle Corporations, 1871-1900,* Summary, Ms. This was the first cattle corporation in New
Mexico and the only one until 1881. Commissioner Drummond paid no heed
to Elkins' plea.

43. Berry Newton Alvis, "History of Union County, New Mexico," *New
Mexico Historical Review,* 22:248.

44. Western Range Cattle Industry Study, *New Mexico Cattle Corporations, 1871-1900.* Summary, Ms.

45. James F. Hinkle, *Early Days of a Cowboy on the Pecos,* 3, 4.

was promptly disapproved because of the previous request for his resignation and because of the excessive number of claims in it.[46] The significance is that each deputy was supposed to make personally all the surveys in each contract; otherwise the deputy might sublet portions of the contract to an inferior surveyor. There was also the possibility that the deputy might remunerate the surveyor general for awarding him a larger contract than he could take care of personally.[47]

Henry M. Atkinson, of Nebraska,[48] took over the office of surveyor general on March 31, 1876.[49] By far the greatest amount of surveying in New Mexico was done under his supervision, and irregular practices were common during his tenure. It was crystal clear that Atkinson operated within a specific framework of instructions as to areas that could be surveyed under the regular annual appropriations. These were:

1. Those lands adapted to agriculture without artificial irrigation.
2. Irrigable lands, or such as can be redeemed and for which there is sufficient accessible water for the reclamation and cultivation of the same not otherwise utilized or claimed.
3. Timber lands bearing timber of commercial value.
4. Coal lands containing coal of commercial value.
5. Exterior boundaries of townsites.
6. Private land claims.[50]

Atkinson did not fulfill these stipulations. There might have been some question as to what constituted *agricultural* land except

---

46. Acting Commissioner, L. K. Lippincott, to Henry M. Atkinson, Surveyor General of New Mexico, 3/8/76 (N.A.). This contract was disallowed.

47. Personal interview, Land Office personnel, December 14, 1954.

48. Atkinson to J. A. Williamson, Commissioner of the General Land Office, 12/4/76 (B.L.M.).

49. Proudfit to Burdett, 3/31/76 (B.L.M.).

50. Williamson to Atkinson, 8/23/76 (N.A.). These categories were repeated each year with the annual instructions. Public Lands Commission, *Final Report,* 1881, 46 Cong., 3 Sess., *H.E.D.* No. 47, 191 (1975), points out that

"It was the custom prior to July 31, 1876, for Congress to make appropriations annually for each surveying district by separate item.

"July 31, 1876 (19 Stats., p. 120), Congress changed the method of appropriation by giving a gross sum for annual surveys, without specifying surveying districts, States, or Territories; which system now exists. The Secretary of the Interior, under this law, annually apportions the same to the several surveying districts as in his judgment is deemed best."

that Commissioner Williamson[51] and Atkinson were clear on the matter: "The classification of surveyable lands made by Congress precludes the survey of portions of this Territory that are valuable for grazing purposes and which could be rapidly sold by the Government were they surveyed and subject to sale."[52]

The special deposit system became a matter of importance in Atkinson's surveys. It was originated by the Congressional Act of May 30, 1862, to reduce the cost to the Government of surveys by authorizing that they be paid for by settlers in townships where they were desired. The law was modified in 1871 to the extent that deposits by settlers could be used in part payment for their lands in the townships, the surveying of which was paid for out of these deposits. On March 3, 1879, the harmlessness of this law came to an end when certificates of deposit became negotiable and could be used in payment for public land anywhere under the terms of the Pre-emption and Homestead laws. Nationally, the total deposits for survey in the seventeen years prior to the modification of 1879 amounted to $368,625.69. The deposits under the act from 1880 through 1884 were $5,813,368.58, and in New Mexico, $13,432.03 through 1879, and $891,707.85 from 1880 through 1884.[53]

The startling increase was the result of regulations adopted by the General Land Office which were not consonant with congressional intention. The application of *one settler* was sufficient to cause the survey of a township, and a form of *settler's application* was adopted that would not overly stretch the conscience of a non-settler to sign. The result was that frequent applications were made for the survey of a township by *one settler* who might be a *non-settler*. The law permitted only the survey of townships; the regulations, however, permitted the survey of connection lines. Assignment of certificates should have been, by law, restricted to those dated subsequent to the Act of 1879; but the regulations permitted such use of earlier certificates, and in localities not authorized by the law. Deputy surveyors secured work on easily surveyable land and individuals who paid for the surveys used the certificates to avail themselves of valuable land. It was even possible, by false

51. *Ibid.,* Williamson.
52. Atkinson to Williamson, 9/30/76 (B.L.M.).
53. *L.O.R.* 10/22/85, 49 Cong., 1 Sess., *H.E.D.* No. 1, 165 (2378), and *S.G.R.* for years quoted.

representation of a lost certificate, to acquire double payment for one deposit.[54]

The situation became so intolerable that on August 7, 1882, a law was passed by which the use of certificates of deposit was confined to the land district in which the lands surveyed were situated.[55] This caused a sharp drop in the amount of money deposited.

It is true that a large proportion of Atkinson's surveys were made under the deposit system and that, for purposes of accounting, special deposits were handled separately from the regularly appropriated survey funds. But surveys under special deposits were subject to the requirements of surveying only entire townships surveyable by law; furthermore, it was specifically stipulated that no surveys were to be extended into townships not already settled.[56]

It is evident that rationalization was used in the interpretation of what constituted a *settled* township. Commissioner William A. J. Sparks, referring to the past use of the deposit survey law, in 1885 stated: "The law is for the benefit of the 'settlers' in a township of unsurveyed lands, not for the benefit of persons not settlers nor yet for the benefit of surveyors."[57] Sparks admitted that the law did not specify how many settlers residing in a township constituted a justification for the survey of that township; therefore, public advantage must be the deciding factor. He scathingly wrote that certainly not *one* settler constituted either a legal or literal justification and added that in many instances in the past the evidence that even *one* person was a settler had been "extremely slight and superficial."[58] "Deposit surveys," continued Sparks, "being restricted by the several provisions of law to surveys for homestead and pre-emption settlers, cannot be made for the benefit of other persons or interests, and it also follows that lands not adapted to nor needed for such settlements are not surveyable under the Deposit System."[59]

---

54. *Ibid., L.O.R.,* 166.

55. *S.G.R.* 7/20/83, 48 Cong., 1 Sess., *H.E.D.* No. 1, 260 (2190).

56. Williamson to Atkinson, 8/23/76 (N.A.).

57. Wm. A. J. Sparks, Commissioner of the General Land Office, to Clarence Pullen, Surveyor General of New Mexico, 6/6/85 (N.A.).

58. *Ibid.*

59. *Ibid.* Henry N. Copp, *The American Settler's Guide,* 22, states that survey deposit certificates could be used only for homestead or pre-emption uses; and, 7, that *"Agricultural Lands* are those that will produce agricultural crops;" also, 51, that land for homestead or pre-emption uses must be cultivated to be held legally.

Atkinson repeatedly blamed the large number of deposits on the failure of Congress to make appropriations sufficient to prosecute the public surveys as rapidly as demanded by the settlement of the Territory.[60] This is demonstrably strange reasoning even if the entire resident population were considered in the need for surveys. It is more reasonable to consider that the bulk of actual and legitimate settlement was demanded by newcomers who had not already acquired land. In 1883 the population of the Territory was about 130,000, three-fourths of whom were natives[61] who presumably had an abode of long standing. Of the remaining one-fourth all but a few foreigners were from the States. Even a large percentage of these had resided in the Territory for some years and had established an agrarian residence. That same year there were 12,847,970 acres of land surveyed in New Mexico; an average, in a single year, of almost 99 acres for each person living there at the time! Of this amount, at least 14/15 was done under the deposit system.

The only possible demand for that amount of surveyed land was that advanced by cattlemen. Two years later Commissioner Sparks reported that "the choicest cattle raising portions of New Mexico . . ." had been surveyed.[62] The land was desired for grazing purposes. Atkinson's own words are proof of that. He had been questioned by Acting Commissioner C. W. Holcomb as to the validity of a contract in the region of the Llano Estacado east of the Pecos River.[63]

Atkinson's answer is revealing: "I presume that but a small portion of this land is suitable for agriculture, but it is adapted for grazing purposes and stockmen are desirous of securing their water and the land embracing same as the nucleus of their stock ranges."[64]

It is evident that the General Land Office accepted this explanation at its face value, because the contract was approved and duly executed.[65] Such flagrant winking at the law can hardly be justified; nevertheless, there is an explanation. Thinking men knew that the national land classification was unrealistic. They knew that large

---

60. *S.G.R.* 8/25/82, 47 Cong., 2 Sess., *H.E.D.* No. 1, 522 (2099).
61. *G.N.M.* 9/6/83, 48 Cong., 1 Sess., *H.E.D.* No. 1, 553 (2191); *G.N.M.* 9/15/90, 51 Cong., 2 Sess., *H.E.D.* No. 1, 595 (2842).
62. *L.O.R* 10/22/85, 49 Cong., 1 Sess., *H.E.D.* No. 1, 168 (2378).
63. C. W. Holcomb to Atkinson, 6/8/81 (N.A.).
64. Atkinson to Holcomb, 6/14/81 (B.L.M.).
65. *S.G.R.* 8/25/82, 47 Cong., 2 Sess., *H.E.D.* No. 1, 528 (2099).

portions of the West were unsuited to anything except grazing, yet there was no classification for grazing land.[66] Such land could not legally be acquired for the only use for which it was suited. Perhaps men became careless, or disillusioned, at the frustration of seeing this condition exist year after year with no attempt at a remedy. At any rate, Atkinson blithely continued to certify that the areas of public surveys were confined to the classifications that had been made by Congress.[67]

Throughout his period in office, Atkinson attempted to show the need for larger appropriations for his surveying district. He used most of the generalities that had been advanced by his predecessor. He stressed the rapid approach of railroad transportation,[68] the desirability of settlers being able to perfect titles in any location at any time they wished,[69] and the fact that all the public domain had already been surveyed in the States.[70]

His surveys were so extensive that they covered nearly every region in the Territory, but a majority of this area was suitable only for grazing cattle (Maps 4-5). Atkinson himself was interested in the cattle business. In 1882 he was an incorporator, with Thomas B. Catron and John H. Thomson, of the Boston and New Mexico Cattle Company. The following year he and William H. McBroom and Joseph H. Bonham formed the New Mexico Land and Livestock Company. In 1884 he joined with Max Frost, W. H. McBroom, and three gentlemen from Kentucky, in forming the New Mexico and Kentucky Land and Stock Company. These three companies operated in Santa Fe County. In 1886 the American Valley Company was incorporated by Atkinson, Thomas B. Catron, William B. Slaughter, and Henry L. Warren. The American Valley is in the area of Salt Lake, Trechado, and Quemado in present Catron County. The combined capitalization of these companies was

66. Public Lands Commission, *Final Report,* 1881, 46 Cong., 3 Sess., *H.E.D.* No. 47, 185 (1975).

67. See the successive *Annual Reports* of his administration. It is of interest also to note that the surveyor general's salary, during Atkinson's administration, was reduced from $3,000 per year to $2,500. Later this salary was raised to the $3,000 that had prevailed from the inception of the office.

68. Atkinson to Williamson, 3/26/78 (B.L.M.).

69. *S.G.R.* 8/15/78, 45 Cong., 3 Sess., *H.E.D.* No. 1, 275 (1850).

70. *S.G.R.* 8/25/76, 44 Cong., 2 Sess., *H.E.D.* No. 1, 229 (1749).

$5,000,000.[71] His associates in all the companies were prominent politically. Equally indicative of his relationship to political interests was his highly questionable approval of the contract with John T. Elkins and R. T. Marmon for the survey of the Maxwell Land Grant in 1878. John Elkins was a brother of Stephen, who in turn was a bondsman for the surveyors as well as a promoter of the grant. The surveyors were responsible to Atkinson and took only twenty-one days for a job that should have taken at least two months for careful work.[72]

Irregularities in surveys under Atkinson were prolific and brought repercussions while he was still in office. Commissioner N. C. McFarland condemned certain survey plats when he pointed out that the topography was poorly and roughly drawn and that the plats were "far below the average of other districts."[73] An examination of survey plats for various periods, comparing them with resurveys, reveals that the early surveys, both in the field and on the plats, were much more accurate than those made in the 1880's under Atkinson.[74]

The early deputy surveyors "carried a good chisel."[75] The surveys

71. Western Range Cattle Industry Study, *New Mexico Cattle Corporations, 1871-1900,* Summary, Ms.

72. Dunham, *Government Handout,* 229.

73. Noah C. McFarland, Commissioner of the General Land Office, to Atkinson, 7/26/83 (N. A.). Ten plats selected at random and compared with resurveys, are summarized in the following table.

| | | | SURVEY | | | RESURVEY | |
| | | Com- | | Date of | | | Date of |
T	R	ment	By Whom	Survey		By Whom	Resurvey
4N	5E	A	Taylor & Holland	1883		C. W. Devendorf	1920
16N	11E	A	Taylor & Holland	1882		Wendell V. Hall	1929
25S	1W	B	A. P. Wilbar	1858		Haste & Tolland	1940
7S	21E	A	Albert W. Steele	1882		Glenn R. Haste	1937
2N	7E	B	G. T. McCullough	1882		Lee S. Miller	1912
15N	11E	A	Wm. White	1882		Wendell V. Hall	1929
16S	2E	B	Garretson & Tivy	1858		O. P. Warner	1930
15S	4E	A	Pearce & Coleman	1882		Donald Harding	1937
17N	12E	A	Taylor & Holland	1882		C. W. Devendorf	1925
15N	10E	A	Wm. White	1884		E. Kimmell	1932

A = inaccurate. B = accurate.

74. Surveyors General, *Survey Plats of Townships,* (B.L.M.).

75. Personal interview, Land Office personnel, March 23, 1954.

in the 1850's were good both for bearing and distance and compare favorably with what would be expected of a competent engineer today. In the 1860's, surveys were not as good as in the 1850's; for example, surveys of Hiram C. Fellows in 1867 were consistently good in bearing but, in many instances, the distances were uniformly one chain long per each half mile. This can best be accounted for by supposing that a surveying assistant (chainman) carried eleven pins, instead of ten, forward from a given monument and used all eleven of them on the first tally. Thus in four tallies, there would be forty-one spaces between the pins instead of forty. The monumentation was also poor. In the early 1870's the surveys were well done; however, the period of the 1880's had some of the worst surveys.[76]

In a resurvey that followed the old Santa Fe Trail, it was obvious that when the original survey had been made the marked monument rocks had been tossed off each side of a wagon as it traversed a winding road. One flat rock, about 18 inches by 18 inches, lay broken as it fell on another rock on the ground.[77] This survey, in T.15N, R.10E, was made by William White in 1884. An examination of the field notes and plat of this survey shows that White was supposed to follow the road, and did, but the field notes do not accurately describe the line.[78] Perhaps Deputy Surveyor White was using a technique sometimes resorted to. This practice consisted of tying a red cloth to a wagon wheel and, by counting the number of revolutions of the wheel, arriving at surveyed distances. As unorthodox as it sounds, this method could be surprisingly accurate on flat ground; however, it was hardly sanctioned by the surveying manual and relied too much on the diligent counting of the revolutions of the wagon wheel.[79]

In many instances it was evident that no original survey had been made at all. One of these was T.15S, R.4E, in southern Socorro County, made by Pearce and Coleman in 1882. The resurvey was made by Donald Harding, *et al.*, in 1936 and 1937. Harding found

76. *Ibid.*, December 14, 1954.

77. *Ibid.*, March 23, 1954.

78. Surveyors General, *Survey Plats of Townships*, (B.L.M.). On other surveys White did a good job.

79. Personal interview, Wallace Bisbee, March 10, 1954.

all the corners of the east boundary of this township but no other monuments, either exterior or subdivisional.[80]

Atkinson did not always follow regulations concerning awarding of surveying contracts. On October 21, 1880, he let a contract to Max Frost.[81] All deputy surveyors were required to certify that they personally, with the necessary assistance, performed all of the surveying work in their contracts. This Frost certified but he did not do the work. He was on hand part of the time, but Charles Easley and William Marland did the surveying. There is doubt that Frost was a surveyor at all; at any rate, his bad eyesight disqualified him from making a Government survey.[82] He was later completely blind.[83]

A similar case occurred in 1882, when Holden R. Warner had contracts for surveys near the southern boundary of the Territory, south of Carlsbad. In the same year he also had contracts in the San Juan River area, in the northwest part of the Territory, as well as in other regions. In each instance he had a different partner. The Territory was too large, and transportation too slow, for him personally to have made all these surveys as he was supposed to have done and as he certified that he did.[84]

Particular inaccuracies sometimes tended to average out over an entire survey. An example is the base line in the vicinity of Fort Sumner. Errors in short distances were greater than the inaccuracy of the entire survey.

There was a feeling among the surveyors of the 1880's that much of the surveyed land would never be used for anything anyhow, so they were inclined to be careless with the surveys. In justice to the deputies, it might be said that the pay was inadequate for really careful work.[85]

---

80. Personal interview, Land Office personnel, December 14, 1954. Surveyors General, *Survey Plats of Townships;* Deputy Surveyors, *Field Note Books* (B.L.M.).

81. Atkinson to Williamson, 10/21/80 (B.L.M.).

82. Secretary of the Interior, *Fraudulent Acquisition of Titles to Land in New Mexico,* 48 Cong., 2 Sess., *S.E.D.* No. 106, 331-332. Report of Inspector Frank D. Hobbs.

83. Personal interview, Land Office personnel, May 10, 1955.

84. *Ibid.,* December 14, 1954.

85. *Ibid.,* December 22, 1954. The idea that the land would not be useful is, of course, at variance with Atkinson's certification that it fell within the classification prescribed by Congress.

In short, the surveys under Atkinson were not conducted in a creditable manner. However, he held office at a time when such practices were characteristic of the entire surveying service and particularly that of the West.[86]

Clarence Pullen succeeded Atkinson on July 29, 1884.[87] His administration was short and a large percentage of the surveys executed under his guidance had already been contracted for by Atkinson. He was still serving under Noah C. McFarland, a Republican Commissioner of the General Land Office, and it was not politically opportune to be too frank in criticism of the fellow Republican he had relieved as surveyor general. He did try to clean up the surveying service in the Territory by ordering some deputies to correct errors in their work and by conducting a number of forthright investigations of surveying contractors. At times, when it would seem hardly avoidable, he voiced cautious condemnation of the work conducted by Atkinson. In relation to contract No. 196 dated August 15, 1883, he wrote, "The original notes I cannot accept as they are so poorly written and unintelligible, and further, the dates show that the survey was made within three days which is an impossibility."[88]

Pullen also tried to clean up irregularities of the deposit system in his district. Deputy Surveyor J. M. McLaughlin, of Tucson, Arizona, wrote and frankly asked if he might be awarded a surveying contract if he could induce some settlers, near the Arizona border, to make deposits for the same. Surveyor General Pullen pointedly informed the deputy that any action on the part of a deputy surveyor to induce settlers to make deposits for surveys was strictly irregular and would subject that deputy to having his commission revoked.[89]

It is evident, though, that his reform policies were not energetic enough to suit William A. J. Sparks, who became Commissioner of the General Land Office in 1885. The latter rebuked Pullen for submitting a group of ten townships, for survey authorization, in which each township had only one settler as an applicant. The only evidence that even this one applicant was an actual settler took the form of a mere formal affidavit. Sparks concluded a long and de-

---

86. Dunham, *Government Handout,* Chap. XII.
87. Pullen to McFarland, 7/29/84 (B.L.M.).
88. *Ibid.,* 8/22/84.
89. Pullen to Deputy Surveyor J. M. McLaughlin, 12/8/84 (F.R.C.).

tailed letter by ordering Pullen to see that the deposit system of survey was "legitimately and lawfully used . . .," and not misused, either for procuring speculative contracts or as an aid in the unlawful acquiring of land to be used for other than settlement purposes.[90]

The General Land Office, by a regulation of June 24, 1885, abolished blank forms in applying for public surveys and reserved the right to pass specifically on each application;[91] furthermore, it required detailed information:

FIRST. The character of the land, whether mineral, cultivable, grazing, timber, desert, swamps, mountainous, rocky, etc.

SECOND. The number of settlers in the township or townships.

THIRD. The character and duration of their inhabitancy of the land.

FOURTH. The extent and value of their improvements.

FIFTH. The uses made of the land and the quantity under cultivation.[92]

The result of this regulation was to abolish entirely the deposit system in New Mexico soon after Pullen left office.

In 1885 President Cleveland, in a letter of May 11, asked George W. Julian to accept either the office of Governor or that of Surveyor General of New Mexico. Cleveland considered the office of surveyor general the more important of the two.[93]

Julian, who had cast his first presidential ballot for General Harrison in 1840,[94] was seventy years old when, on July 22, 1885, he assumed the duties of his new office.[95] He was a politician and a *good* Government man, and tried to comply with the details of the law as he saw it. Above all, he could not be *bought* at any price. It was undoubtedly this unimpeachable honesty that endeared him so little to his contemporaries in New Mexico. Some historians have judged him too harshly.[96] Evidence was everywhere at hand that the

---

90. Sparks to Pullen, 6/6/85 (N.A.).

91. George W. Julian, Surveyor General of New Mexico, to Messrs. McKeyes and Washington, Deming, N.M., 7/1/89 (F.R.C.).

92. Julian to J. A. Armstrong, Joseph, N.M., 2/4/89 (F.R.C.). Julian wrote a large number of letters explaining this regulation of the General Land Office.

93. Julian, "Land Stealing in New Mexico," *North American Review*, 145:2.

94. Julian, *Political Recollections, 1840-1872*, 11.

95. William A. Keleher, *Maxwell Land Grant*, 125.

96. Ralph Emerson Twitchell, *The Leading Facts of New Mexican History*, Vol. II, 462, accuses Julian of being steeped in prejudice against New Mexico and its people and acting in a partisan and political manner.

public domain was being harvested by fraud at an unprecedented rate. "No early problem of his Administration worried Cleveland so much as this wholesale spoliation of the West."[97] This worry was honestly shared by Julian and he acted vigorously to save the public lands so they could be dispensed in the manner prescribed by existing laws.

He was a leading exponent of the homestead principle as it applied to the fertile regions of the Midwest; nevertheless, when he saw conditions in New Mexico for himself, he was realistic enough to realize that much of the land was suitable only for grazing.[98] He was not opposed to the honest settler who desired to make a living, be it raising cows or corn; but he wholeheartedly resented the success of a few in amassing enormous landed estates by the manipulation of the land laws.

His work in relation to the public surveys was particularly trying. The ratio of land settled to land surveyed was much higher under Julian than under his predecessor, Henry M. Atkinson (Appendixes III-VI). This made a difficult problem for Julian. While tremendous acreages had been surveyed, there was a dearth of surveyed areas for the increasing number of settlers. At the same time, appropriations for surveys were meager and the deposit system, which had been productive of much fraud, was sharply regulated by instructions laid down in a Land Office circular of June 24, 1885; furthermore, settlers were urged not to use it.[99] As a result, the deposit system ceased under Julian.[100]

Julian strove earnestly to take care of the demands of actual settlers.[101] On the other hand, he had little patience with requests for surveys not for actual settlers. In one case, ten or fifteen settlers desired to locate in T.22N, R.21E. He replied, "you are informed that I am not authorized, under existing regulations, to make surveys for the accommodation of prospective settlers. Whenever you and your friends become *actual* settlers upon the township men-

97. Allan Nevins, *Grover Cleveland: A Study in Courage*, 225.
98. Julian to Commissioner of the General Land Office, 7/2/89 (B.L.M.).
99. Julian to Mrs. Mary E. Cox, Gila, N.M., 2/18/89 (F.R.C.).
100. *S.G.R.* 7/26/88, 50 Cong., 2 Sess., *H.E.D.* No. 1, 476 (2636).
101. Julian to G. F. Black, Patterson, N.M., 1/31/87 (B.L.M.); Julian to Wm. H. Hugo, Fort Bayard, N. M., 2/7/88; and Julian to O. E. Harney, Springer, N. M., 2/6/88 (F.R.C.). Such specific examples are in sharp contrast to Atkinson's vague references to settlers.

tioned, the survey desired can be made."[102] Again, he received a request for the survey of several townships which stated that some of the settlers were located on the tract and that several settlements had been made within the townships. "This information is not sufficient," he stated, "as I am required to know the exact number of settlers that would be accommodated by any proposed survey."[103]

He was not as careful, however, to survey only areas strictly arable in nature (Maps 4-5). Atkinson had surveyed large quantities of non-arable land and certified that they had been arable. Julian and his superiors in Washington, on the other hand, recognized some grazing land as being within the agricultural class even though the law clearly stated otherwise. Julian thus attained, to a lesser degree, the same results as Atkinson in the matter of surveying grazing land.[104]

The appointment of William A. J. Sparks as Commissioner of the General Land Office, in 1885, set up a storm of controversy with rabid exponents on both sides. He is usually ridiculed for his reform measures. On April 3, 1885, he suspended final action on all land entries. This suspension has generally been given a significance out of all proportion to any real hardship it may have caused actual settlers.[105]

The blanket suspension was modified on December 3 of the same year;[106] nevertheless, suspension of surveys and entries in specified areas was continued for several years. Suspended entries were not new in New Mexico, several having been carried out under Commissioner McFarland;[107] under Sparks they were much greater in numbers and in area covered.

There were two main reasons for the suspension of entries. Filings in areas where fraud was reported or suspected were halted pending the investigation of the suspected cases, and at times entries were stopped until inadequate or fraudulent surveys could be checked.

---

102. Julian to T. W. Fassler, Kendall, Kansas, 4/18/87 (B.L.M.).

103. Julian to C. Toner, Marmelito, N. M., 3/15/87 (B.L.M.).

104. In some instances Julian considered grazing land to be within the legal classification for agricultural use, for example, see Julian to S. M. Stockslager, Commissioner of the General Land Office, 7/2/89 (B.L.M.); and Stockslager to Julian, 5/13/89 (N.A.).

105. Dunham, *Government Handout,* Chap. X, *passim.*

106. *L.O.R.* 9/17/89, 51 Cong., 1 Sess., *H.E.D.* No. 1, 5 (2724).

107. McFarland to register and receiver at Las Cruces, 2/28/84 (F.R.C.), an example suspending entries in T. 6S, R.12E.

Surveys were suspended because examination revealed them to be faulty or because there was reason to believe that they were not made for the benefit of actual settlers. In a great many instances, requests for surveys were never approved if it was felt that they would benefit other than bona fide settlers.[108]

Edward F. Hobart replaced Julian on September 7, 1889,[109] and served until August 2, 1893.[110] He came into office with the Republican administration of Benjamin Harrison, but did not alter policies greatly from those of his Democratic predecessor. Toward the end of his tenure, Julian had been plagued by the need of a number of resurveys of work that either had been poorly done or in which the monumentation had been destroyed. Hobart faced this same problem.[111] Julian's policy of confining surveys to those for actual settlers was continued just as sincerely by Hobart. Furthermore, he probably was even more careful to survey only strictly agricultural land (Maps 4-5).[112] The policy was likewise continued of carefully examining all surveying returns and work in the field.[113] It is evident that the extremely loose practices of the early 1880's were at an end.

---

108. A great deal of correspondence between the commissioner, surveyor general, and registers and receivers, explains these circumstances.

109. Edward F. Hobart, Surveyor General of New Mexico, to Commissioner of the General Land Office, 9/7/89 (B.L.M.).

110. Surveyor General Charles F. Easley to Commissioner of the General Land Office, 8/2/93 (F.R.C.).

111. *S.G.R.* 7/19/90, 431, in *L.O.R.* 9/13/90.

112. Hobart to J. T. McWhirt, Steins Pass, N.M., 12/20/89 (F.R.C.).

113. Lewis A. Groff, Commissioner of the General Land Office, to Hobart, 2/11/90 (N.A.).

3. The Donation Act of 1854

DONATIONS OF LAND to actual settlers were made in Florida and in the territories of Oregon, Washington, and New Mexico as a means of public defense. They were calculated to promote the military strength of settlements exposed to attacks by Indian tribes.[1]

The legislation allowing for donations in New Mexico was contained in the second, third, and fourth sections of the act establishing the office of Surveyor General of New Mexico. By the provisions of these sections, 160 acres of land was granted to every white male citizen of the United States over twenty-one years of age, or to such person who had declared his intention of becoming a citizen, who was residing in the Territory prior to January 1, 1853, and who was resident there at the time the act was passed on July 22, 1854. These conditions were also to apply to persons moving into the Territory between January 1, 1853, and January 1, 1858. Donation claims were filed with the surveyor general until 1860, when the records were transferred to the register and receiver.[2] The most important qualification for securing a donation was continuous residence and cultivation for a period of not less than four years. In addition, the claim was required to be located on surveyed land; and, in case of settlement prior to survey, the land had to be selected by legal subdivisions within three months after the survey. If settlement was made after the survey, the condition of selection had to be made not later than three months after settlement.

In the case of persons living in the Territory prior to January 1, 1853, the four years of continued settlement and cultivation were counted from the date of settlement and might, therefore, have been

---

1. *S.I.R.* 12/2/58, 35 Cong., 2 Sess., *H.E.D.* No. 2, 73 (997).

2. Joseph S. Wilson to Wilbar, 11/8/60 (N.A.). The authority for this transfer was the Act of May 24, 1858, creating the land office at Santa Fe.

completed before the passage of the law. In that case, upon proper application and proof, the person was entitled to a certificate as soon as the land was surveyed. For persons moving into New Mexico after that date, the four-year period started with the date of actual settlement and cultivation. In either case, upon a death prior to the lapse of the four-year period, the right in question descended to the heirs.

Claimants of Mexican or Spanish land grants were not allowed to file for a donation claim. Likewise, holders of donations were excluded from pre-emptions or homesteads, on the grounds that both classes required actual settlement and cultivation and one person could not fulfill these requirements on two claims. A donation claimant could, however, relinquish his claim and file the same land under the Homestead or Pre-emption Laws.[3]

The first application for a donation claim that fulfilled all the requirements stipulated by law, and thus resulted in a notification, was made by Pinckney R. Tulley on December 22, 1858. This was for 160 acres in Section 34, T.18S, R. 4W, in present Doña Ana County. Along with a number of others, it was abandoned and finally forfeited on August 7, 1870. The first donation certificate was issued to James T. Johnson on July 18, 1870, for 160 acres of land in Section 6, T.18N, R.20E,[4] near the south boundary of Mora County.

Actually there were a number of applications for donation claims prior to Tulley's notification. No less than thirteen were made in

---

3. *Stat. L.,* Vol. X, 308-310; McFarland to register and receiver, Mesilla, 1/23/83 (F.R.C.).

4. Registers and receivers, *Abstract of Donation Notifications* (F.R.C. and N.A.). *S.G.R.* 9/30/56, 34 Cong., 3 Sess., *H.E.D.* No. 5, 523, 524 (875), and *S.G.R.* 9/30/57, 35 Cong., 2 Sess., *H.E.D.* No. 11, 260 (919), record 80 applications through September 10, 1857. Six of these are marked as entitled to patent, but merely on the basis of length of settlement. no mention being made of other qualifications. The *Abstract of Donation Notifications* starts with No. 1, indicating that the previous 80 applications were not eligible for notification.

Benjamin Hibbard, *A History of the Public Land Policies,* 354, gives the acreage of donations as 20,105. He does not state the source of his information but it undoubtedly was the Public Lands Commission, *Final Report,* 1881, 297. This figure is through June 30, 1880, only. The final figure for donation certificates was 51,989 acres (338 entries) through the final entry in 1884. There were also 73,298 acres (465 entries) in donation notifications through the final entry in 1882.

1855, the first year that the surveyor general's office was opened. These could not be accepted because the claimants did not actually live on the land they claimed. They lived in settlements, away from the land they cultivated, for the protection of their lives and property from attacks by Indians.

Another difficulty confronting donation claimants was the requirement that the land be surveyed. Most of the land in the vicinity of the settlements had already been reduced to private property, so if settlers removed to a distance from the settlements, there were constant disputes concerning boundaries, which were difficult to settle when the land was surveyed.

A third problem was that donation claims located on private land claims could not be honored due to the extreme slowness with which title to private claims was settled. When making application for a donation, no one could be certain that he was not locating on a private claim.[5]

As early as 1858, Secretary of the Interior Jacob Thompson had urged that the Donation Act be discontinued. It had been initiated as a means of public defense, but proved fallacious as a measure of public policy. The length of residence required and other conditions imposed on claimants caused complications in settling the titles of the donations themselves, as well as trouble and delay in settling titles to adjacent lands.[6] Surveyor General Pelham had earlier reported these troubles to exist.[7]

It also became a potent instrument for fraud. Celso Baca received donation certificate No. 4, in 1870, and made a homestead entry in 1876. It was against the law to acquire a homestead in addition to a donation. Even then Baca was not content, and in 1881 his name appeared on another homestead entry. Related to Baca's activities were the donation entry and homestead entry of Marcelino Moya. The first was filed in 1870, the second in 1876. Neither of these was proved up. In May of 1881 he made another homestead entry and made final proof in June of that year. In December of the same year, his name was on still another entry. Strangely enough, Moya

---

5. *S.G.R.* 9/30/57, 35 Cong., 1 Sess., *H.E.D.* No. 11, 256 (919).
6. *S.I.R.* 12/2/58, 35 Cong., 2 Sess., *H.E.D.* No. 2, 73, 74 (997).
7. *S.G.R.* 9/15/58, 35 Cong., 2 Sess., *H.E.D.* No. 2, 299 (997).

was an invalid who had not been out of bed for several years and who lived in the house of Celso Baca.[8] There is no doubt that Moya was a tool of Baca, who possessed the lands thus entered.

Witnesses swore that Moya had lived on the land since before January 1, 1858, and in the same statement, they mentioned that they had known the applicant for six or seven years only. In other cases different signatures appeared in the same handwriting—many written near the bottom of the sheet, indicating that the proof had been filled in afterward.[9]

On August 21, 1880, John Gwyn made donation entry No. 164, in T.14N, R.8E, southwest of Santa Fe, representing the date of settlement as June 10, 1879. The land involved was marked on the plats in the land office as mineral land; moreover, it was well known that Gwyn had been for years past, and was at the time, a resident of Santa Fe. He was also a large owner in land grants. About this time Gwyn's brother, Thomas, who was in charge of the register's office, filed a pre-emption declaratory statement on land that was also mineral. He likewise had never resided upon the land filed on.[10]

In 1884, Land Inspector Frank D. Hobbs ventured the opinion that not over two per cent of the 457 donation applications on file were valid claims. Of 332 land claims investigated by Special Agent H. H. Eddy in 1883, only that of Juan Martinez, T.19N, R.30E, was a donation. On it were some crumbling walls of an adobe building that had never been roofed and had long been abandoned.[11]

When registers' and receivers' monthly abstracts of donation notifications and certificates are examined, certain entries stand out because they were made in the same township on the same date. This could happen occasionally by chance, but when they appear in this manner regularly it prompts the question, did all the neighbors ride to town the same day to file on donation claims? It is more prob-

8. Secretary of the Interior, *Fraudulent Acquisition of Titles to Land in New Mexico,* 1885, 48 Cong., 2 Sess., *S.E.D.* No. 106, 19 (letter from Elias Brevoort, Receiver of the Land Office at Santa Fe, to Commissioner McFarland, December 5, 1881).

9. *Ibid.,* 23.

10. *Ibid.* In 1871-72, John Gwyn purchased 1,913.60 acres of land at private entry, and with Robert B. Willison, another 938.23 acres during the same period.

11. *Ibid.,* 53, 349.

able that the entries were made in the interest of someone bent on acquiring more land in the township than was legal.[12]

In 1880-81, when the cattle industry was starting its boom,[13] there was a sudden increase in donation entries. In 1880 there were 172 donation notifications and 162 donation certificates. Each group was more than in all the previous years combined (Appendix V). It was required by law that any settler, in order to avail himself of a donation, must have commenced his residence, settlement, and cultivation, in New Mexico not later than January 1, 1858. The question naturally arises as to why there were suddenly so many qualified donation entrants. True, the law did not stipulate when they were to file, but why had they waited 22 years after the final date that residence could be established? The answer is that they were not *bona fide* entrants. In 1882, Secretary of the Interior Teller affirmed that "it was the intent of Congress, in the passage of the New Mexico donation act, that all selections should be made under the act, and settlement and cultivation be commenced by the 1st day of January, 1858, that being the limit of the time within which the necessary residence could be acquired."[14]

As a result, in 1883, there was not a single donation notification or certificate. A lone certificate in 1884 closed the books on this class of land entry in New Mexico.

---

12. Registers and receivers, *Abstracts of Donation Notifications and Certificates* (N.A.).

Typical examples are the following donation notifications in the Santa Fe Land District:

Inclusive No. of Notification	Township and Range	Date
252-265	23 & 24 N - 32 & 33 E	July 31, 1880
344-351	18 N - 26 E	June 8, 1881
374-381	11 & 12 N - 24 E	August 18, 1881
390-398	24 N - 16 E	October 3, 1881
406-414	23 N - 18, 19 & 20 E	October 27, 1881
425-431	17 N - 24 E	November 7, 1881

13. Western Range Cattle Industry Study, *New Mexico Cattle Corporations, 1871-1900*, Summary, Ms.

14. *L.O.R.* 9/29/83, 48 Cong., 1 Sess., *H.E.D.* No. 1, 209 (2190). Decision, November 29, 1882, in the case of Juan Rafael Garcia.

4. The Homestead Act of 1862

THE HOMESTEAD ACT with its principle of free land for actual settlers was the inevitable culmination of national and regional pressures. Tolerance toward squatters, donations to pioneers on the
frontier, and modifications of the pre-emption privileges favorable
to the settler—all pointed to free land. Generosity, subsidization,
natural rights, class struggle, and expediency were coordinately
parts of the pressure.

The 160 acres allowed was based on the theoretical amount of
land required by the head of a family to make a living in a typically
fertile farming community. But New Mexico was arid and 160 acres
was not nearly enough. Therein lay the great weakness of the Homestead Act. The idea of small farms here was a tenacious eastern
dream and wholly untenable, so the Homestead Law became another way of acquiring large amounts of grazing land.

During the decade of the 1880's cattle raising became the great
bonanza. Newspapers, periodicals, and livestock journals pointed
out the large profits to be made in that business. It was said that an
investment of five thousand dollars would net the investor a profit
of forty or fifty thousand dollars in four years. Within that time a
calf worth five dollars could be matured at little cost on the grass of
the public domain and sold for forty or fifty dollars.[1]

Acquiring a stock range was a simple matter in the early days of
the industry before the country became crowded with cattle. It was
only necessary to secure title to an available water supply in order
to control land for miles around as surely as though that land were
actually owned. In this way the public domain was used without
the payment of any tax.[2]

---

1. Dan Elbert Clark, *The West in American History,* 596.
2. *G.N.M.* 9/6/83, 48 Cong., 1 Sess., *H.E.D.* No. 1, 556 (2191).

During the late eighties and early nineties, cattle ranchers began to extend their private holdings. There were several reasons for this. As the ranges became overstocked, not only did the supply of grass dwindle but grazing areas became increasingly hard to control. Surpluses of cattle led to lower prices and droughts and bad seasons made inroads on the vast herds then in vogue. Many cattlemen found they could raise better beeves more economically through selective breeding and supplementary winter feeding. Also, land entries were being more widely made by those desiring to farm where it was possible and by persons desiring to get into the cattle-raising business. To protect their interests, established ranchers had to secure ownership of the land to meet the new competition.[3]

There were a number of ways in which this was done. In New Mexico as elsewhere it was possible for one person to acquire 1,120 acres of land by the legitimate use of the land laws. For instance, a settler could take out a homestead of 160 acres and secure a final certificate either by living on it for five years or by commuting it through payment of cash in six months. It was then possible to move to a pre-emption claim and acquire another 160 acres with six months' residence and the payment of $1.25 per acre. At the same time the settler might be fulfilling the requirements for a timber-culture claim of 160 acres and a desert land claim of 640 acres, neither of which required residence as a condition of securing title. Any person of requisite age, even though in the same family, could take out an additional desert land entry. In some regions another 160 acres was available by application of the Timber and Stone Act of 1878, but this law did not apply in New Mexico. The Donation Law of 1854 provided another means of acquiring land, but both a donation and pre-emption or homestead could not be acquired by the same person. The land laws became so complicated that a shrewd businessman had a decided advantage over a settler in acquiring large properties through their use.[4] These possibilities were well known at the time the laws were being most widely used.[5]

---

3. Clark, *The West in American History*, 597; Hinkle, *Early Days of a Cowboy on the Pecos*, 20; G.N.M. 10/10/88, 50 Cong., 2 Sess., *H.E.D.* No. 1, 844 (2639).

4. Fred A. Shannon, "The Homestead Act and the Labor Surplus," *American Historical Review*, 41:646.

5. John T. Ganoe, "The Desert Land Act in Operation, 1877-1891," *Agricultural History*, 11:144. Both the Public Lands Commission, *Preliminary Re-*

Some land was sold at private entry and public auction, but such sales did not bring a quick turnover of land, which indicates that other available methods were adequate and just as advantageous. These sales were minor in the aggregate.

In amounts in excess of the legal limits established by the land laws, title to public land could be acquired only by purchase from persons who had secured it by compliance with the land laws. The alternative was fraud; nevertheless, there was a legal procedure by which land could be exclusively used without securing title to it. Since final proof of a settler's compliance with the land laws was not required until submission for patent, an applicant (irrespective of the veracity of his application) was protected in the use of the land (providing fraud was not established by Government officials) from the time when he made an original application, until the time when the law required that he apply for a patent. This period ranged from seven years for a homestead entry to thirteen years for a timber-culture claim. Meanwhile, exclusive grazing and watering rights were enjoyed by the applicant. A fraudulent entry was difficult to detect because an application was made with the use of an affidavit and no inspection of the land was made by the register of the land office with whom the affidavit was filed. Accidental discovery of fraud was not likely because of the large size of the district under the jurisdiction of the register. If the register was dishonest, or was not competent in the keeping of his records, and the expiration of an application went unnoticed until someone else made an application for the same land, the period of protected use of the land might in practice be even longer than the time established by law. It was not unusual that an entrant under the land laws would have accumulated by this time enough wealth from the use of the land that it was not a matter of great concern to him if a patent was never issued.[6] As a result of these contingencies, approximately twice as much land benefited applicants under the land laws as was of benefit to them by the securing of patents to land (Appendix VI).

Some of the large holdings of grazing land were procured by purchase from homesteaders or pre-emptors who failed on their claim

---

port, 1879, 46 Cong., 2 Sess., *H.E.D.* No. 46, IX (1923), and *Final Report,* 1881, 46 Cong., 3 Sess., *H.E.D.* No. 47, 411 (1975), note this possibility.

6. J. A. Stinson, ranch superintendent, to J. D. Whitney, president of the New Mexico Land and Cattle Company, 12/3/83, *President's Report,* 5/12/84, 12 (W.R.C.I.S.).

and sold out to ranchers. There were always a number of misin-formed or stubborn settlers who insisted on trying to grow crops where none could be grown.

In the early 1880's, ranchers were usually bitter toward settlers because they were changing the old ways of the free range; but as it became evident that private holdings must be developed to meet competition, the wiser ranchers changed their attitude. Settlers were not then always looked upon with disfavor by the cattlemen, who knew that most of them must eventually give up their efforts to be dirt farmers. If these settlers could be encouraged to remain long enough to prove up their claims before leaving, the ranchers could buy the land, although they could not legally acquire it other-wise. Some settlers had this in mind from the beginning and others were rapidly *educated* by crop failures. This *education* was painful and most settlers were inclined to move away and let their land go back to the Government. If ranchers could encourage them to stay long enough to procure title, both would benefit: the rancher by acquiring the land, and the settler by some remuneration for his patience and effort in acquiring title to it.

An example of this type of encouragement was afforded by the Blanchard brothers west of Roswell. They allowed settlers to haul water from the Blanchard wells, and even invited the settlers' children to attend their own private school. William C. McDonald, later first governor of the state, adopted similar practices, as did the MacGillivray brothers, 50 miles southeast of Estancia.[7] Frederic Gerhardt, an early pioneer near Fort Sumner, told newcomers that they could not possibly make a living on a quarter-section of land. Most would not believe him and settled where not even a well was available. Gerhardt provided these people with water until he didn't have enough for himself.[8] At the Bar T Ranch, near Lords-burg, John and Emma Muir said that they:

---

7. Personal interview, Land Office personnel, December 22, 1954. The first homestead application was made by Henry B. Porter on August 7, 1868. This entry was located in Section 30 of T.20S, R.10W, and was for 160 acres. He pre-empted and paid for his claim on January 21, 1871, becoming the first person in the Territory to own land by virtue of the Homestead Act of 1862. The first five-year homestead that was proved up was claimed by Lawrence G. ✔ Murphy in Sections 32 and 33 of T.10S, R.17E. The certificate for this quarter-section was dated March 3, 1873.

8. Lillie Gerhardt Anderson, "A New Mexico Pioneer of the 1880's," *New Mexico Historical Review*, 29:254.

got on famously with the homesteaders. We sent them beef when we butchered and helped them in every way possible. We really welcomed their coming, but we knew they could not make a living as farmers, no matter how much of that dry land the Government gave them. As soon as they proved up they would be willing to sell, for they did not have enough money to become cattlemen. That is the way it turned out. Because of our friendly attitude, the homesteaders always offered their property to us first.[9]

Another reason for encouraging settlers was that they usually brought a certain amount of money with them when they moved here to settle. Some of it came back to them if they proved up a claim and sold out; meanwhile, it added to the economy of the Territory.

Some homesteaders were farsighted enough to acquire a herd of their own and get into the ranching business, as did the Stratey family, for example, in the vicinity of Ancho, near Corona. They had a store at Ancho and eventually acquired probably 10,000 acres of grazing land.[10]

But not all homesteads were entered by legitimate settlers. In the decade of the 1880's, the population of New Mexico increased by 33,601.[11] Since only 35 per cent of this increase was engaged in agriculture,[12] only 11,760 can be considered as prospective farmers. At a contemporarily calculated figure of four persons per family,[13] 2,940 would be eligible to take out a homestead. But in these ten years, there were 5,740 original homestead entries and in the same period there were 6,937 pre-emption declarations. These required a residence of five years for a homestead and six months for a pre-emption to acquire title. During the same period there were 1,547 timber-culture and 1,207 desert land entries (Appendixes IV and V); for these no residence was required.

Over-all figures are nearly as startling. In 1890, the population of

9. Emma Marble Muir, "Pioneer Ranch," *New Mexico Magazine,* June 1958, 63.

10. Personal interview, Land Office personnel, December 22, 1954.

11. *G.N.M.* 9/15/90, 51 Cong., 2 Sess., *H.E.D.* No. 1, 595 (2842).

12. Richard J. Hinton, *Irrigation in the United States, Progress Report for 1890,* 1891, 51 Cong., 2 Sess., *S.E.D.* No. 53, 62 (2818), adapted from the *Album of Agricultural Statistics,* Department of Agriculture, 1889; *X Census* (Population) 768, 769; *XI Census* (Population) 324, 325.

13. *G.N.M.* 9/15/90, 51 Cong., 2 Sess., *H.E.D.* No. 1, 594 (2842).

New Mexico was 153,076 persons (exclusive of tribal Indians), or about 158,000 in 1891.[14] Since only 35 per cent of the population in the Territory was engaged in agriculture,[15] only 55,300 can be further considered. This figure is further reduced by deduction of residents of the more than 5,000 small-holding claims in the Territory who had a settled place of abode from which they almost certainly would not have removed to prove up a homestead. At four persons per family, their population would be 20,000. In this class were the 8,278 residents of the pueblos who were almost entirely agricultural and were permanently located.[16] Also deducted are the 1,461 soldiers stationed in the Territory at the time. The figure is now 25,561. Allowing a figure of four persons per family, there were 6,390 persons eligible to apply for homesteads. But there were 6,784 homesteads applied for, as well as 465 donations. All eligible persons, to comply with the residence requirements, would have had to leave a former home, move to the new land, build a house, and cultivate the soil. It is absurd to think that this happened; furthermore, the 6,784 homestead applicants would have had to establish six months residence on 7,657 pre-emptions. Of the 6,784 homesteads entered through 1891, only 3,702 were given final certificates through 1896 (when those entered in 1891 would normally be completed). Also, homesteads could be filed only in legally subdivided townships and the clamor for surveys was constant, indicating that many persons desired to make entries where the land was not surveyed. If they were waiting to file on unsurveyed land, it follows that they could not legally have filed on surveyed land.

Of the townships that had original entries by the close of 1891, about 53 per cent were not climatically capable of supporting the growth of crops, so could not have complied with the requirement of cultivation. By the end of 1896, of the townships that had final certificates, about 49 per cent were incapable of supporting crop growth and could not have complied with cultivation requirements (Maps 8-9). It should be borne in mind that much of the area climatically capable of raising crops was not suitable for that purpose because it was mountainous or timbered. The Homestead Law did not apply to timber land.

14. *Ibid.*, 595.

15. Hinton, *Irrigation in the United States*, 1891, 51 Cong., 2 Sess., *S.E.D.* No. 53, 62 (2818).

16. *G.N.M.* 9/15/90, 51 Cong., 2 Sess., *H.E.D.* No. 1, 590, 594, 595 (2842).

There were about 6 original entries per township at the close of 1891, and 5 final certificates at the end of 1896. This is an average. Any township capable of growing crops would have had more than 800 acres homesteaded out of a possible 23,040. Evidently much of the land was acquired in order to control wide-scattered sources of water, which would allow domination of the land for grazing, instead of for cultivation; and, since there were not nearly enough legitimate settlers to account for the amount of land entered, it follows that the entries were illegal.

In the more agrarian sections of the nation, fraud was committed by persons who wished to sell their ill-gotten gains. Fertile cropland was valuable, and speculating in it was frequently lucrative. In New Mexico, however, people wanted land for raising cattle. More particularly, they wanted land so they could control the sources of water for these cattle. In most cases these waterholes were valuable only for watering stock, since they would support little irrigation.

Because control of one waterhole could gain command over thousands of acres of grazing land, such control provided a good living for a family. Control of several watering places controlled more land and might bring wealth. This became the goal and achievement of some persons. Such was their greed that they knowingly broke the law in order to acquire whatever might and cunning would avail them.

The Civil War brought to the Territory a new and hardy breed of enterprising, shrewd, and resourceful young men, many with legal training and all with political acumen. Their goal was not the pittance of a quarter-section homestead.

The Treaty of Guadalupe Hidalgo of 1848 guaranteed property rights of former Mexican citizens. Holdings were of two classes. The great majority of the 80,000 people who became citizens of the United States upon the annexation of New Mexico were comparatively poor. Their chief claim to affluence was generally a small strip of irrigated land along some river or stream.

It was not these meager allotments that were at first sought generally by speculators; rather, they coveted the large grants made to individuals by former Spanish and Mexican governments. The new arrivals saw an opportunity for rapid gains, and life in the Territory became centered around traffic in these grants. Starting with the 1880's, because of a sharp increase in the cattle business, the public domain was to be used more extensively for personal gain;

however, in the earlier years private grants were a riper plum and more sought after for immediate picking. It is unfortunately true that as population increased in settled regions native inhabitants frequently pioneered on the public domain, in areas away from the older settlements, on land with a water supply. Many of them were ignorant of their rights under the land laws and paid for their lack of knowledge when cattle graziers filed on the land they had pio- ✓ neered upon and thus dispossessed them of their homes.

The process by which the United States would guarantee title to former Mexican citizens was, in theory, relatively simple. A grant claimant was required to submit his evidence of title to the surveyor general, who held hearings to determine the validity of the claim and then submitted his findings and recommendations to Congress, which body was responsible for the rendering of a final decision. In practice, this was not so simple, since from the first, numerous claimants suspiciously refused to submit their evidence of title. They believed (in many cases so informed by designing persons) that such action would not secure their titles and could lead to unnecessary labor and expense.[17]

Enter the clever Yankee newcomers. Their method was that of appearing to be benevolent advisors, and it was their practice to exaggerate the complexity of the confirmation process. They, grant claimants were assured, knew the ropes in Santa Fe and Washington and would gladly serve as attorneys to guide claims through the intricacies involved. In the absence of cash, land became the medium of payment for such services and fees came high indeed. Over 80 per cent of the Spanish and Mexican grants were lost to their owners. Not all were relinquished in legal fees; nevertheless, the same manipulators were involved throughout. A small group of politically powerful attorneys controlled Territorial politics, and taxes on real estate imposed after the American occupation became a burden on the land grants. There had been little if any such taxation under the former Governments.[18] With the scarcity of money,

---

17. *S.G.R.* 9/30/57, 35 Cong., 1 Sess., *H.E.D.* No. 11, 257 (919).

18. William A. Keleher, "Land Law of the New Mexico Land Grant," *New Mexico Historical Review,* 4:359, 367; Brayer, *William Blackmore,* 17-19; Public Lands Commission, *Preliminary Report,* 1879, 46 Cong., 2 Sess., *H.E.D.* No. 46, 451 (1923). Had Congress established a commission to adjudicate private land claims soon after the occupation by Americans, as was done in California, the confirmation process could have been relatively simple. As it was, Congress

it is understandable that large areas of choice grant land became available for purchase at prices far below the $1.25 per acre for public domain. Even without the burden of taxes, cash could secure land cheaply in money-hungry New Mexico.[19]

Another inducement for speculators to deal in land grants rather than the public domain was the comparative freedom of grant areas from Indian depredations. Grants were largely on the periphery of the settlements. This traffic in land grants worked to the detriment of the Territory.

The most significant economic factor in the history of territorial New Mexico prior to railroad transportation was the comparative lack of migration in comparison to that of California and Oregon. It may be argued that positive inducements for settlement were greater in the latter areas; nevertheless, there were negative factors in New Mexico of great importance.

Until about 1850, many Americans living east of the Mississippi River believed that because New Mexico lay in the same latitude as the southern states, it would be suitable for a similar economy. However, within a few years, travelers were informing readers otherwise and frequently in a manner that did not invite migration. William W. H. Davis, in his *El Gringo,* described New Mexico as "a desert land . . . almost as unfitted for agricultural purposes as Arabia."[20] Another writer noted the "deserts, parched mountains, poisonous reptiles, and wild Indians."[21] Attention was called to the hostility of the Indians and the low degree of culture of the native inhabitants, and to the fact that in the "rugged mountains and on the waste plains" it was not possible to "support a population in numbers and wealth at all proportioned to its extent of territory."[22]

But of far greater significance, prospective settlers soon learned that Spanish and Mexican grants of land covered most of the arable

---

was dilatory in settling the claims and neglected to appoint a proper commission; consequently, settlement of the claims became extremely complicated.

19. Brayer, *William Blackmore,* 22, 159. Blackmore became the outright owner of approximately 120,000 acres of the Cebolla Grant for $3,000.

20. Loomis Morton Ganaway, "New Mexico and the Sectional Controversy, 1846-1861," *New Mexico Historical Review,* 18:114.

21. *Ibid., Journal of William H. Richardson, a Private Soldier in the Campaign in New and Old Mexico.*

22. *Ibid.,* 120, George A. McCall, *Letters from the Frontier.*

areas upon which settlement was possible without undue danger from Indian attack. In New Mexico it was the spurious claims, instituted largely after American occupation, that proved the greatest deterrent to settlement. In contrast to California, where private claims were settled soon after American occupation, only 22 of 212 claims submitted in New Mexico were patented (and 8 rejected outright) prior to the adjudications of the Court of Private Land Claims, 1891-1904. This left nearly 35,000,000 acres of land privately claimed with consequent unsettled titles.[23]

Federal land laws decreed that any claims be reserved from settlement and public disposal until they were adjudicated by the Federal Government. As a consequence, settlers could never be certain that they were not settling on land that was claimed, or that might later be claimed, as a private grant. This situation was widely known throughout the nation and resulted in a "deep and acknowledged distrust of land titles in New Mexico . . ." that retarded immigration and the rapid settlement of the Territory. Likewise, owners of valid claims could realize only depreciated prices for their property. The only ones who stood to profit by the delay and uncertainty were the holders of doubtful claims, who had use of the land until the true ownership was legally determined.[24] For cattle ranching purposes, even this temporary use of land, in the large quantities involved, was of substantial value.

Then too, there was a large market for this land of doubtful title with foreign cattle-ranch investors, who frequently suffered in the transaction. By the close of the nineteenth century, losses to British and Scotch cattle-ranch investors in the western territories amounted to approximately $17,000,000 or $18,000,000, which they were only partially able to recoup in the twentieth century through the increment on land and profits from the rise in price of cattle.

The initial losses occurred because basically the prices paid for lands and herds were about four times actual value. Frequently the buyers paid for several times as many cattle as were delivered.[25] A tragic example of this shorting of the cattle count was the case of A. E. B. Sparrow. J. W. Lynch secured the Juan de Dios cattle ranch

---

23. *S.G.R.* 7/19/90, 435, in *L.O.R.* 9/13/90. *S.G.R.* 7/22/85, 49 Cong., 1 Sess., *H.E.D.* No. 1, 554-561 (2378).
24. *S.G.R.* 7/22/85, *Ibid.* 527, 528.
25. Maurice Frink, *et al., When Grass Was King*, 315, 264.

and "borrowed" a herd of some eighteen hundred head of cattle from various neighbors. He then negotiated with Sparrow and some associates for the sale of the cattle. On four successive days, followed by nights of partying, the prospective purchasers were taken in the cardinal directions from the ranch to examine the herds. What they did not know was that the "borrowed" herd was driven to a new location each night and that they examined the same herd four different times. Sparrow put $75,000 cash into the deal and was then informed that the cattle had drifted in a storm. They were never recovered. Sparrow was engaged to a young lady in Australia and they were to be married at the end of the year. The wedding never took place since Sparrow, having lost everything he owned, shot himself in the right temple and died instantly.[26]

Foreign investors were also hurt financially because titles to lands sold were frequently invalid.[27] In New Mexico the Court of Private Land Claims, from 1891 through 1904, validated only 1,934,986 acres of grant claims out of the 34,653,340 acres submitted for adjudication.[28]

The thirty-six-year delay on the part of Congress in clarifying titles to these grants was inexcusable. The report of every surveyor general, in that period, urged action in the matter without delay. This urging was, in turn, repeated by Commissioners of the General Land Office and Secretaries of the Interior. It was pointed out that of all known claims reported to Congress, "by far the most important. . ." were those in New Mexico, where the inhabitants were vitally interested in the final quieting of titles.[29]

The individuals who dealt in land grant manipulations came to be known collectively as the "Santa Fe Ring." They were Republican leaders who dominated territorial politics from the period following the Civil War through the 1880's. In the early years of this group's activities, it maintained remarkable cohesion. Political unity was a decided aid in acquiring large quantities of land in the Territory under the most favorable terms, so that it was mutually advantageous for the Ring members to support each other's claims

26. Miguel Antonio Otero, *My Life on the Frontier, 1882-1897*, 37-40.

27. Frink, *et al, When Grass Was King*, 230.

28. U.S. Attorney General, *Annual Report*, 12/1/04, 58 Cong., 3 Sess., *H.E.D.* No. 9, 96 (4811).

29. *L.O.R.* 9/23/91, 133.

to title. It was a common practice to have grants confirmed for much larger areas than was originally intended.[30] This meant adding large quantities of public domain to the original grant.

The former owners were natives who probably would not have thought of claiming more than their papers called for. The Ring, however, taught them new tricks, and the old saying of the Mexicans was verified: *En pais de los ciegos el tuerto es rey.* (In the land of the blind the one-eyed is king.) [31]

The Ring arose out of common interests in land matters, and the remarkable solidarity of the group was eventually shattered by divided concern over land. Their unanimity of purpose could be maintained in the comparative isolation of a railroadless Territory when the group was small and a common desire for riches was stronger than individual differences. The advent of railroad transportation caused a rapid increase in economic development and brought new blood into the Territory, along with new alignments in the ranks of the formerly faithful Ring members.

It has been held that the Democratic administration of Grover Cleveland, in 1885, and the appointment of Edmund G. Ross as Governor, and George W. Julian as surveyor general, marked the decline of Ring influence. Nevertheless, there were important factors in that decline prior to 1885.

It is clear that the solid front of party bosses was cracking from within as early as the Republican Garfield-Arthur administration of 1881-85. This administration set in motion the wheels of land fraud cleanup through local officials in New Mexico. This took time, and the following Democratic administration has too generally been given entire credit for the reforms brought about (Chapter IX).

It must be said that while this book is a severe indictment of the tactics of some American newcomers to the Territory, dilatory and unrealistic procedures by the Federal Government made these tactics possible. These Americans should be judged by the standards

---

30. Harold H. Dunham, "New Mexican Land Grants with Special Reference to the Title Papers of the Maxwell Land Grant," *New Mexico Historical Review*, 30:14. G. B. Anderson, Compl. *History of New Mexico, Its Resources and People*, Vol. 1, 171.

31, Governor's Papers, Edmund G. Ross, State Records Center, Santa Fe, New Mexico. Letter from Ross to John O'Grady, St. Louis, Mo., March 26, 1887.

of that era. National morality was lax and in New Mexico the law was largely what these men made it. By the standards of that day, their reaction to their environment was commonplace.

From 1869 through 1884 the Santa Fe Ring had connections with Republican Land Office officials to their mutual benefit. The more important of these officials were T. Rush Spencer, James K. Proudfit, Henry M. Atkinson (all surveyors general), and Max Frost, register of the Land Office.

Three important members of the Santa Fe Ring were Stephen B. Elkins, Thomas B. Catron and Stephen W. Dorsey. Elkins, Catron's law partner, was a dealer in land grants and was charged with influencing the surveys of these grants so that they appeared to contain hundreds of thousands of acres that did not belong to them. His strongest weapon to that end was manipulation of committees in Congress. He, along with Catron, Frank Springer, Stephen W. Dorsey, and others, was involved with the Maxwell Land Grant, which Secretary of the Interior Cox, in 1869, had decided contained about 96,000 acres. Under the legal guidance and direction of Elkins and his associates, the grant was surveyed and patented for 1,714,764 acres.[32] Furthermore, Elkins attempted to use his influence to have this grant and others surveyed at the public expense.[33]

Catron's land grant dealings laid the foundation for his fortune.[34] He was a recognized captain in this controlling New Mexican industry.[35] "Many of the descriptions of the old Spanish and Mexican land grants had been very loosely worded, and Catron had shown great ingenuity in interpreting them to the advantage of his clients and himself."[36] With over 1,000,000 acres of land, he was one of the largest landowners in the nation. The Tierra Amarilla Grant, with 593,000 acres in New Mexico and Colorado, was his largest single possession.[37] A shrewd and able lawyer, he probably represented more clients in land litigation than any other person in the

32. Anderson, *History of New Mexico*, Vol. 1, 186; Dunham, *Government Handout*, 214-238.

33. *S.G.R.* 9/15/74, 43 Cong., 2 Sess., *H.E.D.* No. 1, 119 (1639).

34. Brayer, *William Blackmore*, 167.

35. Julian, "Land Stealing in New Mexico," *North American Review*, 145:28.

36. Otero, *My Nine Years as Governor of the Territory of New Mexico, 1897-1906*, 142.

37. Vioalle Clark Hefferan, *Thomas Benton Catron*, Ms. (M.A. thesis) 24.

history of the Territory. His influence throughout New Mexico was great. He guarded his interests in Lincoln County in the 1870's,[38] and, at the same time that other territorial officials were fired from various offices late in 1878, he resigned as United States District Attorney after a Federal investigation of the Lincoln County War.[39] Early that year, he had been asked for a detailed explanation of the troubled affairs in Lincoln County. Annoyed by lack of compliance with this request, "official Washington authorized an independent investigation."[40] Catron's reluctance to report on affairs in Lincoln County can be explained by his own involvements there. He held a mortgage on the property of the Murphy-Dolan mercantile and ranching interests (one of the factions in the fighting)[41] and was himself a considerable cattle owner in the vicinity.[42]

Dorsey, who is remembered for his relations with the Star Route mail frauds, was a member of half a dozen cattle corporations in Colfax County,[43] lands of which were carefully selected with the view of encompassing water which would control land for miles around.[44] He claimed the Uña de Gato Grant of about 600,000 acres in Colfax County; and when its forgery was demonstrated in 1879, he thought it unsafe to rely on the spurious title and sought instead to secure

38. Harwood P. Hinton, Jr., "John Simpson Chisum, 1877-84," *New Mexico Historical Review,* 31:193.

39. Frederick W. Nolan, "A Sidelight on the Tunstall Murder," *New Mexico Historical Review,* 31:216,220; C. L. Sonnichsen and William V. Morrison, *Alias Billy the Kid,* 25, 34, 86; Miguel Antonio Otero, *The Real Billy the Kid,* 39, 54; George W. Coe, *Frontier Fighter: An Autobiography,* 71; H. H. Bancroft, *History of Arizona and New Mexico,* 704, 705. Other Federal officials whose terms ended in 1878 were Territorial Governor Samuel B. Axtel, District Attorney William L. Rynerson, Indian Agent Frederick C. Godfroy, Chief Justice Henry L. Waldo, Associate Justice (second district) Samuel B. McLin, Register of the Land Officer at Santa Fe José D. Sena, Receiver of the Land ✓ Office at Santa Fe A. G. Hoyt (1877), Receiver of the Land Office at Mesilla Lawrence LePoint, and Librarian James McKenzie.

40. William A. Keleher, *Violence in Lincoln County, 1869-1881,* 246. This is the most accurate, detailed, and impartial account available of the Lincoln County War.

41. *Ibid.,* 103, *passim;* Nolan, "A Sidelight on the Tunstall Murder," *New Mexico Historical Review,* 31:193.

42. Pat F. Garrett, *The Authentic Story of Billy the Kid,* 35; Chas. A. Siringo, *A Lone Star Cowboy,* 142.

43. Western Range Cattle Industry Study, *New Mexico Cattle Corporations, 1871-1900,* Summary, Ms.

44. Public Lands Commission, *Preliminary Report,* 1879, 46 Cong., 2 Sess., *H.E.D.* No. 46, 446 (1923).

the land by means of homesteading and pre-emptions. He was unable to do this legally, since the land was claimed as a grant and was, therefore, reserved from settlement. Nevertheless, the Commissioner of the General Land Office ordered the land surveyed and opened to settlers. This was now a convenience to Dorsey, who promptly arranged for conveyance of land titles to his ownership in wholesale lots by fictitious persons or those under his influence or in his employ.[45] One person who swore to numerous affidavits was a young gentleman named Kit Carson, Jr., who was employed by Dorsey as a cowboy, teamster, and general utility man.[46]

In the early 1880's there was a great increase in the number of cattle companies.[47] The land dominating sources of water for cattle came into control of owners of these companies largely by fraudulent land entries. The nefarious activities of the American Valley (Cattle) Company become particularly notorious. This company planned to dominate a grazing area roughly 66 miles from north to south and 72 miles east and west in present Catron County. This was from T.8N through T.2S and R.10W through R.21W. The map, facing, does not show all of the area entering into the plans of the company because the water in the townships south of the base line, and the block of townships north of the base line not marked with a "W" or a "+," were already controlled by illegal entries made by employees of the company.

Captain John P. Casey, of Albuquerque, brought cattle into the valley of the Largo, south of Quemado, in the early spring of 1881 after reconnoitering the area the previous autumn. He noted that the area was unsurpassed in its natural advantages for raising cattle and promptly named it the American Valley, after which he set about carving out a cattle kingdom.[48]

The first step in that direction was to arrange for the surveying of the townships so that land entries could be filed on areas controlling the water. This was done by depositing money that could later be used as part payment for land entered under the land laws. It was required by law that actual settlers must reside in a township

45. *S.G.R.* 7/20/87, 50 Cong., 1 Sess., *H.E.D.* No. 1, 666 (2541).
46. Secretary of the Interior, *Fraudulent Acquisition of Titles to Land in New Mexico,* 1885, 48 Cong., 2 Sess., *S.E.D.* No. 106, 312.
47. Western Range Cattle Industry Study, *New Mexico Cattle Corporations, 1871-1900,* Summary, Ms.
48. *Albuquerque Daily Democrat,* April 30, 1883, 2.

A portion of the Surveyor General's map of 1882. On the original, in the possession of Mr. Fletcher Catron, Santa Fe attorney, the township lines and "+" marks are in pencil. The "W" marks are in red ink. The penciled marginal notation is in the hand of Fletcher Catron's father, T. B. Catron, who was the attorney for the American Valley Company at this time.

for it to be surveyed. This requirement was partially fulfilled by early settlers in the region, and for the rest, it was ignored. The entire area was surveyed from March through August 1882. During this period, Casey formed a verbal partnership with Surveyor General Atkinson. Atkinson was considered a good man to have as a partner because through him they could get possession of land in the American Valley regardless of who settled it, while Casey secured the range by arranging entries to cover the water in the area. To facilitate these arrangements, he was provided by Atkinson with plats of the American Valley long before they were approved or filed in the Land Office at Santa Fe.[49]

Control over almost all the land on both sides of Largo Creek was attained from October through December 1882, by homestead and pre-emption entries made in the names of John Doyle, Washington Jones (a Negro cook), Eugene Ohara, Thomas Reynolds, Matthew Drya, Dr. Thomas J. Wright (Dodge City, Kansas, physician who never resided in the territory; father-in-law of W. C. Moore), William C. Moore, Thomas Cassaday, James Casey, Hank Andrews, and Annie Casey. This land promptly came into the ownership of John P. Casey.[50]

In the area north of the base line around Salt Lake, Trechado, and Quemado there were only six springs, and several claims entered in behalf of the newly forming American Valley Company covered nearly all of the water in the vicinity. Claims were entered by Morton Crossman, James Casey, Robert McAntire, James E. Reynolds, Edward McGinty, Hank Andrews, Daniel H. McAllister, Daniel C. Casey, John J. Patton, Richard Mitchell, and Thomas J. Wright. These were consecutively entered as numbers 1596 through 1606, all on January 2, 1883. They were entered variously in townships 1, 2, and 3 north, and ranges 14, 15, 16, 17, and 18 west. Furthermore, on March 15, 1883, six of these claims were entered for commutation to cash by Daniel C. Casey, Daniel H. McAllister, Richard Mitchell, Hank Andrews, Edward McGinty, and James E. Reynolds with consecutive entry numbers of 721 through 726. A number of these entries were made on land upon which settlers other than the appli-

---

49. *Survey Plats* (B.L.M.). John P. Casey, Sr., *Notarized Statement*, October 15, 1892. Secretary of the Interior, *Fraudulent Acquisition of Titles to Land in New Mexico*, 1885, 48 Cong., 2 Sess., *S.E.D.* No. 106, 326.

50. *Tract Books* (B.L.M.). Various records also spell Drya as Deye.

cants already resided and the original settlers were dispossessed of their homes. Other applications were made on land where no one lived and the applicants did not establish a residence as was required by law.[51]

Daniel C. Casey, Wright, Patton, and McAntire were never on the ranch up to this time and Reynolds signed papers in blank. Andrews, a full-blooded Ute Indian, never signed any papers. Indians were allowed to take out a homestead only under certain conditions and were not allowed to commute a homestead. Surveyor General Atkinson and Register Frost were well aware that "Indian Hank" was indeed an Indian. Andrews was hanged by a mob the following winter (1883-84) for alleged cattle stealing.[52]

Edward McGinty authorized no one to use his name and did not even know where he was supposed to have located until Surveyor General Atkinson showed him. He had never been in Santa Fe until after the entry was made. He was also represented as having made commutation proof before Register Max Frost and as having signed his name in full when actually he could sign by mark only. Later he was promised a sum of money (which he never received) for signing an affidavit that he had never made a homestead entry.[53]

Richard T. Mitchell worked for the American Valley Company, but swore that he never made the alleged entry which was later commuted to cash. After he discovered the supposed entry, Mitchell went to Atkinson about the matter. The latter told him that if he would give him a quitclaim to the land he (Atkinson) would give him $600. Mitchell agreed to this, since the entry was in his name and he didn't know how else to reclaim his right to make another entry. They went to the office of T. B. Catron, where the papers were made out and he was given $300 in cash and the balance in paper.[54]

D. H. McAllister was the manager of the American Valley Company starting in June of 1882. He put in what cattle he had, and it was agreed that W. C. Moore was to furnish money to increase the

---

51. Secretary of the Interior, *Fraudulent Acquisition of Titles to Land in New Mexico,* 1885, 48 Cong., 2 Sess., *S.E.D.* No. 106, 309, 326, 327. Registers and Receivers, *Abstracts of Original Homestead and Cash Sales Entries* (N.A.). *Survey Plats* (B.L.M.).

52. Secretary of the Interior, *Ibid.,* 327.

53. *Ibid.,* 325.

54. *Ibid.,* 325, 326. When Mitchell deeded the land to Atkinson, he had no legal right to make another entry, as he was evidently led to believe, unless the original entry was canceled with no willful act on his part.

stock and run the ranch. The profits were to be divided. Moore was employed by Casey and ran the business during the extensive intervals when Casey was away; consequently, McAllister did not at this time know that Moore owned no interest in the ranch, and in September, Moore informed McAllister that he had just bought a one-third interest from John P. Casey and Surveyor General Atkinson.[55]

Casey knew procedures in the General Land Office in Washington and knew all about land laws, but McAllister was entirely ignorant in such matters. As a consequence, he left all such matters to Casey, who obliged by making out entry papers (along with the others of January 2, 1883) for McAllister to sign and told him it was useless for him to go to Santa Fe to make entry. McAllister swore that he paid out nothing to enter or to commute the entry and that Atkinson or Moore must have paid it.[56]

In May 1883, McAllister severed his relations with the company, allegedly because he became satisfied of its fraudulent operations. More likely, he was disgruntled by the treatment accorded him by Casey, Atkinson, and Moore, and became the chief prosecution witness in the trial for two murders that he alleged were committed by employees of the American Valley Company. Two settlers, Alexis Grosstet and Robert Elsinger, made the mistake of settling on land needed to round out this company's holdings and, earlier in May, they were assassinated. These "American Valley" murders became the most famous unsolved crime in the history of Territorial New Mexico, not because of those murdered, but on account of the important names surrounding the American Valley cattle ranching. The Santa Fe Ring is reported to have been much interested in this case.[57]

To summarize, the company was started by Casey and Atkinson, while Moore later purchased a one-third interest from them. McAllister entered the picture by joining with Moore in the company although the latter, at the time, had no interest in it, and T. B. Catron became involved in the association as attorney for the group. The next member (in the month preceding the murders) was General John A. Logan,[58] who, the following year, in the elec-

---

55. *Ibid.*, 326. John P. Casey, *Statement.*
56. *Ibid.*, 326, 327.
57. *Ibid.*, 341. Otero, *My Life on the Frontier, 1882-1897,* 93. The author is preparing a book on these American Valley murders.
58. F. Stanley, *Longhair Jim Courtright,* 101, *passim.*

tion of 1884, became the vice presidential candidate under James G. Blaine. Logan died in 1886, the same year the small fry were eliminated and the American Valley Company was incorporated by Atkinson (no longer surveyor general), Catron, William B. Slaughter, and Henry L. Warren.[59]

When McAllister severed his connection with the company, he went to Atkinson with a view to selling his interest. McAllister wanted $3,000, but Atkinson said he already had $24,000 in the business and could not afford to pay that much. After consultation with Atkinson's attorney, T. B. Catron, McAllister agreed to accept $1,600 for the stock he had put in and the land that had been entered in his name. A quitclaim deed was given for the land. McAllister was certain that Register Max Frost was a party to the fraud, because he had heard Casey say that it would only take three words from him to put Frost out of office.[60]

The American Valley case was by no means isolated. Fraudulent entries were common throughout the Territory and those in Colfax County were among the most prevalent. Special Agent John M. Dunn made some investigations in this area as well as elsewhere in the Territory. When he could find but very little fraud, at a time when other inspectors were finding almost nothing else, the General Land Office became suspicious and sent Inspector Frank D. Hobbs to check the cases already covered by Dunn. Hobbs found many people who believed that Dunn had not acted in the best interests of the Government and that he had devoted his time to protecting the interests of stockmen who were parties to illegal entries. Dunn spent much of his time at the home of S. W. Dorsey, used Dorsey's horses at will, and enjoyed himself generally. Upon one occasion he inspected fraudulent entries at the Dubuque Cattle Company and was picked up at Dorsey's ranch by a four-horse rig belonging to the Dubuque outfit. A few days later he returned in the same comfortable manner. Inspector Hobbs unearthed convincing evidence that a great deal of land was entered by illegal means and straightway came into the ownership of Mr. Dorsey and other ranchers in the area.[61]

59. Western Range Cattle Industry Study, *New Mexico Cattle Corporations, 1871-1900,* Summary, Ms.

60. Secretary of the Interior, *Fraudulent Acquisition of Titles to Land in New Mexico,* 1885, 48 Cong., 2 Sess., *S.E.D.* No. 106, 327.

61. *Ibid.,* 312-315.

The Prairie Cattle Company, owned entirely in Scotland, pre-empted and homesteaded most of present Union County without making a dollar's worth of improvements. The Palo Blanco, Dubuque, and Portsmouth cattle companies and J. S. Taylor, E. J. Temple, H. M. Porter, W. E. Corbitt, J. W. Dwyer, and John Delano, all had numerous entries.[62]

Few if any of the original entrymen complied with the law. For example, José Ma. Martínez transferred seven claims to the Dubuque Cattle Company by quitclaim deeds in an impossibly short length of time.[63]

In 1883 more than 150 Spanish-name settlers along the Rio Pecos sent a petition to the Secretary of the Interior requesting that an investigation be conducted regarding lands there. They were being dispossessed of their homes:

> we have settled on the public land, many of us years ago, when the Indians were bad and when we had to defend our homes with the rifle; . . . most of us were ignorant of the homestead laws at the time, but upon the land whereon our homes were situated being surveyed, we sent up our filings to the register at Santa Fé, and they were returned by him with statements that the land upon which we had been living on for ten and twelve years had been taken up by parties which we know have never been on the land. We would also call your attention to the number of entries made by either men who have been dead for years, or non-residents, unknown to us, and have never settled on the public lands along the Pecos or the Salado.
>
> We also beg that you will investigate the claims of homesteads made by one W. H. McBroom in T. 4 N., R. 24 E., in names of fictitious parties.
>
> We know that this McBroom and others have made false statements, and have fraudulently filed and now hold the lands of some of our best settlers, who have been residing on their lands for years, but who cannot get their filings accepted at the Land Office on account of the filings of this said McBroom.
>
> We would also call your honorable attention to the fraudulent filings of one Orcott and one Goodwin on the Lower Pecos.

---

62. *Ibid.,* 129, *passim; L.O.R.* 9/28/87, 50 Cong., 1 Sess., *H.E.D.* No. 1, 160 (2541).
63. *Ibid., L.O.R.*

These parties have hired men in their employ who make it a business to file on land under assumed names and enter them in the land office at Mesilla, thereby preventing citizens of the United States from exercising their legal rights thereon under the provisions of the homestead and pre-emption laws.[64]

In 1882 and 1883, 7,200 acres of public domain in the eastern part of the Territory were taken up by one individual for grazing purposes through homestead and pre-emption claims entered in the names of fictitious persons under conditions that made it impossible for them to be legal. In southern New Mexico the Vermont and Rio Grande Cattle Company acquired 3,000 acres of land by similar methods.[65]

By 1883 the famous Chisum clan had acquired a strip of 160-acre tracts from near Bosque Grande, about thirty-five miles north of Roswell, down the Pecos to Artesia. Prior owners of these homesteads were friends, relatives, and employees of the Chisum family. "It is very probable the initial filings had been at the suggestion of the Chisums, for by the early 1880's they were utilizing every means to retain control of the well-watered range along the frontage of the Pecos."[66] In 1885 all southeast New Mexico was devoted exclusively to cattle ranching.[67] There was no intent of complying with the land laws by growing crops.

Another case involved 6,500 acres of fraudulent pre-emption and homestead claims. Ninety-one entries, embracing 14,000 acres, were acquired by another cattle company. In San Miguel County 84 entries of 160 acres each were found to have been made in behalf of still another cattle company. In the Las Cruces district 56 entries covering 10,500 acres were acquired illegally by a firm of cattlemen. A case in Colfax County involved 7,000 acres and 45 entries. Commissioner Stockslager reported that "While the entries in the above-mentioned [five] cases . . . only cover about 52,000 acres, they actually control an immense territory by appropriating all the

---

64. Secretary of the Interior, *Fraudulent Acquisition of Titles to Land in New Mexico*, 1885, 48 Cong., 2 Sess., *S.E.D.* No. 106, 29.

65. *L.O.R.* 10/7/86, 49 Cong., 2 Sess., *H.E.D.* No. 1, 91, 92 (2468).

66. Hinton, "John Simpson Chisum, 1877-84," *New Mexico Historical Review*, 32:63.

67. Hinkle, *Early Days of a Cowboy on the Pecos*, 3.

water in the respective localities. The cattlemen are masters of the country, and they domineer and rule the people in their vicinity in such a way as to make it exceedingly difficult to induce parties to give evidence of the fraudulent transactions."[68]

There is further evidence that homestead entries were made in the interest of parties other than settlers. Often groups of entries were made in a single township on the same day. Preceding and following these groups are completely random entries. It is evident that groups of neighbors filed on the same day or else the land was filed upon by several persons in the interest of the party or parties desiring to consolidate holdings in that area. The latter is more likely.[69]

In 1883, Special Agent Eddy investigated 200 homestead claims, only 65 (32.5 per cent) of which met with homestead regulations. In determining the legality of these claims, he gave every possible advantage to the claimants. In a number of cases in which improvements had been partially or completely destroyed by Indians, he recommended that a patent be issued. In other instances when affidavits substantiated that settlers had been forced to leave their homes because of danger from Indians, he likewise urged that the

---

68. *L.O.R.* 10/4/88, 50 Cong., 2 Sess., *H.E.D.* No. 1, 48 (2636). All the cases mentioned did not necessarily come to light in the year of this report, at least one having been mentioned in an earlier report.

69. Registers and receivers, *Abstracts of Final Homestead Certificates* (N.A.). The following are some examples of this phenomenon:

LAS CRUCES LAND OFFICE FINAL HOMESTEAD CERTIFICATES

Inclusive No. of Certificate	*Township and Range*	*Date*
41-52	17, 18 S - 10, 11 W	October 1, 1879
80-88	8, 9 S - 8 W	November 1, 1882
95-108	5 S - 19 W	December 23, 1882
123-129	2 S - 14 W	March 28, 1883
135-140	5 S - 20 W	April 21, 1883
259-267	10 S - 3 W	July 15, 1884

SANTA FE LAND OFFICE FINAL HOMESTEAD CERTIFICATES

226-244	10 N - 30, 31 E	June 15, 1881
250-265	9 N - 29, 30 E	June 25, 1881
327-339	23 N - 18, 19, 20 E	November 4, 1881
395-406	13 N - 36 E	December 30, 1881
484-499	23 N - 19, 20 E	April 10, 1882
668-677	17 N - 29, 30 E	September 11, 1882

settlers receive a patent. This was also his feeling in certain cases in which settlers had been forced to vacate because of illness.[70]

The chief factor in noncompliance with the law was the complete absence of any settlement or improvements on the land of any kind whatsoever. In other instances the land had been abandoned for years; the applicant was under legal age; a house had been built by a party other than the applicant; or the resident on the land had never filed a claim and was unaware that one had been filed. Frequently settlers in the neighborhood had never heard of the supposed claimant.[71]

Eddy concluded that "An honest investigation would result in the cancellation of hundreds of fraudulent entries, and many thousand acres of land would be thrown open to entry by actual settlers. . . . the office should send at least six agents into this Territory without delay. . . ."[72]

Only 58 per cent of original homestead entries were patented (Appendix V). An application provided the use of the land, and for grazing purposes frequently this is all that was desired. It was estimated in 1885 that 40 per cent of five-year homesteads in New Mexico were fraudulent,[73] which is probably conservative in view of Eddy's findings of 67.5 per cent in 1883.

The Homestead Law was not suitable for any except limited portions of New Mexico, and it was greatly abused; nevertheless, no essential change was made in the system until the Stock-Raising Homestead Act of 1916. Halfway attempts at compromise had been made with the Enlarged Homestead Act of 1909 and the Three Year Homestead Act of 1912. It was not until the act of 1916 that grazing land was recognized as such, by classification, in a homestead law. Before that the idea of a homestead as a crop-raising farm unit had basically prevailed.

---

70. Secretary of the Interior, *Fraudulent Acquisition of Titles to Land in New Mexico,* 1885, 48 Cong., 2 Sess., *S.E.D.* No. 106, *passim.*
71. *Ibid.*
72. *Ibid.,* 315.
73. *L.O.R.* 10/22/85, 49 Cong., 1 Sess., *H.E.D.* No. 1, 223 (2378).

5. Cash Sales of Land

WHY WOULD SETTLERS buy land when free land was available through homesteading? There is no single answer to this question. An obvious answer is that a homesteader could secure additional land, through pre-emption, after completing a homestead entry by means of a five-year residence or by commutation to cash in six months. Many settlers did this. The homesteader could also purchase lands that were, from time to time, offered for sale by the Government.

Another answer is more unpleasant. It was easier for the unscrupulous to find a bogus entryman to stay six months on a pre-emption claim than five years on a homestead, and less difficulty was encountered in concealing the nature of a false pre-emption entry for the shorter time.

The Act of 1854, establishing the office of Surveyor General of New Mexico, extended the pre-emption privilege to unsurveyed areas, and until the Homestead Acts of 1878 and 1880 gave homesteaders every privilege enjoyed by pre-emptors, a settler protected his rights by pre-empting rather than by waiting for a survey and homesteading.[1] It should be added, though, that in New Mexico a comparatively small amount of land was disposed of prior to 1880 (Appendixes IV-V).

Cash sales of land were out of harmony with the homestead principle,[2] and there were repeated and strenuous efforts to have the

---

1. Roy M. Robbins, *Our Landed Heritage: The Public Domain 1776-1936*, 237, is only partially correct in stating that the pre-emption privilege was extended to unsurveyed land in 1862. Earlier statutes of 1853 and 1854 (as well as 1862) extended pre-emption to certain unsurveyed areas, *L.O.R.* 1868, 97.

2. Paul Wallace Gates, "The Homestead Law in an Incongruous Land System," *American Historical Review*, 41: 654.

Pre-emption Law repealed. Advocates of this measure named it the "speculator's law" in a disparaging effort to distinguish it from the "settler's law."[3] Many believed that "The policy of disposing of public lands as a means of raising revenue [had] long since been rejected by enlightened views of public economy."[4]

Land could be acquired for cash in New Mexico through public auction, private entry, pre-emption, commuted homesteads, land scrip, and sale of military and Indian reserves.[5]

In the spring of 1870, there was considerable excitement in the Territory occasioned by a coming public auction sale of areas in certain townships, principally along the Canadian and Hondo rivers (Map 12). Some of these townships were fractional; and all portions were excluded that had been reserved by law for schools, Indians, the military, and other uses. This included areas within private grants.[6] The sale was to continue for no longer than two weeks, then the land was to be opened to private entry. Pre-emption claimants in the designated areas were required to establish their claims to the satisfaction of the register and receiver at Santa Fe, where the sale was to be held, commencing August 8. They were, furthermore, required to make payment on their claims before the date of the sale or forfeit their rights to any land they claimed.[7] They were unable to do this in every instance because some of the land had not yet been subdivided.[8]

It is evident that the publicity attending the public sale of 1870 gave a comparatively large impetus to the land disposal program in New Mexico, small as it was in actual amount. In the two years prior to 1870, there were only 10 original homestead entries filed, and in that year there were 96. From 1858 through 1869 there were

---

3. Robbins, *Our Landed Heritage,* 285.

4. *L.O.R.* 10/22/85, 49 Cong., 1 Sess., *H.E.D.* No. 1, 227 (2378).

5. The Graduation Act of 1854 need not be considered, since it was repealed in 1862, and the first cash sales of land in New Mexico were in 1868.

6. President of the U.S., *Order for the Sale of Land,* May 3, 1870 (N.A.). This was the only public sale in the Territory.

7. *Ibid.* Public sales were auction sales and differed from private entry in that the latter was for land offered at public sale and upon which no one had bid during the designated period of the sale. Copp, *The American Settler's Guide,* 8.

8. *S.G.R.* 8/20/70, 41 Cong., 3 Sess., *H.E.D.* No. 1, 418 (1449).

13 donation notifications, and in 1870 there were 14. The first mineral land sales were made in 1870; there were 21 of them. In the same year there were 26 cash sales. The only previous sales were three pre-emptions in 1868 (Appendixes IV and V).

The sale itself was not immediately a great success, since only 1,958.23 acres were sold for $2,447.79. No one would bid over the going rate of $1.25 per acre for pre-emption land.[9] After the sale, the unsold land was placed in the offered[10] class and was eventually disposed of through sale at private entry.

Among the largest purchases at the sale were those of Wilson Waddingham along the Canadian River and Ute Creek near their confluence. In 1871 he bought 6,589.58 acres of land from the Government and the following year 5,427.79.[11] Their strategic location for controlling water is apparent (Map 13). These purchases became part of the domain which was to be known as the famous Bell Ranch.[12] Settlers in the region had been repeatedly urged by the register at Santa Fe to enter their lands; nevertheless, many of them failed to heed the warning, and consequently lost the tracts that they had settled upon when Waddingham bought the land.[13]

Waddingham's purchases were not looked upon with favor by some of the people in New Mexico: "In my judgment the lands put in market for private entry should be limited in quantity to each purchaser. It is a common practice in this Territory to enter the smallest legal subdivisions bordering on streams, with the view to speculation and to secure the public land adjacent thereto for grazing purposes without purchase."[14] This point of view was shared in Washington.[15]

Other extensive purchases at private entry were made by Joseph C. Lea along the Rio Hondo from its source to its junction with the Pecos River. From 1879 through 1885, he bought 13,386.98

9. Eben Everett, register at Santa Fe, to Joseph S. Wilson, 8/21/70 (F.R.C.).
10. Lands proclaimed for sale but not sold. Copp, *The American Settler's Guide*, 8.
11. Registers and receivers, *Abstracts of Cash Entries* (N.A.).
12. Wilson Waddingham, *Bills and Invoices,* 1887-1890 (W.R.C.I.S.).
13. Eben Everett, Register at Santa Fe, to Charles Ebel and Gotfried Gauss, Red River, N.M., 5/5/72 (F.R.C.).
14. Public Lands Commission, *Preliminary Report,* 1879, 46 Cong., 2 Sess., *H.E.D.* No. 46, 450 (1923), statement by William McMullen, civil engineer.
15. *S.I.R.* 11/1/85, 49 Cong., 1 Sess., *H.E.D.* No. 1, 38 (2378).

acres.[16] Other members of the Lea family bought more than 2,400 acres in the same area.[17]

Sales made under the Proclamation of May 3, 1870 were suspended on July 10, 1886, pending a determination of its legality. On June 9, 1890, Secretary of the Interior Noble rendered an affirmative decision based on the Act of July 22, 1854, establishing the office of Surveyor General of New Mexico, Kansas and Nebraska. The last clause of section 13 of this act gave the President authority to make sales of land in Nebraska. Since the whole act included New Mexico, it was ruled that this authority also extended to that Territory. J. C. Lea was one of the persons whose land was in question and, as demanded, he filed an affidavit that he had made various private entries in good faith and that his improvements on the land had cost not less than $20,000. In view of the lapse of time and the expenditures made on the faith of the offering, the Proclamation was ordered to be held legally as *res judicata* and the titles to the lands involved were no longer questioned.[18]

During the years there was considerable effort on the part of local Land Office officials to make known to the nation what New Mexico had to offer in the way of land available for purchase. They stressed pre-emption and private entry rather than homestead.[19] It was natural that they should do so since a major part of their income depended on fees from their business. There was also a certain amount of pride in the "Sunshine State."[20] In correspondence regarding the possibility of buying land from the United States, it was frankly stated that there was good grazing

---

16. Registers and receivers, *Abstracts of Cash Entries* (N.A.). His purchases were, in acres: 1879, 321.69; 1882, 165.96; 1883, 559.56; 1884, 519.24; and 1885, 11,820.53. Part of the city of Roswell is located on portions of this land. At $1.25 per acre, it was a good investment.

17. Registers and receivers, *Tract Books* (B.L.M.). Part of this was under the Desert Land Law. Numerous other persons purchased land made available by the Proclamation of May 3, 1870, but none in as large quantities as Waddingham and Lea.

18. S. V. Proudfit, *Decisions of the Department of Interior Relating to Public Lands,* Vol. X, 652-655.

19. Everett to Charles Troll, Louisville, Kentucky, 8/21/70; and to A. D. Ottarson, Nashville, Tennessee, 2/17/71 (F.R.C.).

20. First so designated in the *Annual Report* of Governor L. Bradford Prince, 9/15/90, 51 Cong., 2 Sess., *H.E.D.* No. 1, 634 (2842).

land available and some excellent land susceptible to irrigation. "New Mexico," it was pointed out, "is very different from any other part of the Republic. Cultivation is wholly consequent upon irrigation and where water cannot be brought, the soil is unfit for cultivation."[21]

Cultivation of the soil was a requirement for pre-emption, yet it was reported that 60,000,000 acres of land were available in New Mexico for pre-emption.[22] This was more public domain than was available in the Territory,[23] and a majority of it would grow no crops (Map 10).

Land officials of that day did not consider this a contradiction. They reflected that most of the land was fit only for grazing, and that the law should so allow. It was their duty to administer the land laws as they were written, but they saw the hopelessness of a literal interpretation of that duty and tempered their actions with the realities of the arid domain under their jurisdiction. It was not generally their intention to condone unlawful entries, but rather to make it possible for lawful entrants to secure land. Without a liberal interpretation of arability, this could not often be done.

Nevertheless, lawlessness did prevail. It was estimated that, based on reports of special agents, from 75 to 90 per cent of pre-emption claims in New Mexico were fraudulent.[24] This may be somewhat high. Findings of Special Agent H. H. Eddy indicate 56.7 percent. Of 111 cases examined by Eddy, 63 in no way complied with the law.[25] In one case in T.15S, R.17W, northwest of Silver City, James Voss was the pre-emptor but never lived on the land; furthermore, he did not know nor care which of three claims

---

21. Everett to James Eastman, and others, Tecumseh, Nebraska, 1/4/71 (F.R.C.).

22. Everett to Charles Troll, Louisville, Kentucky, 8/21/70 (F.R.C.).

23. It is evident that Everett made a rough estimate of all the public domain in the Territory and classified it as available for pre-emption. His estimate was high by about 15,000,000 acres. Total acreage is 77,568,640. Land already claimed under the land laws, private land grants claimed at that time, grants to the Atlantic and Pacific Railroad (later partially forfeited), Texas and Pacific Railroad (later completely forfeited), railroad rights-of-way, military reservations, and Indian reservations, accounted for about 32,500,000 acres, leaving a balance of approximately 45,000,000.

24. *L.O.R.* 10/22/85, 49 Cong., 1 Sess., *H.E.D.* No. 1, 222 (2378).

25. Secretary of the Interior, *Fraudulent Acquisition of Titles to Land in New Mexico,* 1885, 48 Cong., 2 Sess., *S.E.D.* No. 106, *passim.*

he supposedly owned because J. W. Fleming was going to give him $300 for proving up. Later Voss said he did not want to pre-empt a claim but Fleming told him he had to do so because his name was already in Washington.[26] Such blackmail tactics were typical of the fraudulent cases.

Land scrip was a transferable certificate, in lieu of land, awarded to individuals by the Government as awards for various services or for obligations incurred.[27] The homestead idea largely superseded the awarding of land bounties for services rendered and, since most of the land disposals in New Mexico occurred subsequent to the beginning of the homestead era, scrip was only a minor phase of the public land disposals in that Territory (Appendix IV).

By the four categories of free land (homestead, timber-culture, donations, and soldiers' and sailors' homesteads), there were 622,684 acres deeded to individuals. On the other hand, settlers paid cash for 648,028 acres of Government land (Appendix VI). The railroads also sold 356,260.56 acres during this period and a large amount was purchased from grant owners by individuals. It is evident that many people preferred to buy their land rather than get it free from the Government with the strings that were attached by the latter.

---

26. *Ibid.,* 140.

27. Both Hibbard, *A History of the Public Land Policies,* and Robbins, *Our Landed Heritage,* deal with this subject extensively.

6. The Timber Culture Law of 1873

THE TIMBER CULTURE ACTS were "in substance, a subsidy paid in lands to encourage the planting and culture of timber."[1] They were in operation from 1873 until their final repeal in 1891. They were a mistake in arid New Mexico. Except in rare instances it was impossible to comply with the law since nature controlled the balance here. Where there were trees, timber-culture was illegal. Where there were no trees, none were destined to grow without irrigation, and irrigated land was more valuable for crops than for trees.[2]

Compared to other states and territories where the Timber Culture Act was tried, little land was disposed of under this law in New Mexico (Map 14). Still, considering the difficulty of compliance, an amazing number of persons took steps to avail themselves of this class of national bounty. There were nearly eighteen times as many original entries as final certificates. By 1891, the year the law was repealed, 1,609 entrants had filed original papers for 230,335 acres. By 1903 the final returns were all in and there were only 91 certificates with 12,937 acres.[3]

---

1. *S.I.R.* 11/1/85, 49 Cong., 1 Sess., *H.E.D.* No. 1, 39 (2378).

2. See Maps 15 and 16. In most of the areas shown in Zone 4, and better, trees were already growing. In virtually all the rest they would not grow without irrigation. Maker and Dregne do not deal specifically with timber growth, but a comparable land classification map compiled by Charles E. Linney, *et al., Climate as it Affects Crops and Ranges in New Mexico,* 6, shows timber growth in essentially the same localities as Maker and Dregne's Zone 4 and better except that the entire eastern part of the state is basically devoid of timber.

3. See Appendix V. The first original timber-culture entry was filed by Dumas Provencher in Section 26, T.10N, R.10W, in present Valencia County, in 1875. The first final certificate was issued to Oregon Bell in Section 6, T.11S, R.25E, near Roswell, on July 29, 1887.

This shows that frequently the law was used only to hold possession with no intent to acquire title.[4] There was more interest in the immediate use of the land than in ultimate ownership. A timber-culture entry ran for thirteen years before it lapsed. Eight years were required for final proof and five more years were allowed to complete the entry, and even longer if failure to complete the entry did not come to the attention of local land officials. During this time the entryman had use of the land "free of rent, interest or taxes."[5]

Fraud in timber-culture entries was widespread. Land Inspector A. R. Greene, after a scathing denunciation of the entire timber-culture system, concluded that "The experiment has approximated success about as nearly as an effort to make water flow up hill. I doubt if the trees standing on any timber-culture entry west of the hundredth meridian would retard a zepher."[6]

The fault was chiefly in the system. Human nature was too weak to refrain from violating a law which was so easy to circumvent. So lightly was the law regarded that it became neighborly to exchange services as witnesses to affidavits. The more innocuous method of evasion was simply the failure of careless entrymen to obey the law. It was a common practice for homestead and other settlers to take up an adjoining quarter-section of land as a timber-culture claim with no intention of growing trees.[7]

A more flagrant practice was that carried out by cattle corporations, which arranged for entries by persons other than corporate members, with no pretense of complying with any part of the law. Numerous persons were asked what kind of timber was planted in their locality. In twenty-one pages of testimony, not a single person knew of any timber being planted, let alone being able to name the kind.[8] The object was to secure valuable grass land by controlling water for stock. It was accomplished by requiring herd-

---

4. *S.I.R.* 11/1/85, 49 Cong., 1 Sess., *H.E.D.* No. 1, 39 (2378).

5. William F. Raney, "The Timber Culture Acts," *Mississippi Valley Historical Association (Proceedings)*, 10:223; Copp, *The American Settler's Guide*, 64.

6. *L.O.R.* 10/22/85, 49 Cong., 1 Sess., *H.E.D.* No. 1, 203 (2378).

7. *Ibid.*

8. Public Lands Commission, *Preliminary Report*, 1879, 46 Cong., 2 Sess., *H.E.D.* No. 46, 441-461 (1923).

ers to take out entries covering these watering places. The adjoining land was valuable only to those who controlled the water. In this way entire townships were dominated by cattle interests.[9]

Registers and receivers monthly abstracts of timber-culture entries show numerous entries in the same township on the same date. These groups stand out because they are surrounded by random entries. Chance cannot account for these claims occurring so close together in time and location in thinly settled New Mexico. It is easier to believe that the consecutive entries were made in the interest of an individual, or corporation, who was trying to acquire more land than this law allowed.[10]

In 1883 Special Agent H. H. Eddy examined 332 land claims in the Territory. Only seven were timber-culture claims. None of these complied fully with the law. William W. Conkling, T.17S, R.16W (an area reasonably subject to timber-culture entry), had recently located his claim and seemed to be acting in good faith, but had as yet done nothing to comply with the law. Frank L. Orcutt's claim, T.8N, R.22E, showed no evidence of improvement or occupation and was located on a mesa where there was no water to irrigate and where trees would not grow without irrigation. The claim of Erastus J. Wilcox, T.1N, R.26E, showed no improvements or occupation, but he declared his intention of planting trees in the spring, and Eddy recommended that action be deferred in this case. The entry of O. L. Houghton, T.1S, R.25E, was made in his own behalf. He had plowed five acres of land but had planted no trees; nevertheless, Eddy recommended that the entry be not disturbed. The entry of Leedra R. Savage, T.2S, R.25E, conflicted with an earlier homestead entry on which there were five acres of plowed land but no trees. Robina J. Smith had filed a timber-culture entry on grazing land in T.3S, R.25E, that was

---

9. *L.O.R.* 10/22/85, 49 Cong., 1 Sess., *H.E.D.* No. 1, 204 (2378).

10. Registers and receivers, *Abstracts of Original and Final Entries* (N.A.). Original entries at the Las Cruces office:

Inclusive Numbers of Entry	*Township and Range*	*Date*
162-175	18, 19, & 20 S - 26 E	May 12, 1883
181-186	21 S - 26 E	June 1, 1883
381-388	17 S - 19 E	April 3, 1885
635-639	23 S - 27 & 28 E	November 14, 1888
687-697	11 & 12 S - 23 & 24 E	March 9, 1889
777-782	23 S - 27 E	October 10, 1889

occupied by Richard Lowery. Lowery had built a house and said he had filed a pre-emption claim on the land. David H. Rust also filed in T.3S, R.25E. There was no evidence of occupation or cultivation and Eddy recommended that the entry be held for cancellation.[11]

The wisdom of the Timber Culture Act is open to question.[12] It was passed at a time when the subject of promoting timber resources was coming to the public attention. It was thought possible to transform the bleak plains of the West by having land-hungry men cultivate trees in exchange for a farm. This was a visionary dream and no more. It was a failure as far as accomplishing what Congress had in mind[13] and, in New Mexico, it was the least successful of all the land laws.

---

11. Secretary of the Interior, *Fraudulent Acquisition of Titles to Land in New Mexico,* 1885, 48 Cong., 2 Sess., *S.E.D.* No. 106, *passim.*

12. Robbins, *Our Landed Heritage,* 218.

13. Hibbard, *A History of the Public Land Policies,* 422.

7. The Desert Land Act of 1877

WITHIN A FEW YEARS after the passage of the Homestead Law, it was evident that its application to the arid lands of the West was not practical. A quarter-section of land where rainfall was plentiful was valuable to its owner, but an area of the same size west of the 100th meridian was usually of value for growing crops only if irrigation was applied.

It was to cope with this situation that the Desert Land Act was passed on March 3, 1877. It applied to any citizen of the United States of requisite age, or to such person who declared his intention to become a citizen. Only one entry of 640 acres, in compact form, was permitted to any one person. The price of the land was $1.25 per acre, but only twenty-five cents per acre was required to be paid when the entry was filed. The entrant was required to reclaim this land within a period of three years. At any time within that period, after producing satisfactory proof, he could pay the balance and secure title to the claim. A patent could be obtained on unsurveyed land. All lands not timber or mineral, which could not produce an agricultural crop without irrigation, were considered desert lands within the meaning of the law.[1] No assignments were to be made under the terms of the act.[2]

The law had weaknesses that made its application difficult from the start. One of these was the size of the area sold. The passage of the act was attended by much debate on this point. It was pointed out that well-tended, irrigated land is exceedingly productive and the question was raised as to why a person should be allowed 640 acres of such land and only 160 acres under other

---

1. *L.O.R.* 11/1/77, 45 Cong., 2 Sess., *H.E.D.* No. 1, 41 (1800). Text of the act.

2. Public Lands Commission, *Final Report,* 1881, 46 Cong., 3 Sess., *H.E.D.* No. 47, 415 (1975).

land laws. The Senator who sponsored the bill illogically replied, "Simply because it is very expensive and difficult to conduct water to the land."[3]

That view was all the more reason for limiting the size of the tract because allowing the larger amount was simply an inducement to acquire it for grazing purposes. This was a purpose of promoters of the law.[4] Existing laws prohibited the sale of public lands except in a few instances. This bill allowed for purchase and the amount allowed was more worthwhile for grazing than the previous maximum of 160 acres. But this was an irrigation and not a grazing law.[5]

The value of small tracts intensively cultivated was well recognized in New Mexico, where irrigation had been practiced for centuries. For the average settler, large acreage meant a large mortgage and the interest took much of the profit. More land than a farmer could care for himself meant hiring help and payments on the mortgage might preclude this. A good living could be had on 60 or 80 acres and often persons who had more than that sold part of it.[6]

Another weakness was the looseness with which the bill was drawn. A liberal construction would allow title to pass with very little water put on the land while a strict interpretation would require that all the land be irrigated. Except in rare instances it was impossibly expensive to irrigate fully the entire 640 acres. In New Mexico easily irrigated land had long been privately owned and what was left required more cash for reclamation than the average person could afford.

The General Land Office adopted a strict interpretation of the law from the start, although Commissioner Williamson recognized that it would probably defeat its operation and beneficial results. On the other hand, a liberal construction was certain to permit easy evasion of the law and render it a mockery.[7]

The tract allowed was too small for a stock range and too large for most persons to irrigate by using only their own resources. It

---

3. Hibbard, *A History of the Public Land Policies*, 427.

4. *L.O.R.* 11/1/77, 45 Cong., 2 Sess., *H.E.D.* No. 1, 33 (1800).

5. The Stock-Raising Homestead Act of 1916 also allowed 640 acres.

6. Richard J. Hinton, *A Report of Irrigation and Cultivation of the Soil Thereby*, 1891, 52 Cong., 1 Sess., *S.E.D.* No. 41, 214 (2899).

7. *L.O.R.* 11/1/77, 45 Cong., 2 Sess., *H.E.D.* No. 1, 33, 34 (1800).

was held that all the land must be irrigated within the required three years for a patent to be legally issued.[8] "This was expecting a miracle second only to the rain-making act of 1873."[9] On the other hand, the area was too small to attract investment capital to develop the large-scale storage of water needed to irrigate the arid regions.

The General Land Office had misgivings about the application of the Desert Land Law in New Mexico. Eight months after it was passed, all entries under the act were suspended and hearings were ordered to determine their legality. These were to be most thorough and were to reveal whether any of the land entered would produce an agricultural crop without irrigation, whether any had been previously cultivated by residents or semi-residents, and whether entries had been made by parties other than real applicants. Such development of the facts was to be made as would "fully protect the interests of the United States, prevent the success of fraud and secure the rights of all persons who [had] made entries in good faith under said law."[10]

This order for suspension was revoked within a month at the insistence of Secretary of the Interior Schurz. At the same time, however, specific instructions were issued that any cases suspected of fraud were to be reported immediately to the General Land Office.[11]

There was justification for these suspicions. The law specified that entries must be in compact form; yet, it was less than a year old when numerous persons desired to take out entries in contiguous subdivisions of 40 acres.[12] The obvious purpose was to control a maximum acreage adjacent to a stream or series of springs. This could be important for irrigation purposes, but even then to irrigate the whole claim would be expensive and difficult to accomplish in three years. Far more important, such control of a source of water gained the owner dominion over large quantities of grazing land in areas back from the water. For example, "Senator Dorsey [owned]

---

8. William B. Mathews, *Mathews's Guide for Settlers upon the Public Lands,* 159. Case of Geo. Ramsey, 5 L. D., 120.

9. Ernest S. Osgood, *The Day of the Cattleman,* 195.

10. Williamson to register and receiver, Mesilla, 10/8/77 (F.R.C.).

11. *Ibid.,* 11/8/77.

12. Atkinson to Williamson, 11/10/77 (B.L.M.).

all the springs on 160 acres, and this [controlled] the whole 10,000 acres back of it."[13]

The matter of contiguous entries was dealt with by Land Office ruling. Desert land entries could be made on unsurveyed land; and without survey lines as a guide, a great deal of looseness arose as to what constituted *compact form*. Even in surveyed areas entries frequently followed streams in a comparatively narrow strip.[14] It was ruled that entries must be made as nearly as possible in the shape of a legally subdivided section which was, of course, a square. Parts of more than one section might be admitted if they conformed to the proper shape. Merely contiguous small pieces of land, joined end to end, were ruled to be illegal whether on surveyed or unsurveyed land.[15]

But this did not end fraudulent use of the land. Since it was required that only twenty-five cents per acre be paid at the time of entry, and since the entryman had three years to make proof of reclamation and complete the payment, and could relinquish areas and make entries in other names, a way was opened to control large bodies of land along streams at what amounted to a nominal rental.[16] In this way thousands of acres of land in New Mexico were held as a lease for three years by the payment of twenty-five cents an acre. Officials there regarded desert land entries as a fruitful source of a great deal of "crookedness."[17]

Through 1891 there were 415,203 acres in original entries and 66,725 acres in final certificates. Through 1894 (when entries made in 1891 would normally have been completed) acres in final certificates had more than doubled to 139,622. Thus only about 33 per cent of entries made by 1891 were proved up by the end of 1894 (Appendix IV). Since two-thirds of the entries were never completed by conducting water upon the land, it is evident that it was used for other than irrigating purposes. This could only be for grazing on 57 per cent of it, that being the percentage of entries

13. Public Lands Commission, *Preliminary Report*, 1879, 46 Cong., 2 Sess., *H.E.D.* No. 46, 446 (1923).

14. *L.O.R.* 10/22/85, 49 Cong., 1 Sess., *H.E.D.* No. 1, 226 (2378).

15. *L.O.R.* 10/28/81, 47 Cong., 1 Sess., *H.E.D.* No. 1, 408 (2017).

16. *S.I.R* 11/24/88, 50 Cong., 2 Sess., *H.E.D.* No. 1, XII (2636).

17. *L.O.R.* 10/4/88, 50 Cong., 2 Sess., *H.E.D.* No. 1, 76 (2636). Reports of Register Edmund G. Shields and Receiver James Brown, Las Cruces Land Office.

made in townships where crops could not be grown without irrigation and where there was no irrigation. A large percentage of even
the remaining 43 per cent of townships that would support crop
growth without irrigation was in mountainous or forested areas
where crops could not be grown because of the terrain. Also, 75 per
cent of entries made through 1891 were made in townships where
there was no irrigating in any part of the township at that time
(Maps 17-18). Furthermore, by 1891 only about 47,000 acres had
been added to the total under cultivation by irrigation during the
fifteen years the law was in force,[18] as opposed to 415,203 acres in
original entries, so there were nearly nine times as many acres in
original entries as were added to the irrigated total. By 1894 there
were nearly three times as many acres in final certificates as were
added to the total brought under cultivation by irrigation through
1891 (Appendix IV).

But all the land brought under irrigation was not public domain.
Conservatively estimated, 40 per cent was irrigated by private irrigation companies operating on land purchased from grants and individuals.[19] So almost fifteen times as much land was entered, and
nearly five times as much acquired by certificates, as public domain
brought under irrigation while the law was in effect.

Registers were not very discerning in the entries they allowed to
be filed. The practice of making a number of consecutive entries in
the same township on the same day was common.[20] These groupings
are bound to stand out when they are surrounded by completely
random entries.

Although the Desert Land Law was badly misused, the fifteen-year
period during which the original law was in existence was practi-

---

18. Estimate based on table of irrigated areas, p. 81.

19. Estimate based on data in Hinton, *A Report on Irrigation and Cultivation of the Soil Thereby*, 1891, 52 Cong., 1 Sess., *S.E.D.* No. 41, *passim* (2899).

20. Registers, *Abstracts of Desert Land Entries and Certificates* (N.A.).
Typical original entries at the Las Cruces Land Office:

Inclusive Numbers of Entry	Township and Range	Date
286-290	6 S - 16 E	May 5, 1884
338-347	5 S - 2 E	September 24, 1884
393-399	17 S - 18, 19 E	April 2, 1885
660-665	14 S - 9 E	June 7, 1888
679-685	22, 23 S - 27 E	October 23, 1888
686-690	13 S - 26 E	October 23, 1888

cally concurrent with a mushroom growth of the cattle industry. The intention of a large element in this industry was to make a quick return on an investment while the use of free or inexpensive grazing land was made available by means of control of a water supply in the vicinity of the land. This segment of the industry stopped at nothing to acquire land controlling water for their operations; however, some of the cattlemen themselves deprecated these tactics.[21]

Along with fraudulent use of desert land entries there was a steady growth of legitimate irrigation. Records of the amount of land irrigated are by no means complete and those available are contradictory. The first census to contain irrigation records was that of 1890. This was actually for 1889. The figure for that year was 91,745 acres of irrigated land.[22] That same year there were 263,106 acres in improved farms.[23] Approximately 40 per cent of improved farms were irrigated, so using this percentage as an index for figures prior to 1890, the acreages through 1900 follow:[24]

Year	Acres in improved farms	Acres irrigated (estimate)	Increase in acres irrigated over previous decade
1860	136,358	54,500	
1870	143,007	57,200	2,700
1880	237,392	94,900	37,700
1890	263,106	105,000	10,100
1900	326,873	229,000	124,000

Nationally there was a marked decrease in desert land entries by 1887. The cattle industry reached its maximum development by the middle eighties and the demand for land fell off. Profits of the industry showed a sharp decrease beginning with 1885 because of overstocking and the severe winters.[25] In New Mexico the decrease in desert land entries did not come until 1891, when original entries

---

21. The Avarica Cattle Company (Arizona), *Prospectus,* (W.R.C.I.S.).

22. *XI Census* (Agriculture by Irrigation), 193.

23. *XI Census* (Agriculture), 74.

24. *VIII Census* (Agriculture), 178 [Arizona deducted]; *IX Census* (Compendium), 688; *X Census* (Compendium), Vol. I, 718; *XI Census* (Agriculture), 74; *XII Census* (Crops and Irrigation), 852. Hinton, *A Report on Irrigation and Cultivation of the Soil Thereby,* 1891, 52 Cong., 1 Sess., *S.E.D.* No. 41, *passim* (2899), shows larger figures than these but they are incomplete and contradictory.

25. Ganoe, "The Desert Land Act in Operation, 1877-1891," *Agricultural History,* 11:146.

dropped to 19,548 acres from the figure of 55,534 in 1890 (Appendix IV). Likewise the depressed period in the cattle industry came to New Mexico in the early 1890's.[26] The winter of 1886-1887 was unusually severe on the northern plains and cattle losses in some herds were as high as 80 per cent.[27] The winters were milder in New Mexico and losses not heavy; consequently, the cattle depression came later here than in the North, and when it came, was caused by droughts, overstocking, and low prices.[28]

The decline of the cattle industry brought a new epoch to irrigation. "In 1882, there were no irrigation works built on sound engineering principles, but by 1888, investors were turning from ranching to the rapidly developing irrigation companies."[29]

In New Mexico there were 19 irrigation companies incorporated in 1888; 32 in 1889; 23 in 1890; and 14 in 1891—a total of 88.[30] Conservatively estimated, 40 per cent of the land brought under irrigation during the decade of the 1890's was irrigated by these companies. Purchases under the Desert Land Act were minor because these companies needed land in large quantities for economical development of irrigation facilities. Land in excess of amounts allowed by desert land entry was acquired from individuals and from land grants. The Springer Land Association purchased 130,000 acres from the Maxwell Land Grant Company. Other areas of successful development were along the Rio Pecos, the Rio Grande, the San Juan, and in the Mimbres Valley. Some companies chose areas that were impractical for irrigation development and failed. Two of these were in Bernalillo County; one in Tijeras Canyon and the other along the Rio Puerco.[31]

---

26. Hinkle, *Early Days of a Cowboy on the Pecos,* 20.

27. Clark, *The West in American History,* 597-598.

28. Hinkle, *Early Days of a Cowboy on the Pecos,* 20.

29. Ganoe, "The Desert Land Act in Operation, 1877-1891," *Agricultural History,* 11:146, 147.

30. *G.N.M.* 10/10/88, 50 Cong., 2 Sess., *H.E.D.* No. 1, 843 (2638); 10/12/89, 51 Cong., 1 Sess., *H.E.D.* No. 1, 459 (2726); 9/15/90, 51 Cong., 2 Sess., *H.E.D.* No. 1, 609 (2842); and 10/12/91, 52 Cong., 1 Sess., *H.E.D.* No. 1, 339 (2935).

31. *Ibid., passim.* See also Hinton, *Irrigation in the United States, Progress Report for 1890,* 51 Cong., 2 Sess., *S.E.D.* No. 53, *passim* (2818); Hinton, Nettleton, and Hay (*Irrigation; Underflow Investigation;* and *Geology,* respectively), 52 Cong., 1 Sess., *S.E.D.* No. 41 (Pts. 1, 2, and 3 respectively), *passim* (2899). Many of the statistics in the last two mentioned documents seem exaggerated, and to some extent, so do the Governor's Reports.

A person who made a desert land entry for irrigation purposes rather than grazing had four possible ways of achieving his purpose:

1. His own individual effort.
2. A co-operative, with the owners of the land holding the stock.
3. A state-sanctioned irrigation district with a comparatively large number of members.
4. Purchase of water from an irrigation company at a specified rate.[32]

Irrigation by individual effort was generally unsatisfactory because few persons had the capital to do more than divert water from easy-access streams in short ditches to land near the watercourse. Without storage facilities, water was quite limited. Even if it were not, as soon as all the land along a stream was appropriated, others on higher ground could not gain access to the water. Title to land not adjacent to streams did not give title to water. "The separate control of land and water tended to create water monopolies . . . ," with the owners of land not adjacent to water dependent on the owners of the streams.[33]

This was a problem in New Mexico even before the advent of the Desert Land Law. In 1872, for example, ten homestead entrants requested permission to move the location of their entries from the Rio Hondo to the North Spring River some 18 miles to the north. Other settlers above them had taken all the water from the Rio Hondo and left none for irrigation downstream.[34]

Irrigation by small co-operative groups was hardly more satisfactory than individual effort because the individuals of these groups generally had little but labor to offer to the enterprise.

State-controlled irrigation districts were also hardly possible because the Government retained title to the land until final proof was made, and final proof could not be accomplished until the land was irrigated. As a consequence, title to land could not be put up as

---

32. Ganoe, "The Desert Land Act in Operation, 1877-1891," *Agricultural History*, 11:149, 150.

33. *Ibid.*, 150. New Mexico later officially rejected the riparian doctrine and adopted the "Colorado doctrine" which recognized only priority of use as the basis for acquiring a water right. Clyde O. Martz, *Cases and Materials on the Law of Natural Resources*, 69. The native custom had recognized priority of use.

34. Everett to Drummond, 1/8/72 (F.R.C.).

security for the tax issues that would in turn secure the bonds that would raise money to construct the irrigation works.[35]

The dream of vast fortunes from irrigation companies was largely just a myth. These companies learned through bitter experience that the land laws did not operate in their favor.[36] Then too, many of these companies built reclamation projects as cheaply and as quickly as they could in order to bring in revenue as soon as possible. The resulting maintenance cost soon forced many into bankruptcy.[37]

It was evident that a land law which gave no consideration to the problem of water needed substantial revision. Congress took a half-hearted step in that direction in 1888, when it passed an act providing for the withdrawal of irrigable land from entry.[38] By this act, 39 reservoir sites totaling 40,170.20 acres were selected in New Mexico.[39]

These withdrawals (repealed in 1890) were very unpopular with the people of New Mexico, who felt that the Territory was as much entitled to national aid for irrigation purposes as other sections were entitled to aid for rivers and harbors. It was granted that the withdrawals covered potentially irrigable lands but it was the feeling that nothing would eventually come of this action and the immediate result would be to keep settlers from filing entries and making developments on their own initiative.[40]

Starting in 1877, there had been a determined movement to repeal the entire desert land policy. This movement was not successful and a new era in irrigation started in 1891 with the problems of operation still unsolved.[41]

---

35. Ganoe, "The Desert Land Act in Operation, 1877-1891," *Agricultural History*, 11:151, 152.

36. *Ibid.*

37. Ganoe, "The Desert Land Act Since 1891," *Agricultural History*, 11:266.

38. Robbins, *Our Landed Heritage*, 294, 295.

39. *L.O.R.* 9/23/91, 51.

40. *G.N.M.* 9/15/90, 51 Cong., 2 Sess., *H.E.D.* No. 1, 608 (2842).

41. Ganoe, "The Desert Land Act in Operation, 1877-1891," *Agricultural History*, 11:153, 157.

8. Other Disposals of the Public Domain

MILITARY RESERVATIONS

A number of abandoned military reservations in New Mexico remained in an unsettled state for years because there was no authority for their restoration to the public domain. A Congressional Act of June 12, 1858, interdicted the sale of lands in a military reserve without a special act of Congress, and provided that they were not subject to pre-emption or homestead entry.

Special acts of Congress for the sale of military reserves usually provided for appraisers to evaluate the land, after which it was sold for not less than the appraised value, or for less than the minimum price of $1.25 per acre.[1] This was the case under the Act of February 24, 1871, when 13,645 acres at Fort Sumner were declared for sale. Meanwhile, in 1870, Lucien B. Maxwell had purchased the buildings and improvements on the abandoned military reservation and, together with some forty families, had moved there to live. Soon thereafter, Eben Everett, the register at Santa Fe, placed a request with the General Land Office to have the land transferred to the Interior Department so that it might be surveyed to enable the people living there to acquire title to the land.[2]

In 1872 Maxwell, through his attorney, J. Houghton of Santa Fe, requested permission to purchase the land within the limits of the reserve at private sale. He was informed that although he was the purchaser of the buildings he had no right to the land on which they were situated. The land could be disposed of only in accordance with the provisions of the Act of February 24, 1871,[3] which called for appraisal of the land and sale at public auction.[4]

---

1. Public Lands Commission, *Final Report*, 1881, 46 Cong., 3 Sess., *H.E.D.* No. 47, 249 (1975).
2. Everett to Joseph S. Wilson, 11/25/70 (F.R.C.).
3. W. W. Curtis, Acting Commissioner, to J. Houghton, 10/31/72 (N.A.).
4. See note 1.

By 1873 there were a hundred or more settlers on the reserve and Maxwell was still pressing the General Land Office for permission to buy the land on the grounds that the settlers had located there before the passage of the act providing for its disposal. The Land Office, however, still refused to recognize the right of the settlers to live on the reserve.[5]

Meanwhile Lucien Maxwell's son, Peter, deposited $2,500 for the survey of the townships within which the military reservation was located. The deposit was made in April 1872.

Early in 1874 a petition was sent to the General Land Office requesting that office to seek relief from Congress for the settlers on the reservation in the form of a law granting them homestead and pre-emption privileges. Commissioner Drummond ruled against this petition because "the settlers went upon the lands without authority of law. The deposit was made by Mr. Maxwell who purchased the Government buildings of the War Department, and not the settlers. This would indicate that the settlements were made in the interest of Mr. Maxwell, and that the lands [might] pass into his hands."[6]

In the spring of 1874, the reservation was appraised by Surveyor General James K. Proudfit[7] and Abram G. Hoyt, register of the Land Office at Santa Fe.[8]

In making deposits for survey, it was Maxwell's evident intention to use the receipt for the money deposited in payment for the land surveyed.[9] His intention was thwarted when the Land Office discovered that the deposit was for the survey of a military reservation. The money thus deposited then became an entire loss until the Act of March 3, 1879, made certificates of deposit for the survey of public lands assignable by endorsement and receivable in payment for any lands entered under the Homestead or Pre-emption laws. Meanwhile Maxwell had lost the triplicate copies of the certificates of deposit; nevertheless, after considerable maneuvering he was able to get a refund of his money, but he was not able to acquire the land he had sought.[10]

---

5. Drummond to Houghton, 2/8/73 (N.A.).
6. Drummond to J. W. Nesmith, House of Representatives, 1/12/74 (N.A.).
7. Drummond to Proudfit, 3/9/74 (N.A.).
8. *Ibid.*, to Abram G. Hoyt, 3/11/74.
9. See Chapter II.
10. J. M. Armstrong, Acting Commissioner, to Atkinson, 9/26/79, and Williamson to Atkinson, 3/29/80 (N.A.).

Most of the land in the Fort Sumner Military Reservation was eventually sold at public sale on January 15, 1884. A small portion, however, did not find buyers until 1914.[11]

Fort Sumner was the only reservation reverting to the public domain by a Special Act of Congress. Forts Butler, Cummings, Craig, McRae, and an unnamed reserve in T.18N, R.20E, were relinquished by the Regular Act of July 5, 1884, which provided for "the survey, appraisal and sale of abandoned Military Reservations, [such areas] to be appraised and sold at public sale, to the highest bidder for cash, at not less than the appraised value, nor less than $1.25 per acre."[12] All but Fort Cummings were either partially or wholly within private grants and no action was taken to dispose of those portions on the public domain prior to 1891.

Fort Thorn was never officially declared, yet its status was such that it was considered necessary to invoke official action for it to revert to the public domain. This authority was given by a decision of the Secretary of the Interior. All official declarations of forts in New Mexico were made by order of the President except Fort Butler, which was originally sanctioned by order of the Secretary of War (Appendix VII).

Forts still officially activated at the end of 1891 were Selden, Bayard, Marcy, Stanton, Union, and Wingate.[13] Fort Selden was relinquished on March 17, 1892, by authority of the Act of 1884. Fort Union reverted to the owners of the Mora Grant, where it was located, on April 1, 1894,[14] and Fort Marcy was relinquished on June 15, 1895.[15] Forts Bayard, Stanton, and Wingate are still in use (Appendix VII). Others such as Bascom, Conrad, Fillmore, Lowell, Fauntleroy (renamed Lyon), Tularosa, Webster, and West, and Camps Cook, Mimbres, and Vincent, were never officially declared to be military reservations but were simply appropriated from the public domain or private grants as the need arose and reverted to the same without official action.

The only military reservation in New Mexico that was not originally surveyed by military personnel was Fort Thorn. At the request

---

11. Registers and receivers, *Tract Books* (B.L.M.).

12. Julian to J. W. Virgin, San Marcial, N.M., 8/2/87 (B.L.M.).

13. *L.O.R.* 9/23/91, 52 Cong., 1 Sess., *H.E.D.* No. 1, 145 (2933).

14. F. Stanley, *Fort Union (New Mexico)*, 57.

15. Survey Records Section, *Survey Field Notes and Executive Documents of Military and Indian Reservations*, 119 (B.L.M.).

of General Garland, Surveyor General Pelham let a contract for the survey of that reserve to Deputy Surveyor John W. Garretson.[16] Other military reserves were included in Garland's request but were so distant from the lines of public surveys that Pelham considered their survey would entail a greater expense than he felt authorized to incur.[17] It was fortunate that none of these other surveys were made because the General Land Office decided that such surveys were not the function of that office and disallowed the account of Deputy Garretson for his survey of Fort Thorn.[18]

INDIAN RESERVATIONS

The Jicarilla Apache Indian Reservation, in present Rio Arriba and Sandoval counties, was first established by Executive Order of March 25, 1874, in accordance with treaty stipulations of December 10, 1873.[19] The reservation was twice restored to the public domain and the situation was finally clarified by President Cleveland on February 11, 1887, when 129,313.35 acres were allotted to 845 Indians, and 280.44 acres were reserved for mission, school, and agency purposes. The balance of 286,400 acres was unallotted.[20]

After considerable delay, in which at least two deputy surveyors rejected the work, a contract was finally let for the survey of the reservation to Mr. Hugh Hartman.[21] The contract was dated October 1, 1887.[22] The survey was duly made; but after much further delay, accusations, and recrimination, on February 14, 1890, it was finally rejected as being unsatisfactory. On October 23, 1890, a contract was made with James P. Harper for this same survey and for the allotments. To insure adequate work, the survey was made under the supervision of Special Agent J. K. Rankin.[23].

A reservation for Mescalero Apache Indians was first set aside

16. Pelham to Hendricks, 4/30/58 (B.L.M.).

17. *S.G.R.* 9/30/57, 35 Cong., 1 Sess., *H.E.D.* No. 11, 256 (919).

18. Hendricks to Pelham, 6/16/58 (N.A.).

19. Survey Records Section, *Survey Field Notes and Executive Documents of Military and Indian Reservations,* 65 (B.L.M.).

20. Public Lands Commission, *Report,* 1905, 58 Cong., 3 Sess., *S.E.D.* No. 189, 295 (4766).

21. Julian to Commissioner, General Land Office, 11/22/87 (F.R.C.).

22. Julian to Henry R. Martin, Santa Fe, 4/11/89 (F.R.C.).

23. Groff to Hobart, 2/14/90, 11/24/90 (N.A.).

south of Fort Stanton, by the Executive Order of May 29, 1873.[24] The upper part of the Ruidoso River Valley was excluded from the reservation in an attempt to avoid conflict with the settlements there.[25] This did not satisfy the Indians, as they were reluctant to live in the mountains during the winter, "although they desired that region for hunting." Then too, they had to live too far from the agency.[26]

In an attempt to correct these shortcomings, a new Executive Order of February 2, 1874, cancelled the old order and designated new boundaries.[27] In order to enlarge the reservation and to remove some of the ambiguities of the former metes and bounds descriptions,[28] a new boundary was designated by the Executive Order of October 20, 1875.[29] This boundary did not meet with the approval of certain miners within the territory.[30] Rich mineral deposits had been found in the western part of the reserve as it was then constituted. Surveyor General Atkinson suggested that both the miners and the Indians might be placated if a portion of the west edge of the reservation should be removed and some land added south of the 33d parallel.[31]

As it developed, some land was taken from the western edge of the reservation but none was added to the south, thus the reserve was reduced in size.[32] The area was finally established at 474,240 acres in 1883.[33]

The present Navaho[34] Reservation consists of about 15,000,000 acres of land in northwestern New Mexico, northeastern Arizona, and southeastern Utah. It has had a complex history, starting with

---

24. Frank D. Reeve, "Federal Indian Policy in New Mexico, 1858-1880," *New Mexico Historical Review,* 13:267, 268.

25. Drummond to Proudfit, 6/23/73 (N.A.).

26. Reeve, "Federal Indian Policy in New Mexico, 1858-1880," *New Mexico Historical Review,* 13:268.

27. *Ibid.*

28. Burdett to Proudfit, 11/19/75 (N.A.).

29. Reeve, "Federal Indian Policy in New Mexico, 1858-1880," *New Mexico Historical Review,* 13:269.

30. Williamson to L. A. Russell, U.S. Indian Agent, South Fork, N.M., 3/19/81 (N.A.).

31. Atkinson to Gen. J. H. Hammond, U.S. Indian Inspector, 10/15/79 (B.L.M.).

32. McFarland to register and receiver at Mesilla, 7/15/82 (N.A.).

33. Acting Commissioner William Walker to Julian, 8/25/85 (N.A.).

34. Berard Haile, O.F.M., "Navaho or Navajo?" *The Americas,* 6:85-90.

the treaty of 1868 between the United States and the Navaho In
dians, which set apart 3,414,528 acres, as a reservation.[35]

After a series of complicated orders, amendments, and cancella-
tions, an amendment of 1884 provided for the exemption of all
those portions of irrigable land in T.29N, R.14, 15, and 16W, south
of the San Juan River in New Mexico.[36] But the Navaho refused
to give up the land; what is more, the Indians needed this land "in
order to have access to water for their flocks." Its economic value
to the Navaho was above question, while "to the white people in
general, its occupancy by a handful of settlers could be of little
importance, either to the general economy or to the progress of
civilization. . . ." The Navaho knew little of the white man's practice in such matters so he relied upon his own sense of justice and
doggedly clung to the land until it was returned two years later.[37]
Adjustments continued until as late as 1934.[38]

On June 15, 1880, Congress ratified an agreement with the Ute
Indians in Colorado which provided for the survey of unoccupied
grazing and agricultural lands for the Southern Utes on the La
Plata River in Colorado. If enough land was not found in Colorado,
then the balance of the allotments were to be selected in the vicinity
of the La Plata River in New Mexico. In accordance with the act,
on October 18, a contract was made with J. Alexander Tyler and
Thomas B. Medary for these surveys.

As was expected, not enough agricultural land was found in Colorado, so the surveys were continued in New Mexico in the vicinity
of the La Plata River and also on the San Juan. The total amount
surveyed for these allotments in New Mexico was 120,349.47 acres.[39]

The land of the Pueblo Indians was confirmed by United States
patents in 1864 under old Spanish grants validated by the Acts of
December 22, 1858, and June 21, 1860. Additional lands were
allotted to San Felipe and Nambé pueblos by Executive Orders
of June 13, and September 4, 1902. By Executive Orders of March

---

35. H. J. Hagerman, *Navajo Indian Reservation*, 72 Cong., 1 Sess., *S.E.D.*
No. 64, 3.

36. *Ibid.*, 4.

37. Reeve, "A Navaho Struggle for Land," *New Mexico Historical Review*,
21:1-21. This article is an interesting account of the entire Navaho struggle
for this region.

38. Sanford A. Mosk, *Land Tenure Problems in The Santa Fe Railroad
Grant Area*, 14.

39. *L.O.R.* 10/11/82, 47 Cong., 2 Sess., *H.E.D.* No. 1, 81, 82, 84 (2099).

16, 1877; May 1, 1883; and March 3, 1885, 215,040 acres were set aside for the Zuñi Indians. The area of the original Spanish grant was 17,581.25 acres.[40]

INDIAN RESERVATIONS RESTORED TO THE PUBLIC DOMAIN

The Bosque Redondo Reservation, consisting of 1,024,000 acres surrounding Fort Sumner, was created by Executive Order on January 15, 1864.[41] It was never surveyed while a reservation and became subject to survey and entry on July 24, 1871,[42] at which time it was officially abandoned by order of the Act of February 24, 1871.[43]

The Hot Springs Reservation for southern Apache and other Indians, of 448,000 acres, was created by Executive Order on April 9, 1874, and the boundaries were defined December 21, 1875.[44] It was located in T.8-9S, R.7-8W, in the southwest corner of present Socorro County.[45] It was never surveyed while a reservation and, except for five sections on which the buildings were located, it was restored to the public domain by Executive Order of August 25, 1877.[46]

The Gila Apache (Santa Lucía) Reservation, in T.15, 16, 17S, R. 16, 17, 18, 19W,[47] in present Grant County, was selected on May 11, 1860, by Indian Agent Steck for the Gila Apaches, including the Mimbres, Mogollon, and Chiricahua bands of that tribe. No executive order was ever issued in the case and no steps were ever taken to settle Indians on the reservation.[48] It was surveyed in October 1860, to include 144,000 acres.[49] On January 19, 1882, it was

40. Public Lands Commission, *Report*, 1905, 58 Cong., 3 Sess., *S.E.D.* No. 189, 295 (4766). For the story of the Pueblo land grants, see Herbert O. Brayer, *Pueblo Land Grants of the "Rio Abajo," New Mexico.*

41. Survey Records Section, *Survey Field Notes and Executive Documents of Military and Indian Reservations, passim* (B.L.M.).

42. Drummond to J. M. Gallegos, House of Representatives, 5/17/72 (N.A.).

43. Drummond to Spencer, 6/10/71 (N.A.).

44. Survey Records Section, *Survey Field Notes and Executive Documents of Military and Indian Reservations, passim* (B.L.M.).

45. Reeve, "Federal Indian Policy in New Mexico, 1858-1880," *New Mexico Historical Review,* 13:303.

46. Williamson to Atkinson, 9/8/77 (N.A.).

47. Atkinson to McFarland, 11/17/81 (F.R.C.).

48. Survey Records Section, *Survey Field Notes and Executive Documents of Military and Indian Reservations,* 59, 60 (B.L.M.).

49. Clark to Edmunds, 11/30/61 (B.L.M.).

restored to the public domain by order of the Secretary of the Interior.[50]

The Tularosa Reservation of 384,000 acres was located on the Tularosa River, beginning at the headwaters of the Tularosa and extending down the river 30 miles for 10 miles on each side.[51] It was established by Executive Order on November 9, 1871, and officially abandoned, also by order of the President, on November 24, 1874.[52] It was never surveyed while a reservation.[53]

RAILROAD LANDS

Railroads received a large amount of the public domain in grants and rights-of-way. The one grant in New Mexico which was ever legally earned by a company to which it was granted was that to the Atlantic and Pacific Railroad Company (later acquired by the Atchison, Topeka and Santa Fe), and only to the A. & P. was title to land conveyed by the United States. Of this grant, 3,565,730.91 acres, exclusive of railroad right-of-way, was acquired by the A. & P. in New Mexico.[54]

The grant was made on July 27, 1866. Another line, the Texas and Pacific, was awarded a grant on March 3, 1871.[55] The A. & P. reorganized by the A. T. & S. F. and the Frisco, laid tracks from Isleta, New Mexico, to Needles, California, and thus earned that

50. McFarland to register and receiver at Mesilla, 1/30/82 (N.A.).

51. Commissioner of Indian Affairs, *Annual Report,* 11/15/71, 83.

52. Burdett to Proudfit, 1/18/75 (N.A.).

53. Map to accompany *L.O.R.* 11/1/76, 49 Cong., 2 Sess., *H.E.D.* No. 1 (1749).

54. James P. Reinhold, assistant to the president of the Santa Fe Railroad, to the author, September 16, 1955. The information was supplied by J. W. Higgins, valuation engineer system. Valuable studies on railroads are: William S. Greever, *Arid Domain: The Santa Fe Railway and its Western Land Grant;* Greever, "Railway Development in the Southwest," *New Mexico Historical Review,* 32:151-203; Sanford A. Mosk, *Land Tenure Problems in the Santa Fe Railroad Grant Area;* John Bell Sanborn, *Congressional Grants of Land in Aid of Railways;* David Maldwyn Ellis, "The Forfeiture of Railroad Land Grants, 1867-1894," *Mississippi Valley Historical Review,* 33:27-60; George W. Julian, "Our Land Grant Railways in Congress," *International Review,* 14:198-212; Julian, "Railway Influence in the Land Office," *American Review,* 136:237-256; and John B. Rae, "Commissioner Sparks and the Railroad Land Grants," *Mississippi Valley Historical Review,* 25:211-230.

55. *Stat. L.,* Vol. 14, 293; Vol. 16, 573.

portion of the grant.[56] The balance of the A. & P. grant was for-feited on July 6, 1886. The Texas and Pacific grant was likewise forfeited by a statute of February 28, 1885.[57]

Although the Texas and Pacific was not successful in acquiring title to its grant of land, this grant was still important in the disposal of the public domain in New Mexico, as was the unearned portion of the A. & P. grant. These grants tied up millions of acres of land and thus prevented actual settlement thereon.[58]

By 1891 the A. & P. had met with but little success in selling its grant land. In New Mexico, it sold 41,592.19 acres of grazing land to the Cebolla Cattle Company at 50 cents per acre. It also sold, in 1890, 314,668.37 acres of timber land, and the timber on it, to the Mitchell brothers. The price was $1.425 per acre. Outside of a few possible minor tracts, this was the extent of the railroad land sales in New Mexico.[59]

This failure to sell land can be accounted for by scarcity of water, troubles connected with unsurveyed land, and droughts during the early 1890's. Then too, ranchers used the land almost at will be-cause of traditional range rights and their success in preventing the passage of any effective Territorial trespass laws.[60]

Prior to the turn of the century, the Atlantic and Pacific also failed in its attempt to rent grazing rights. "In 1887 it announced that anybody using its acreage must take out a lease, but nobody did; under existing laws, the company could take no effective action against trespassers. In 1892 the railroad again attempted to interest renters but succeeded in making only one small lease for one year."[61]

Another item of the public domain related to railroad corpora-tions was the matter of rights-of-way. The Right of Way Act of

---

56. Greever, *Arid Domain*, 29, *passim.*

57. *Stat. L.*, Vol. 23, 337, 338; Vol. 24, 123, 124; Ellis, "The Forfeiture of Railroad Land Grants, 1867-1894," *Mississippi Valley Historical Review*, 33:42.

58. C. W. Holcomb, Acting Commissioner, to register and receiver at Mesilla, 4/14/81 (F.R.C.), is typical of the voluminous correspondence on this subject. This letter alone suspended fifteen entries because they conflicted with the lands withdrawn for the benefit of the Texas and Pacific Railroad Company.

59. Greever, *Arid Domain*, 48, 52; Greever to the author, January 16, 1956.

60. *Ibid.*, 43, 48.

61. *Ibid.*, 49.

March 3, 1875, provided for a 200-foot right-of-way and twenty acres for station grounds every ten miles. This rule of a 200-foot right-of-way was the general practice and was followed in the grant to the A. & P., except that the amount per station and proximity of stations were not specified. The one exception to the 200-foot right-of-way was allowed the Texas and Pacific, which was granted 200 feet on each side of the railroad and ground for stations not to exceed 40 acres each. The number of stations was not specified.[62]

The Southern Pacific (El Paso to the Colorado River) took over the Texas and Pacific prior to the revoking of the latter's grant,[63] but it was not entitled to the original 400-foot right-of-way and 40-acre lots for stations. The Southern Pacific's right-of-way was governed by the terms of the Act of 1875, subject, however, to any rights then existing of the Texas and Pacific.[64] Through 1891, there were 22,670 acres in rights-of-way taken from the public domain in New Mexico.[65]

In the matter of station grounds, the Right of Way Act of 1875 allowed one tract of 20 acres every 10 miles, but the A. & P. grant did not specify the amount. As an approximation, however, the amount allowed by the Act of 1875 should not be far off. Railroads for which data is available specified, on plats filed with the Interior Department, as much land for stations as they were allowed,[66] as did, in all probability, the rest. In 935.15 miles (Appendix VIII) there would be 94 twenty-acre tracts of 1,880 acres in station grounds. Combining rights-of-way and station grounds, there were about 24,550 acres granted to railroads in New Mexico for rights-of-way through 1891. This figure, added to the area granted to the A. & P. Railroad, makes a total approximating 3,590,281 acres of land granted for railroad purposes in New Mexico by the Federal Government.

In the entire Territory through 1891, there were only 622,684

---

62. *Stat. L.,* Vol. 14, 294; Vol. 16, 576; Vol. 18, 482.

63. James P. Reinhold to the author, September 16, 1955.

64. C. W. Holcomb, Acting Commissioner, to register and receiver at Mesilla, 6/16/81 (F.R.C.).

65. Acreage of rights-of-way can be calculated from Appendix VIII by the following formulae: 935.15 miles × 5,280 (feet in a mile) × 200 (width of right-of-way) ÷ 43,560 (square feet in an acre) = acres of right-of-way on the public domain in New Mexico.

66. McFarland to register and receiver at Las Cruces, 5/22/84 (F.R.C.), is an example that concerns the Silver City, Deming, and Pacific Railroad Co.

acres of land granted to individuals by virtue of the land laws. An additional 648,028 acres of public domain were sold to individuals; but, even this total of 1,270,712 acres (Appendix VI) is insignificant compared to the amount granted to railroads.

MINERAL AND COAL LANDS

When Surveyor General Pelham arrived in New Mexico to institute the surveying system there, his only precedent regarding mineral lands was contained in his original instructions, and it informed him that mineral lands could not be acquired under the provisions of the Donation and Pre-emption laws.[67] This left no method for people to acquire title to mineral lands under the land laws of the United States.

From his first year in office, Pelham had to deal with this problem. The first effort in New Mexico to acquire title to mineral land was made in 1855, when Hugh Stephenson filed a pre-emption claim for the land covered by his furnaces and machinery for extracting ore. Stephenson's claim was located in T.22S, R.3E, in the Organ Mountain Mining District in Doña Ana County. There was no provision of law allowing this filing, so the claim was withdrawn.[68]

Pelham, who filled the offices of register and receiver during the first years of his incumbency as surveyor general, summed up the problem in 1859:

> the Government does not recognize the vesting of title to individuals in mines discovered on the public lands. In California it has been customary to allow the discoverer of a mine to work it, if on public land until he abandons it when it then is liable to be worked by another but no title is vested in either and it is the opinion of this office that the same custom holds good in this Territory. When this country was ceded to the United States all the laws of Mexico then existing were declared to be in force excepting such as conflicted with those of the United States. As the Mexican Laws in regard to mines are directly opposed to those of this government in their principle and practicable application they are virtually repealed.[69]

67. *L.O.R.* 11/30/54, 33 Cong., 2 Sess., *H.E.D.* No. 1, 100, 102 (777).
68. Pelham to Bvt. Maj. J. T. Sprague, Ft. Fillmore, 3/24/60 (B.L.M.).
69. Pelham to John Donaldson, Calabasas, N.M., 5/21/59 (B.L.M.).

Prior to 1866 there was no general mineral legislation. In lieu of such legislation, there grew up a system of local regulations controlling the size, location, and possession of mining claims and the water rights appurtenant thereto. These regulations, applying at first only to placer claims, varied in different localities. Regulations governing lode mining were established as soon as required. It was customary for miners in various localities to organize mineral districts and elect recorders whose duty it was to record the location of all claims filed with them. Filing was generally required in order to make the claim valid. These regulations grew from the mutual consent of their makers and became recognized as binding in the courts in all matters relating to mining claim titles.[70]

The first national mineral land legislation was the Mining Act of July 26, 1866, providing that both surveyed and unsurveyed land was to be open to exploration and occupation by all citizens of the United States or persons declaring their intention to become citizens. The act was subject to regulations prescribed by law and also local miners' rules that did not conflict with national laws. The law applied only to lode mines. This act was followed by the Placer-Mining Act of July 9, 1870, which provided for the survey and sale of placer-mining claims at $2.50 per acre.

The next mining legislation was passed on May 10, 1872, and it amended the original act of 1866. It recognized mineral lands as a distinct class and provided for the survey and sale of placer lands at $2.50 per acre and $5.00 per acre for lode claims.[71]

The first coal land legislation was the Act of July 1, 1864. Under this act, coal lands became subject to pre-emption at a minimum price of $20 per acre. The law required that such lands first be proclaimed for sale by the President to the highest bidder in legal subdivisions. The following year, on March 3, the law was supplemented so that citizens of the United States engaged in coal mining as a business could enter 160 acres of coal land, or less, at $20 per acre.

Finally, the Act of March 3, 1873, allowed for a pre-emption of 160 acres of coal land to an individual and 320 acres to an asso-

---

70. Public Lands Commission, *Final Report,* 1881, 46 Cong., 3 Sess., *H.E.D.* No. 47, 321 (1975).
71. *Ibid.,* 321, 322.

ciation. The price was fixed at $10 per acre for lands *more* than 15 miles from a completed railroad and $20 per acre for coal land *within* 15 miles from a railroad. Furthermore, an association of no less than four persons, having expended at least $5,000 in improving a mine on their claim, might take out an additional entry of 640 acres at the stated prices.[72]

The laws covering mineral lands on the public domain did not extend to private grants; consequently, there arose a difficult problem in this connection. The Treaty of Guadalupe Hidalgo of 1848 obligated the United States to honor only such regulations as were in force under the former government, providing they did not conflict with national policy and welfare. Mineral rights did not extend to land grants under the governments of Spain and Mexico. There were many who felt that, in this matter, the largess of the United States should spread no further than that of the former governments. In the grants originally confirmed, Congress failed to withhold mineral rights; therefore, they passed to the grantees.[73]

After 1879 Congress confirmed no more grants in New Mexico until 1891. This presented another problem. The Act of July 22, 1854, provided that unconfirmed grants be held in a state of reservation; thus they were closed to miners as well as to settlers, and the failure of Congress to act gave grant claimants the use of large areas of land without ownership of the same.[74]

The situation was settled to some extent by the Act of March 3, 1891, establishing a Court of Private Land Claims. By the third section of this act, gold, silver, and quicksilver mines, or minerals of the same, on grants subsequently confirmed, were reserved for the United States. However, the same act provided that no such mine could be worked, on any property confirmed under the act, without the consent of the owner of the property unless otherwise arranged by subsequent legislation. Other mineral rights were not mentioned and, consequently, went with the confirmed grant.[75]

This condition was not settled until 1926. On June 8 of that year, the Secretary of the Interior was authorized to lease the right to mine such metals to the grantee of any claim confirmed by the Court

---

72. *Ibid.*, 292; Copp, *The American Settler's Guide,* 72-76.
73. *S.G.R.* 8/20/86, 49 Cong., 2 Sess., *H.E.D.* No. 1, 537, 538 (2468).
74. *L.O.R.* 9/23/91, 133.
75. *Stat. L.,* Vol. 26, 860.

of Private Land Claims. The royalty for this right was assigned at from 5 to 12½ per cent of the net value.[76]

The greatest impetus to mining development came with the advent of railroad transportation in 1880 (Appendix IV). There was also a better knowledge of mineral resources in the Territory by this time. As early as 1857, the Secretary of the Interior had suggested the propriety of a geological survey of New Mexico, and in 1860 an unsuccessful attempt was made to achieve Congressional action to that end; however, the Civil War halted further activities in the matter.[77] The first decisive step in the direction of a geological survey was taken by Major James W. Powell, who followed more than a decade of geological studies in the West with his monumental "Report on the Arid Regions of the United States," in 1878.[78]

By 1871, Indian dangers had lessened in many parts of the Territory; and surveyors, settlers, and miners alike were appreciative of the better progress that was consequently promised;[79] nevertheless, mining did not increase greatly until the decade of the 1880's.[80]

LANDS FOR EDUCATIONAL PURPOSES

The Act of July 22, 1854, establishing the office of surveyor general, reserved sections 16 and 36 in each township for the benefit of schools in the Territory, and a quantity of land equal to two townships was reserved for the establishment of a university.[81] Subsequently sections 2 and 32 were also reserved for common schools.[82]

The Morrill Act of 1862 provided for 30,000 acres of land for each senator and representative in Congress at the time. The purpose of this grant was to establish a college for instruction in agri-

---

76. Emilio D. DeSoto and Arthur R. Morrison, *Mining Rights on the Public Domain,* 396.

77. Edmunds to John Watts, House of Representatives, 12/16/61 (N.A.).

78. Dunham, *Government Handout,* 35.

79. *S.G.R.* 11/19/71, 42 Cong., 2 Sess., *H.E.D.* No. 1, 178 (1505). Indian depredations continued in the southwest part of the Territory until the middle of the next decade.

80. Westphall, "Albuquerque in the 1870's," *New Mexico Historical Review,* 23:264.

81. *Stat. L.,* Vol. 10, 308-310.

82. George A. Graham, *Know New Mexico: Acquisition of State Lands,* 3.

cultural and mechanical arts;[83] nevertheless, none of this land was actually granted to the Territory until the passage of the Ferguson Act of June 21, 1898. The Enabling Act of June 20, 1910, made additional grants and later legislation added still more (Appendix IX).

---

83. Simon Peter Nanninga, *The New Mexico School System*, 98.

9. Federal Prosecution of Fraud

LARGE-SCALE PROSECUTION of fraudulent practices came with the advent of the Democratic administration in 1885; nevertheless, there was warning by 1879 that title to much public land was being acquired in a manner and under conditions not contemplated by law largely because the land laws were not being adapted to the arid West.[1]

The decade of the 1880's in New Mexico saw the expansion of the railroad and a boom in land entries and the cattle business. Land for grazing purposes was needed in ever increasing quantities — far more than could legally be acquired under the land laws. Competition for grazing rights on the public domain was becoming so keen that it was ever more desirable to acquire title to land — especially to land that controlled water. The consequence was an epidemic of fraudulent manipulation of the land laws. Prior to this decade there had been only four indictments for land fraud in the Territory, none of which had resulted in a conviction.[2]

By 1881, the incidence of fraud was such that Elias Brevoort, receiver of the Land Office at Santa Fe, on December 5, informed Commissioner N. C. McFarland, in a letter of far-reaching consequence, "that I have quite recently become impressed with the belief there has been for some months past a system of frauds perpetrated in making entries of lands."[3] He named as principal suspected parties José de Sena, former register at Santa Fe; Antonio

1. Public Lands Commission, *Preliminary Report*, 1879, 46 Cong., 2 Sess., *H.E.D.* No. 46, IX (1923).

2. United States, *Transcript Record of District Court Cases.* First Judicial District, Nos. 382 and 383. *Criminal Docket (Old)* June 1877-March 1886. Third Judicial District, Nos. 334 and 390.

3. Secretary of the Interior, *Fraudulent Acquisition of Titles to Land in New Mexico*, 1885, 48 Cong., 2 Sess., *S.E.D.* No. 106, 19.

Ortiz y Salazar, former probate judge of Santa Fe County; John Gwyn and Thomas Gwyn of Santa Fe, the latter a former register; Miguel Salazar, Las Vegas attorney; Alexander Grzelachowski, better known as "Polaco"; Celso Baca of San Miguel County; and Miguel Martin, Leandro Urtadio, José Trejora, Luis F. García, Hilario Montana, Ignacio Valdez, Tarivio Martin, Frank Unruh, and B. F. Houx, all residents in the vicinity of Cimarron in Colfax County. There were also, he believed, many others.[4]

The practice was to have witnesses furnish false affidavits, dating back the time of settlement to suit the case, and the entrant then acquired the land without ever having seen it, after which the principal manipulators and advisors purchased it for a nominal sum. Another practice was for stock-raisers to have their laborers make false entries for their employers' benefit.[5]

Brevoort suggested that a special agent of the Interior Department be sent to the Territory at once to investigate. He should be "a man firm and resolute, and beyond the reach of bribery, who should be paid *double* or *treble* the usual salary of special agents, with all expenses paid, for the reason that the risk of life [was] great, not only to him, but to persons giving information of the frauds in question...."[6]

Brevoort left office on December 8, 1881, three days after his communication with the Commissioner.[7] He had been a dealer in land grants; but, at this time, it seems he had no axe to grind on the troubled wheel of Territorial politics, since his name drops completely from the resulting investigations, charges, and countercharges.

As a direct result of Brevoort's charges, on August 5, 1882, Robert S. Graham, a clerk in the General Land Office, was appointed for a period of one month to investigate fraud in New Mexico. This was later extended for an additional thirty days. He found that conditions warranted a much more extensive scrutiny than originally

---

4. *Ibid.,* 19-21.

5. The Donation Law required four years of residence and cultivation and a certificate was acquired by presenting proof of such. In 1881 there were 172 donation notifications and 162 donation certificates; more than in all previous years combined. See Appendixes IV and V for complete statistics on all land laws.

6. Secretary of the Interior, *Fraudulent Acquisition of Titles to Land in New Mexico,* 1885, 48 Cong., 2 Sess., *S.E.D.* No. 106, 19.

7. *Ibid.,* 22. He took office in July 1878.

contemplated. By the end of 1884, at least seven special agents of the General Land Office had conducted investigations in the Territory. These were Richard J. Hinton, H. H. Eddy, John M. Dunn, Frank D. Hobbs, John G. Evans, A. R. Greene, and Charles A. Walker.[8]

With the evidence unearthed by these agents, Secretary of the Interior Teller and Commissioner McFarland set in motion the wheels of justice through indictments for the widespread fraudulent practices in the Territory.

Through 1891 there were 3,633 criminal cases in the five Federal District Courts in New Mexico. Of these, 641 involved land fraud; however, there were only four such cases prior to 1883. Exclusive of these four, land fraud cases were initiated in the first and second districts in 1883, the third district in 1884, and the fourth district in 1887. None of the 69 cases in the fifth district initiated in 1891 involved land fraud. The first district had 1,431 cases, with 388 land fraud; second district, 894 cases, with 33 land fraud; third district, 933 cases, with 149 land fraud; and the fourth district, 306 cases, with 71 land fraud.[9]

Perjury accounted for the most cases, with a total of 442. Unlawful inclosures followed with 78 cases, and violation of timber laws accounted for 64. Other categories were subornation of perjury, con-

---

8. *Ibid.*, 23-25, *passim.*

9. United States, *Territorial Court Records.* Transcript Records and Dockets of District Court Cases. The first district consisted of the counties of Santa Fe, San Juan, Rio Arriba, and Taos; second district, Bernalillo, Valencia, and Socorro; third district, Doña Ana, Sierra, and Grant; fourth district, San Miguel, Colfax, Mora, and Lincoln; fifth district, Socorro, Lincoln, Chaves, and Eddy. Some changes were made from time to time in the counties within the various districts, which accounts for overlapping. The cases by years follow:

Year	No. 1	No. 2	No. 3	No. 4	Total
1871	2	—	—	—	2
1876	—	—	1	—	1
1878	—	—	1	—	1
1883	52	1	—	—	53
1884	3	—	48	—	51
1885	10	—	1	—	11
1886	275	15	61	—	351
1887	40	6	16	14	76
1888	4	8	7	23	42
1889	2	3	14	5	24
1890	—	—	—	29	29
	388	33	149	71	641

spiracy, official misconduct, abstraction of records, bribery, forgery, false certificate, and unlawful obtaining of land (Appendix XI).

There were only 15 cases with a jury verdict of guilty, but this does not tell the entire story. In 82 cases the defendant was not found by a United States Marshal, and these marshals repeatedly wrote on subpoenas that after a diligent search they were unable to find the defendant and did not believe the person existed. This was probably true, because one grand jury foreman pointed out that many entries were made with fictitious names.[10] Some of these defendants may have skipped the country, but in either instance they were presumably guilty. Also, in 209 dismissed cases, all or part of the records are missing from the transcript. Many dismissed cases were not prosecuted by the U. S. Attorney because records were lost or stolen from the files.[11] At that time this was a serious difficulty, because all affidavits, etc., were in longhand, and only single copies existed. Thus, if they were missing, it was difficult to duplicate them. Without the missing transcripts, it is impossible to say how many of these cases were not prosecuted because the record had already been stolen at the time for prosecution. The fact that the records were lost or stolen is a strong presumption of guilt in all these cases. Then too, in 28 cases the verdict is in neither the docket nor the transcript, and here also there is a possibility of guilt.[12]

The Democrats came into power in 1885, and with Commissioner Wm. A. J. Sparks leading the way, they intensified the prosecution of land fraud cases in the Territory. In 1886 there were 351 cases — far more than in any previous or subsequent year.[13] The Republicans, nevertheless, under Secretary of the Interior Teller and Commissioner McFarland, had not only pressed charges in numerous indictments, but also had conducted the investigations that were used as the basis for Democratic prosecutions.[14] In Washington,

---

10. *L.O.R.* 10/7/86, 49 Cong., 2 Sess., *H.E.D.* No. 1, 470 (2468). This foreman was R. W. Webb.

11. The dockets give this information in a number of cases.

12. United States, *Territorial Court Records.* Transcript Records and Dockets of District Court Cases. Appendix XI is a summary of all cases.

13. See Note 9.

14. Names of persons indicted by the Democrats were almost entirely those investigated by the Republicans. In the years after 1884, Land Office Reports mention only four special agents by name as having investigated fraud in the Territory. These are: Clark S. Rowe, *L.O.R.* 10/7/86, 49 Cong., 2 Sess., *H.E.D.*

Commissioner Sparks gave his Republican predecessors due credit for collecting information on land fraud;[15] but in New Mexico this courtesy was sorely lacking.[16]

There was loud lamenting in Democratic Washington that convictions were almost impossible to secure in New Mexico. The sparseness of English-speaking people bore the brunt of the blame. Native New Mexicans were accused of being unreliable witnesses who would swear to anything, and native juries were charged with never returning a verdict of guilty regardless of the evidence. Sympathy was expressed for these people, however, because they were unaware of the law and could be deceived into signing fraudulent papers in the interest of others. Natives with honest intentions were frequently taken advantage of, it was pointed out, by unscrupulous manipulators, who gave them false descriptions of the land they lived on prior to the time they filed this description in the land office. These descriptions were for worthless land and the settler filed the spurious description thinking it was for the land he had settled upon. His home was then filed upon by a person representing the party who supplied the false description and the settler was deprived of his valuable land in exchange for the worthless acreage he had filed upon. If he complained he was told that he had committed perjury by entering land he had never lived upon and that if he did not keep quiet he would be arrested and prosecuted.[17]

No. 1, 273 (2468); J. N. Smithee, E. R. Stafford, *Ibid.*, 471; and Clayton G. Coleman, *L.O.R.* 9/28/87, 50 Cong., 1 Sess., *H.E.D.* No. 1, 159, 160 (2541). Only isolated examples of the work of these agents are given. One particularly telling and widely quoted indictment against fraud in the nation, contained in part in the Annual Report of Commissioner Sparks for 1885, *L.O.R.* 10/22/85, 49 Cong., 1 Sess., *H.E.D.* No. 1, 202-205 (2378), was originally written at the request of Sparks' predecessor by Inspector A. R. Greene from Santa Fe, N.M., on November 3, 1884: Secretary of the Interior, *Fraudulent Acquisition of Titles to Land in New Mexico,* 48 Cong., 2 Sess., *S.E.D.* No. 106, 378-381.

    15. Dunham, *Government Handout,* 185.

    16. *L.O.R.* 10/7/86, 49 Cong., 2 Sess., *H.E.D.* No. 1, 470 (2468).

    17. *Ibid.*, 90, 91, 272. Commissioner Sparks' opinions were based on a letter from Special Agent H. H. Eddy to Commissioner McFarland, 5/17/83, Secretary of the Interior, *Fraudulent Acquisition of Titles to Land in New Mexico,* 1885, 48 Cong., 2 Sess., *S.E.D.* No. 106, 49. The practice by which settlers were deprived of their land is confirmed by numerous letters between commissioners and registers, receivers, and surveyors general (N.A., B.L.M., and F.R.C.).

It is true that the native inhabitants were used by clever schemers who took advantage of their ignorance of laws and customs they were not acquainted with. It is also true that native juries returned few verdicts of guilty, but this must be explained. At that time juries had to be selected largely from native inhabitants because they composed the bulk of the population. There were two reasons why a verdict of guilty was seldom returned: fear of reprisal,[18] and sympathy for anyone accused of a crime.[19]

It was well known also that a majority of the accused were innocent as to interest. They did not understand the English language, were ignorant of the land laws, were confiding, and were "mere tools in the hands of designing men as well as the betrayed of official corruption."[20]

Far more important, though, is the fact that many cases with damaging possibilities never got to the jury. There is not a shred of evidence indicating that Washington officials were aware of the many times that United States Marshals were unable to find defendants, or of the really amazing number of records that were lost or stolen from the files (Appendix XI). To blame juries for these conditions is utterly unfair since the theft of the missing records had to be the work of persons who had access to the files; largely the attorneys in the cases. The United States Attorneys themselves are not blameless in the matter.[21]

Persons and corporations against whom indictments were returned represented all classes in the Territory; Charles Ilfeld, Max Frost, Pedro Sánchez, Dubuque Cattle Company, Wm. H. McBroom, Luciano Baca, Red River Cattle Company, Lake Cattle Company, Palo Blanco Cattle Company, Prairie Cattle Company, Portsmouth Cattle Company, Stephen W. Dorsey, Miguel Martin, Cimarron

---

18. Personal interview, Land Office personnel, March 23, 1956.

19. Paul W. Robinson to the author, March 26, 1956. Mr. Robinson is a prominent Albuquerque attorney and he points out that even today "predominantly Spanish juries are perhaps a little more sympathetic than Anglo juries, and are inclined to be more lenient as far as accused persons in criminal matters are concerned, and are likewise inclined to be perhaps more lenient in granting awards to plaintiffs in civil damage cases."

20. *L.O.R.* 10/7/86, 49 Cong., 2 Sess., *H.E.D.* No. 1, 470 (2468). Address of R. W. Webb, foreman of the grand jury, First Judicial District, to Chief Justice Long.

21. Personal interview, Land Office personnel, March 23, 1956.

Cattle Company, Wm. F. Purmont, George H. Purmont, Theo. Maxwell, Charles Blanchard, and M. A. Upson, to name only a few.[22]

But one person was singled out over all the others; Max Frost, register of the Land Office at Santa Fe and reportedly a conspicuous and successful manipulator of the Santa Fe Ring.[23] He came to New Mexico as a sergeant[24] in charge of the military telegraph line built into Santa Fe.[25] During the years 1881-1883 he was Adjutant General of New Mexico, from which position his title of "Colonel"[26] derived. By 1884 he was prominent in politics and once unwisely boasted to Inspector John G. Evans that he had great influence with the grand jurors of his county and would have persons indicted who made an affidavit against him. He was likewise secretary of the San Mateo Cattle Company, interested in a mining company, connected with four newspapers,[27] as well as being an incorporator, in 1883, of the San Mateo Cattle Company, together with Amado Chaves and Simón Vivo. In 1884 he joined with H. M. Atkinson, W. H. McBroom, and three gentlemen from Kentucky in forming the New Mexico and Kentucky Land and Stock Company.[28]

As a result of charges preferred by Francis Downs, a Santa Fe attorney, on October 30, 1883, and by R. W. Webb on January 8, 1884, Frost's conduct in office was thoroughly investigated by Inspector Frank D. Hobbs. On the basis of Hobbs' reports in the matter, Commissioner McFarland presented charges to Frost on September 24, and requested that he make any showing he might desire before the case was turned over to the Secretary of the Interior.[29]

---

22. United States, *Territorial Court Records.* Transcript Records and Dockets of District Court Cases.

23. *L.O.R.* 10/7/86, 49 Cong., 2 Sess., *H.E.D.* No. 1, 470 (2468); Secretary of the Interior, *Fraudulent Acquisition of Titles to Land in New Mexico,* 1885, 48 Cong., 2 Sess., *S.E.D.* No. 106, *passim.* Governor's Papers, Edmund G. Ross, State Records Center, Santa Fe, New Mexico. Letter from Ross to John O'Grady, St. Louis, Mo., March 26, 1887.

24. *S.G.R.* 8/15/78, 45 Cong., 3 Sess., *H.E.D.* No. 1, 277 (1850).

25. Paul A. F. Walter, "New Mexico's Pioneer Bank and Bankers," *New Mexico Historical Review,* 21:224.

26. M. A. Otero, Jr., to the author, May 27, 1955.

27. Secretary of the Interior, *Fraudulent Acquisition of Titles to Land in New Mexico,* 1885, 48 Cong., 2 Sess., *S.E.D.* No. 106, 83, 387.

28. Western Range Cattle Industry Study, *New Mexico Cattle Corporations, 1871-1900.* Summary, Ms.

29. Secretary of the Interior, *Fraudulent Acquisition of Titles to Land in*

Two months later, on November 24, Frost had not presented a defense and McFarland laid the matter before Secretary Teller recommending Frost's dismissal. McFarland pointed out that a large number of persons expressed want of confidence in Frost's official integrity and openly charged that his office was not honestly conducted. They also expressed fear of volunteering evidence out of court because of Frost's political influence.

Among specific charges investigated by Inspector Hobbs, and reported to Secretary Teller, was that L. J. Orcutt paid Frost $700 for furnishing him aid in enlarging his ranch by means of a number of fraudulent entries. In numerous other cases Frost was charged with attaching his signature to fraudulent entry papers without the affiants being present. Another case involved nineteen fraudulent homestead entries made in the interest of Pedro Sánchez, Indian Agent at Santa Fe. Nine of the entries were in the names of fictitious persons, and in the rest the persons in whose names the entries were made swore under oath that they had not signed the papers. He was charged with being a silent partner of M. Salazar, a land attorney at Las Vegas. Salazar was able to pass entries through the land office without bothering entrymen to make affidavits or to sign papers. It was learned by the inspector that Frost did a great deal of work at night, the mornings after which the clerk would find many final proofs that had not been there on the evening before. Frost was charged with being a party to many illegal final proof notices that were printed in two or three copies of a newspaper and omitted from the regular edition. He had assumed entire charge of the receiver's office and the latter did nothing but sign his name while Frost received all money sent by mail and made returns by personal check contrary to official instructions. A number of irregularities in the method of keeping records of entries were noted, raising the suspicion that certain lands were held on the books long after they should have been relinquished. Finally, Frost had raised the fee for publishing final proof notices, and the newspapers in which he had an interest had received most of the business.[30]

On December 9, Frost belatedly answered the charges, giving as an excuse for his tardiness that he had been injured in a fall from a buggy and had been unable to perform any active physical

---

New Mexico, 1885, 48 Cong., 2 Sess., *S.E.D.* No. 106, 149, 203, 204, 386, 387, *passim*.

30. *Ibid.*, 381-384.

or mental labor. He addressed his letter to Secretary Teller instead of to Commissioner McFarland, who had presented the charges. The following circumstance sheds light on his reason for doing this. On October 30, 1883, Francis Downs had preferred charges against Frost in a letter to Secretary Teller. The letter was registered and marked "private." Even before Teller acknowledged the letter, Frost was in some manner informed not only of the charges but also of their language.[31] However, Frost's influence had run its course and he was permitted to resign in March 1885.[32]

It is evident that the numerous investigations of land fraud in the Territory were a deterrent to this type of activity. In 1884, the first year that the numbers of reported fraud cases were published by the General Land Office, New Mexico led the nation with 827 cases, followed by California with 574. Late that year the pressure of investigation reached a climax when Max Frost was put on the carpet by the Interior Department. The following year New Mexico dropped to eleventh place with only 63 cases and during subsequent years, the entries reached their average of fifth place (Appendix X).

On July 14, 1886, an indictment was returned against Max Frost by the grand jury on a charge of official misconduct. On July 30, 1886, an additional fourteen charges were filed, wherein Frost was either named as sole defendant or was named with others on conspiracy charges. Five of the total number of cases filed against him were based upon misconduct; one was based upon a false certificate given; another was for subornation of perjury; and eight were for conspiracy. In the examination into the complete record of the case, it appears that the first case filed was the key case of the United States Attorney, who was Thomas Smith. This case came on for trial first on February 24, 1887, and the jury verdict was guilty. Edward Miller was the foreman of the jury, and the jury verdict assessed a penalty against Frost of imprisonment for one year and a fine of $5,000. Immediately following this, Frost's attorneys moved for a new trial. A hearing was held upon their motion and a new trial was denied. Following that, Frost's attorneys submitted a long series of affidavits and filed a motion for a rehearing on the

31. *Ibid.*, 175, 176, 387-389.

32. *L.O.R.* 10/7/86, 49 Cong., 2 Sess., *H.E.D.* No. 1, 470 (2468); Anderson, *History of New Mexico,* Vol. I, 189. Frost signed his last Abstract of Entries in that month. Charles F. Easley signed for April, *Monthly Abstract of Homestead Entries* (F.R.C.).

question of whether or not he was entitled to a new trial. The affidavits in question relate to the fact that the foreman of the jury, Edward Miller, had a great deal of animosity toward Frost's attorney, who was Henry L. Waldo, and other affidavits attempted to show the proper disposition by Frost of the funds which he was charged to have accepted in the nature of a bribe.

The basic indictment of the grand jury charged him with the acceptance of $60 as a bribe, and at the time of the first trial a receipt was offered in evidence that Frost had receipted for a total sum of $225. These affidavits went to the point that Frost had no way of knowing, nor did his attorneys, prior to the time of the first trial, that anything more than the $60 would come up; and when the receipt was introduced into evidence it placed a burden upon Frost to show the proper disposition of the entire sum of $225, which Frost alleged he could do and submitted affidavits to show a partial proper distribution of this money. It appears that the United States District Judge was impressed with the affidavits, and upon rehearing granted Frost a new trial, which was held on August 17, 1888, and which resulted in a jury verdict of not guilty. In the first trial, for which the list of jurors appears, the only Anglo name on the list was that of the foreman, Edward Miller. The list of jurors in the second trial does not appear in the official record of the proceedings; however, the jury verdict is in Spanish and signed by David Velarde as the foreman of the jury. It would appear from this jury verdict that the trial proceeded through an interpreter.

Immediately following the jury verdict of August 17, 1888, whereby Frost was found not guilty, a series of other cases against him were dismissed, apparently upon motion of the United States Attorney, though no record of his motion or any order of dismissal appears in the official record of the file, these appearing only in the docket in the office of the Clerk. Other cases against Frost, a total of five, were dismissed on August 18, 1888, giving the United States Attorney leave to reinstate them at any time. The reason for this was that the official files were missing from the office of the Clerk. It is assumed that in those days the indictments rendered by the grand jury were by original copy only and that no duplicate was retained; someone apparently had taken a number of these cases against Max Frost and others out of the office of the United States District Court Clerk. It is more than coincidence that these files are missing. It would not be uncommon to have one case misfiled; however, even in those days, anyone taking a file out of the office of the Clerk was required to receipt for the same, and no receipt or other document appears in the records in the office. The cases which are missing involved one of official misconduct against Max Frost; two others were conspiracy charges against Max Frost and P. H. Kuhn. The other two were conspiracy charges against Max Frost and Pedro Y. Jaramillo.

Frost did stand trial in three other cases, two of which were based upon conspiracy, the co-conspirators being Luciano Baca and Amado Chaves, and the jury verdict in those cases was not guilty. The other case involved official misconduct, and the court apparently instructed a verdict in favor of Frost because the alleged act was barred by the statute of limitations of the day. The five cases which the United States Attorney made subject to reinstatement were dismissed from the record in 1904.[33]

Max Frost was extremely fortunate in having all the charges against him disposed of in one way or another since the records in the case show that it was a real battle all the way.

It is also evident that his case was related to the indictment of a number of persons other than those named in indictments with him. The key case against Frost was No. 975a. Forty-two other cases appear with the suffix "a" immediately following 975a. These numbers break into the regular sequence of numbers following No. 1026. All of these were perjury cases and all were either dismissed or returned with a verdict of not guilty. Apparently the basis for the dismissal or acquittal was that the people involved, while committing an act of perjury, did so either unknowingly or through coercion of their employer or some other person.[34]

New Mexico's leading newspaper stoutly defended Frost and bitterly condemned the grand jury indictments. Surveyor General Julian and Governor Ross were vilified and ridiculed for pressing the matter. It was charged that the United States Attorney would

33. United States, *Criminal Docket,* Vol. I, First Judicial District, August 1, 1882-May 2, 1896; *Transcript Record of Cases,* First Judicial District, Nos. 975a, 1086, 1092, 1093, 1095, 1101, 1103, 1104, 1105, 1107, 1109, 1140, 1141, 1142 and 1149. Paul W. Robinson aided materially in assembling the facts of this case.

34. Paul W. Robinson to the author, March 26, 1956. Mr. Robinson is of the opinion that Mr. Frost was related to even more cases than the 42 linked to key case No. 975a, but the evidence here is not conclusive.

reap a rich harvest in fees if he didn't have to "divvy" too much.[35]
This stand on the part of the *New Mexican* is understandable because Frost was president, manager, and editor of both the daily
and weekly editions.[36] These papers were editorially powerful in
the Territory and most other news sheets followed their lead. Only
a few supported the Democratic administration's fraud prosecutions.[37]

Another matter of concern to the Government was the unlawful
inclosure of the public domain. As early as 1879 this was an issue
with the Public Lands Commission. Inquiries revealed that there
was then very little fencing in New Mexico, but that in most parts
of the Territory, cattle could safely be confined during the winter
months when they were inclined to drift and break wire fences.
Ranchers did not desire to fence the range because it was not
crowded and there seemed to be plenty of room for all.[38]

Early in the next decade this situation was changed when large
cattle corporations were formed[39] and land entries were taken out
in ever increasing numbers (Appendixes IV-V). The fight was now
on to control water and range facilities.

The first complaint against large-scale fencing in the Territory
was made in 1883. On February 24 of that year, some two dozen
petitioners complained of the unlawful inclosure of large tracts
of land in Colfax and Mora counties. Named in the petition were
the Cimarron and Renello cattle companies.[40] On March 15 of
the same year, more than 50 persons complained of fencing along
Ute Creek and other parts of the country by large stock companies
and others.[41] The chief offender in this case was the Dubuque Cat-

35. *Santa Fe Weekly New Mexican and Livestock Journal,* August 5,
1886, 1.

36. Anderson, *History of New Mexico,* Vol. 1, 469.

37. *The Santa Fe Weekly Leader,* November 20, 1886, 2.

38. Public Lands Commission, *Preliminary Report,* 1879, 46 Cong., 2
Sess., *H.E.D.* No. 46, 447-459 (1923).

39. Western Range Cattle Industry Study, *New Mexico Cattle Corporations, 1871-1900.* Summary, Ms. There was only one corporation previous to
1881.

40. Secretary of the Interior, *Unauthorized Fencing of Public Lands,* 1884,
48 Cong., 1 Sess., *S.E.D.* No. 127, 24. Earl W. Hayter, "Barbed Wire Fencing,"
Agricultural History, 13:196, says that barbed wire was first used in New Mexico in 1884. The correct date was earlier than this; nevertheless, the whole
article is an excellent history of barbed wire fencing.

41. Secretary of the Interior, *Fraudulent Acquisition of Titles to Land in
New Mexico,* 1885, 48 Cong., 2 Sess., *S.E.D.* No. 106, 28, 29.

tle Company. The fenced area was some of the best grazing land in the Territory. The only pretense of ownership to any of this land was held by virtue of certain fraudulent homestead claims.[42]

It has been said that barbed wire fencing was not economically a sound practice in New Mexico because of the comparatively large amount of land required to be inclosed to feed a given number of cattle.[43] Statistics indicate otherwise. Reports of the General Land Office from 1885 through 1888 show that New Mexico, reporting 3,438,830 acres as being acted upon or awaiting investigation, ranked third in the nation, behind only Colorado and Kansas. New Mexico was well ahead of Nebraska, Montana, Utah, Wyoming, California, Nevada, Oregon, Idaho, and Dakota (Appendix XII).

There were 78 indictments in the Territory for unlawful inclosure, of which 6 were returned with a verdict of not guilty and 63 were dismissed without trial. In only one case was there a verdict of guilty, but in 6 cases the defendant was not found by the marshal who attempted to serve a subpoena. In one other dismissed case the records are missing from the transcript in the office of the District Court Clerk, which may have been the reason for dismissal. In another case the verdict is in neither the docket nor the transcript record of court cases (Appendix XI).

In 1884 the General Land Office mailed a letter of inquiry to registers and receivers requesting information on land fraud in general as well as the effect of inclosures in their respective districts. The matter had attracted wide public attention and had been brought prominently before Congress.[44] In 1885 Congress passed an act making the inclosure of public lands a punishable offense,[45]

---

42. Secretary of the Interior, *Unauthorized Fencing of Public Lands,* 1884, 48 Cong., 1 Sess., *S.E.D.* No. 127, 25.

43. Clara M. Love, "History of the Cattle Industry in the Southwest," *Southwestern Historical Quarterly,* 20:9. The Prairie Cattle Company reported, in 1883, that it was not to their best interests to fence the public domain (Secretary of the Interior, *Fraudulent Acquisition of Titles to Land in New Mexico,* 1885, 48 Cong., 2 Sess., *S.E.D.* No. 106, 51) and were not reported as having done so in New Mexico; but they controlled so much of the land in the northeast part of the Territory that it was probably not necessary for them to do so. In Colorado they were accused of fencing 1,000,000 acres of public land, *L.O.R.* 10/22/85, 49 Cong., 1 Sess., *H.E.D.* No. 1, 472 (2378).

44. Acting Commissioner L. Harrison to register and receiver at Las Cruces, 10/4/84 (F.R.C).

45. Hibbard, *A History of the Public Land Policies,* 478.

and a vigorous campaign was started by the General Land Office to stop the practice.

By 1889 acreage inclosed was small,[46] and only a few cases remained to be acted upon in 1890[47] and 1891.[48]

Timber depredation was another matter of surveillance by the Federal Government. Until 1878, there was no law by which timber could be legally acquired from the public domain except for railroad use where trees could be cut from public land adjacent to the right-of-way. People had tried to buy timber or timber land, but were unable to do so; consequently, it became the practice to appropriate it by trespass, trusting that the Government's terms would not be too severe in settling for the depredation.[49] In recognition of this situation Congress passed, on June 3, "An Act authorizing the citizens of Colorado, Nevada, and the territories to fell and remove timber on the public domain for mining and domestic purposes."[50]

But the depredations continued and even increased. In New Mexico, as early as 1880, agents had "investigated and reported upon cases involving 1,169,984 feet, 23,000 shingles, 41,050 laths, which [was] but a small portion of the depredations upon the public timber." Mills with a capacity of 15,000 feet per day were located on unsurveyed public lands and upon unconfirmed private land grants. Some of the trespassers showed a willingness to settle for the timber they had taken while others claimed that it was for domestic purposes, when it was obviously being sold on the open market.[51]

In one case parties had large contracts to supply railroad ties, bridge timbers, etc., to the Mexican Central Railroad Company, for constructing a railroad in the Republic of Mexico. This timber was supplied from the public domain in New Mexico.[52]

With but one exception the 64 persons who were indicted for violation of timber laws in the Territory were Anglos.[53] Since they

---

46. *L.O.R.* 9/17/89, 51 Cong., 1 Sess., *H.E.D.* No. 1, 275 (2724).

47. *L.O.R.* 9/13/90, 51 Cong., 2 Sess., *H.E.D.* No. 1, 79 (2840).

48. *L.O.R.* 9/23/91, 52 Cong., 1 Sess., *H.E.D.* No. 1, 316 (2933).

49. Hibbard, *A History of Public Land Policies*, 463.

50. Williamson to register and receiver, Mesilla, 3/29/79 (F.R.C.). The Timber and Stone Act of the same date allowed for the purchase of such land but did not apply to New Mexico.

51. *L.O.R.* 10/18/80, 46 Cong., 3 Sess., *H.E.D.* No. 1, 580 (1959).

52. *L.O.R.* 10/28/81, 47 Cong., 1 Sess., *H.E.D.* No. 1, 373 (2017).

53. United States, *Territorial Court Records*. Transcript Records and Dockets of District Court Cases.

were a definite minority at the time, this proportion would not have held had the timber been universally cut for domestic purposes as was allowed.

Of the 64 indictments returned the defendants in 8 cases were judged not guilty and 31 were dismissed without trial. While only 3 were found guilty, 9 others were not located by marshals who attempted to serve them with subpoenas. In 10 cases the records are missing from the transcript record of court cases, and in 3 cases the disposition cannot be determined, because the verdict is in neither the docket nor the transcript (Appendix XI).

10. Conclusion

THE ECONOMIC, social, and political life of territorial New Mexico centered around agriculture, stock raising, and mining. Manufacturing was limited to jewelry and such home manufactures as were common to any frontier community.

The greatest impetus to economic development in the Territory was the advent of railroad transportation. By December 7, 1878, the Atchison, Topeka and Santa Fe Railroad had reached the northern boundary of New Mexico and a subsidiary, the New Mexico and Southern Pacific, started to build south from there. Progress was slow. It was not until April 5, 1880, after a burst of activity, that the line reached Albuquerque.[1]

There followed immediately an unprecedented increase in land entries. The largest number of original homestead entries previous to 1880 was in 1870, when there were 96, while in 1880 there were 181 entries. In 1876 there were 35 final homestead certificates, the largest number in any year previous to 1880, and in 1880 there were 98. The high for donation notifications prior to 1880 was in 1877, when there were 38, and in 1880 there were 172. The increase was even greater in the case of donation certificates. The largest number previous to 1880 was in 1873 when there were 27; in 1880 there were 162 (Appendixes IV-V).

This increase was permanent and steady, as is shown (see p. 116) by a comparison of the entries in the dozen years following 1880 with the same number of years previous to 1880.

Yet, in the 1880's, these land entries brought no appreciable gain to agriculture, the very thing they were, by law, calculated to foster. The raising of crops was still one of the requirements for com-

---

1. Westphall, "Albuquerque in the 1870's," *New Mexico Historical Review,* 23:257, 265.

Kind of entry	Inclusive years prior to 1880			Inclusive equivalent number of years after 1880		
	Years	Entries	Acres	Years	Entries	Acres
Original homestead	1868-79	441	63,515	1880-91	6,343	877,313
Final homestead	1873-79	88	12,951	1880-86	1,538	199,372
Original timber-culture entries	1875-79	38	5,422	1880-84	385	52,240
Donation notifications	1858-79 (22 yrs.)	168	26,101	1880-82 (3 yrs.)	297	47,197
Donation certificates	1870-79 (10 yrs.)	64	8,840	1880-84 (5 yrs.)	274	43,149
Pre-emption declarations	1861-79 (19 yrs.)	616		1880-91 (12 yrs.)	7,041	
Mineral land applications	1869-79	62		1880-89	546	
Original desert land entries	1877-79	45	16,668	1880-82	122	30,484
Mineral land sales	1870-79	8	129	1880-88	377	6,438
Cash sales	1868-79	352	47,142	1880-91	3,398	437,231

(See Appendixes IV-V)

pliance with the land laws, therefore "the arrival of the railroad in New Mexico did not provide the degree of immediate impetus to agrarian development that occurred in California and several other states and territories in the west. Not until the 1890's did agriculture in New Mexico begin to make substantial gains from a total profit point of view."[2] The table following supports this conclusion:

IMPROVED FARMS

	1870	1880	1890	1900
Total acreage	143,007	237,392	263,106	326,873
Irrigated acreage	57,200	94,900	105,000	229,000
Value excluding livestock	2,381,253	5,769,561	8,431,940	22,040,424

The figures above are compiled from census reports.

What accounts for the lower increases in the 1880's than the 1870's and 1890's? Most of the arable land in the Territory was in

---

2. Jim F. Heath, *A Study of the Influence of the Atchison, Topeka, and Santa Fe Railroad upon the Economy of New Mexico, 1878 to 1900*, Ms. (M.A. thesis) 86, 87.

areas claimed as private grants.[3] There were indications as early as 1872 that land grants were becoming depleted as a source for the purchase of land;[4] nevertheless, traffic in these grants continued to augment agricultural development through the 1870's. By the 1880's grant land was becoming more costly because of the approach of railroads. Newcomers, with improved agricultural methods, could reasonably have been expected to increase the agricultural economy; nevertheless, this did not happen to any great extent, because title to grant land was extremely uncertain and the increasing cost made its purchase unwarranted. Furthermore, more claims to grants were continually being advanced. Of the 77,568,640 acres of land in New Mexico, 34,653,340 acres were finally submitted to the Court of Private Land Claims for adjudication between 1891 and 1904. Of this, the Court confirmed only 1,934,986 acres. (Congress had previously confirmed 45 claims for 6,676,831 acres, 22 of which were patented for 4,780,894 acres.) Thus the Court rejected 32,718,354 acres that actual settlers could feel free to settle on with certainty of securing a patent.[5] Before this there had been little room, in semi-arid New Mexico, for settlers who desired to pursue agriculture.

The release of this land to the public domain was concurrent with the accelerated growth of agriculture. Over 95 per cent of the acreage was rejected by the Court between 1891 and 1900. The peak years were 1894, 1895, and 1898, with about 5,000,000 acres each year.[6]

The situation is all the more striking when it is observed that both stock raising and mining showed immediate and substantial gains upon the arrival of railroad transportation and the resulting increase in land entries (see table, p. 118).

The close parallel between railroad building progress through the Territory, compared to phenomenal increases in surveys and entries and, by comparison, a relatively steady increase in population, is startling, as is the rapid decline of these categories after the initiation of land fraud prosecutions in the Territory, culminating when charges were preferred against Max Frost for land fraud on

---

3. Public Lands Commission, *Preliminary Report,* 1879, 46 Cong., 2 Sess., *H.E.D.* No. 46, 451 (1923).

4. *S.G.R.* 10/7/72, 42 Cong., 3 Sess., *H.E.D.* No. 1, 123, 124 (1560).

5. U. S. Attorney General, *Annual Report,* 12/1/04, 58 Cong., 3 Sess., *H.E.D.* No. 9, 96 (4811); *S.G.R.* 7/19/90, 435 in *L.O.R.* 9/13/90; *S.G.R.* 7/22/85, 49 Cong., 1 Sess., *H.E.D.* No. 1, 554-561 (2378).

6. U. S. Attorney General, *Annual Reports,* 1891-1903.

	1870	*1880*	*1890*	*1900*
Number of cattle	57,534	347,936	1,631,533	803,097
Number of sheep	619,438	3,938,831	2,474,494	3,333,743
Pounds of wool	684,930	4,019,188	7,980,998	15,209,199
Value of livestock	2,389,157	10,914,800	25,111,201	31,727,400
Value of mining products	343,250	441,691	4,611,764	2,686,473

The figures above are compiled from census reports.

October 30, 1883 (Appendix XIII). It would seem that illegal entrants were noticing these prosecutions and being more careful of the entries they made, as witnessed by the decline in land entries; but, it was also true that they merely switched to a new gimmick. The year 1883 saw the arrival of illegal inclosures of the public domain (Chapter IX); however, the Federal Government took stern measures against this practice and it largely ended by 1888 (Appendix XII).

A number of things account for the dramatic increase in surveys and land entries over the amount indicated by no more than the ready market afforded by the railroad. It was becoming increasingly unprofitable and risky to purchase land claimed as private grants.[7] At the same time, there was a growing tendency on the part of cattle ranchers to acquire deeded land, in contrast to the old system of common use of the public range. Land which controlled a water supply was especially desired (Chapter IV). This became possible on a large scale, in 1879, when a modification of the Special Deposit Law made certificates of deposit negotiable and useful for payment of public land anywhere under the terms of the Pre-emption and Homestead laws (Chapter II). The sudden surge in public domain business was not, however, accounted for by legitimate settlers under the land laws. It was, rather, the avaricious demands of cattle raising interests supplemented by the acquisitions of land speculators that accounted for the bulk of public domain business.

Federal regulations of August 1882 caused a sharp drop in special deposits the following year and annual appropriations were too meager to continue more than a fraction of the previous surveys; in fact, surveys declined more than entries after 1883 (Appendix XIII). Land entries, while diminishing sharply, continued at a

---

7. See note 4.

higher rate than previous to the arrival of railroad transportation. Public pressure for land disposal continued and the policy in New Mexico changed to temper the law with the reality of the arid nature of the Territory. In the years of peak disposals and surveys (1879-1883), Republican Surveyor General Atkinson repeatedly certified that surveyed land complied fully with all the requirements of the law including the strategic requirement that it would support crop growth. In the last years of the decade, Democratic Surveyor General Julian, faced with continuing demand for surveys and entries, recognized certain areas to be within the agricultural class, although the law had in no way changed. This rationalized interpretation was supported by Julian's superiors in Washington. It was obvious official temporizing with the law to satisfy public demand; nevertheless, it must be stated that surveillance of the situation was more thorough than in preceding years.

While it is true that cattle graziers persistently violated the land laws of the United States, many of them did so knowingly and with the firm conviction that they had a strong moral, if not legal, right to do so. The Federal land laws were not applicable to most of the arid land in the Territory because the land in New Mexico was suited principally for grazing, which required large amounts of land for successful operation. Yet the laws were designed to limit the amount of the public domain that could be acquired by one person, and these stipulated that the land must be cultivated by that person.

A water supply was an absolute necessity for the raising of stock. Water was scarce and if the springs and streams were taken up by settlers, the adjacent public domain was useless except in localities where water for stock could be obtained from wells. It was recognized that ten or twelve head of cattle on 160 acres was the general maximum and that as few as four was more often correct. These would not begin to support a family. Available watering places should have been calculated to serve as the nucleus for a suitable quantity of grazing land adjacent to it. This adjacent land should have been made available for adequate homesteads or sold at graduated prices so that the full potential value of the land would have been realized.

Since the bulk of the land was good only for grazing, it was natural that cattle ranchers sought the widely scattered springs and streams to water their stock. There was logic in their convictions

that such water was more valuable for watering a large quantity of
stock than for the possible garden patch that might be irrigated by
that water. Large-scale storage of water for irrigating purposes did
not begin until the late 1880's, and irrigation before that was largely
confined to areas where water could be diverted from living streams.
Marginal irrigation was less valuable to the economy of the Territory than the same water used to support a large grazing area.

The real fight in New Mexico was over water and was as much
between the have and have-nots in ranching as between ranching
and agrarian interests. The land laws, limiting to an inadequate
amount the quantity of land that could legally be acquired, encouraged the struggle over the really valuable land—the land with
water. Had there been devised a system of parceling land in accordance with the nature of the country, much of the fraud in land
matters would have been averted. Given a sensible system, sensible
people would largely have followed it. Given an impossible system,
even sensible people rebelled against it and, like a small force that
can cause an avalanche, this rebellion grew to unmanageable
proportions.

The situation encouraged the strong and the firstcomers. It was
impossible to make a living on the amount of land that could legally
be acquired under the land laws so there was provocation to break
the law to some degree in order to make a living. Once this step was
taken, who was to say how much was enough? Had cattle graziers
been permitted to homestead land up to some such amount as the
2,560 acres recommended by Major James W. Powell in his monumental report on the *Lands of the Arid Regions of the United
States,* and had they been required to buy the arid land (even at a
nominal price) to obtain a share in the water, the great baronial
holdings of cattle interests carved from the public domain would
not have become a reality. There would have been far less cause to
break the law in the first place and persons whose duty it was to
police these laws would have had a less disillusioning task in doing
so. There were always the greedy and deliberately lawless, but the
widespread breakdown in morality would not have had a reason to
exist and a heartened law enforcement body could surely have been
able to cope with the incorrigible element.

If this seems to place too much faith in the innate justice of
human nature, there is the realistic consideration that land in the
sensible quantity of sixteen times what was allowed would have

meant only one-sixteenth the amount of checking for harassed land office officials who could have devoted the time saved to closer supervision of the larger amounts. This might as well have been done because many persons secured larger amounts by one method or another anyway. It was common for hired hands to take out land entries for the benefit of their employers. Since the quantity allowed was hardly enough to do these hired hands much good, and since they received some remuneration for their service, there was reason to turn it over to their employers. Had they been able to secure enough land to make a living, many would have been reluctant to let it go. Indeed, large ranchers would have had more difficulty finding help with which to make such a bargain in the first place. The alternative would have been a larger number of smaller ranches with consequent benefit to the economy of the Territory and a more rational serving of human justice. As it was, a comparative few early acquired most of the water, and without that commodity, it was pointless for others to acquire land.

APPENDIX I

TERRITORIAL AND NATIONAL OFFICIALS

Year	Surveyor Gen'l of New Mexico	Commissioner, Gen. Land Office	Secretary of the Interior	President of U.S.	Party of U.S. Admin
1854	W. H. Pelham	John Wilson	R. McClelland	F. Pierce	Democrat
1855	do.	T.A. Hendricks	do.	do.	do.
1856	do.	do.	do.	do.	do.
1857	do.	do.	J. Thompson	J. Buchanan	Democrat
1858	do.	do.	do.	do.	do.
1859	do.	S.A. Smith	do.	do.	do.
1860	A.P. Wilbar	J.S. Wilson	do.	do.	do.
1861	J.A. Clark	J.M. Edmunds	C.B. Smith	A. Lincoln	Republican
1862	do.	do.	do.	do.	do.
1863	do.	do.	J.P. Usher	do.	do.
1864	do.	do.	do.	do.	do.
1865	do.	do.	J. Harlan	A. Johnson	Nat'l Union
1866	do.	J.S. Wilson	O.H. Browning	do.	do.
1867	do.	do.	do.	do.	do.
1868	B.C. Cutler	do.	do.	do.	do.
1869	T.R. Spencer	do.	J.D. Cox	U.S. Grant	Republican
1870	do.	do.	C. Delano	do.	do.
1871	do.	W. Drummond	do.	do.	do.
1872	J.K. Proudfit	do.	do.	do.	do.
1873	do.	do.	do.	do.	do.
1874	do.	S.S. Burdett	do.	do.	do.
1875	do.	do.	Z. Chandler	do.	do.
1876	H.M. Atkinson	J.A. Williamson	do.	do.	do.
1877	do.	do.	C. Schurz	R.B. Hayes	Republican
1878	do.	do.	do.	do.	do.
1879	do.	do.	do.	do.	do.
1880	do.	do.	do.	do.	do.
1881	do.	N.C. McFarland	S.J. Kirkwood	J.A. Garfield	Republican
1882	do.	do.	H.M. Teller	(C.A. Arthur)	do.
1883	do.	do.	do.	do.	do.
1884	C. Pullen	do.	do.	do.	do.
1885	G.W. Julian	W.A.J. Sparks	L.Q.C. Lamar	G. Cleveland	Democrat
1886	do.	do.	do.	do.	do.
1887	do.	do.	do.	do.	do.
1888	do.	S.M. Stockslager	W.F. Vilas	do.	do.
1889	E.F. Hobart	do.	J.W. Noble	B. Harrison	Republican
1890	do.	L.A. Groff	do.	do.	do.
1891	do.	T.H. Carter	do.	do.	do.

APPENDIX II

NEW MEXICO DISTRICT LAND OFFICES

The first Land Office for New Mexico was established on May 24, 1858, and opened in Santa Fe on November 24.[1] It continued to serve the entire Territory until March 3, 1874, when all that part of New Mexico south of the base line became a separate district to be called La Mesilla land district.[2] The office continued at Mesilla until May 1, 1883, when it was transferred to Las Cruces.[3]

A new district office was opened in 1888 and another in 1889. The first of these, for the Colfax district, with office at Folsom, was created on December 18, 1888. The boundary was as follows:

> Commencing at the northeastern corner of said Territory and running thence west on the northern boundary line of said Territory to the line dividing ranges numbered twenty-four and twenty-five; thence south on said range line to the principal base-line running east and west through said Territory; thence east on said base-line to the eastern boundary line of said Territory; thence north on said eastern boundary line to the place of beginning. . . .[4]

The Lincoln land district, with office at Roswell, was created on March 1, 1889:

> Beginning at a point on the line running north and south between the State of Texas and the Territory of New Mexico, where such line would be intersected by the township line between townships numbers one and two, north of the base line, and running thence west to the southwest corner of San Miguel county along the line between the counties of Lincoln and San Miguel, said southwest corner being on said line in range number nineteen west (east) of the New Mexico principal meridian, thence north to the southeast corner of Valencia county, a distance of about 4 miles, thence west on the south line of Valencia county parallel with the line between townships numbers one and two through township number two north to the east line of range number eight, east of the New Mexico principal meridian, thence south along said range line between ranges numbered eight and nine east of said principal meridian to the second standard parallel south on the line between townships numbered ten and eleven south of the base line, thence east along said parallel to the line between ranges numbered ten and eleven south (east) of the base

1. Hendricks to Pelham, 10/1/58 (N.A.).
2. Burdett to Proudfit, 7/7/74 (N.A.).
3. McFarland to register and receiver, Mesilla, 3/2/83 (F.R.C.) .
4. *L.O.R.* 9/17/89, 51 Cong., 1 Sess., *H.E.D.* No. 1, 112 (2724).

line (principal meridian), thence south along said range line to the township line between townships numbered twelve and thirteen south, thence east along said last-named line to the meridian of longitude number twenty-eight degrees thirty minutes west from Washington, thence south along said meridian line to the line of the State of Texas, thence east along said line to the southeast corner of the Territory of New Mexico, and thence north along the boundary line between the State of Texas and the Territory of New Mexico to the point of beginning. . . .[5]

This changed the southern boundary of the previously established Colfax land district.

5. *Ibid.*, 114.

APPENDIX III

ANNUAL SURVEYS IN NEW MEXICO

[Compiled from Land Office reports for the years involved.
All measurements are in acres]

Fiscal year (ending June 30)	*Public land surveyed during fiscal year*	*Public land surveyed, not previously reported*	*Public land surveyed and reported in fiscal year*	*Cumulative total of public land surveyed*	*Unsurveyed public land*
1855					77,568,640
1856	20		20	20	77,568,620
1857	928		928	948	77,567,692
1858	800,217		800,217	801,165	76,767,475
1859	767,214		767,214	1,568,379	76,000,261
1860	453,555		453,555	2,021,934	75,546,706
1861 a	220,337		220,337	2,242,271	75,326,369
1862 a	50,871		50,871	2,293,142	75,275,498
1863	—		—	2,293,142	75,275,498
1864	—		—	2,293,142	75,275,498
1865	—		—	2,293,142	75,275,498

a. Figures for 1861 and 1862 were given in lineal miles, chains, and links of surveys rather than acres, so the acreage figures in this chart are only approximate, based on the proportionate amounts for the two years.

Fiscal year (ending June 30)	Public land surveyed during fiscal year	Public land surveyed, not previously reported	Public land surveyed and reported in fiscal year	Cumulative total of public land surveyed	Unsurveyed public land
1866	—		—	2,293,142	75,275,498
1867	39,413 [b]		39,413	2,332,555	75,236,085
1868	650,198		650,198	2,982,753	74,585,887
1869	—		—	2,982,753	74,585,887
1870	1,258,106		1,258,106	4,240,859 [c]	73,327,781
1871	161,414	—	161,414	4,402,273	73,166,367
1872	2,991	17,712	20,703	4,422,975	73,145,665
1873	391,341	46,093	437,434	4,860,410	72,708,230
1874	625,775	—	625,775	5,486,185	72,082,455
1875	722,907	—	722,907	6,209,092	71,359,548
1876	1,080,686	—	1,080,686	7,289,778	70,278,862
1877	630,972	—	630,972	7,920,750	69,647,890
1878	541,429	9,701	551,130	8,471,880	69,096,760
1879	333,822	38,189	372,011	8,843,890	68,724,750
1880	1,624,156	75,604	1,699,760	10,543,650	67,024,990
1881	3,179,216 [d]	916,217	4,095,433	14,639,083 [e]	62,929,557
1882	1,287,308	7,584,319	8,871,627	23,510,710	54,057,930
1883	8,361,741	4,486,299	12,847,970	36,358,680	41,209,960
1884	2,162,490	5,152,381	7,314,871	43,673,551	33,895,089
1885	—	1,693,728	1,693,728	45,367,279	32,210,361
1886	—	679,524	679,524	46,046,803	31,521,837
1887	—	533,682	533,682	46,580,485	30,988,155
1888	240	766,275	766,515	47,347,000	30,221,640
1889	25,990	1,028,189	1,054,179	48,401,179	29,167,461
1890	58,698	178,434	237,132	48,638,311	28,930,329
1891	—	157,136	157,136	48,795,441	28,773,193

b. Private claims.

c. Of the surveys in New Mexico Territory, 959,841 acres are Navaho Indian lands reserved by the second article of the Treaty of June 1, 1868 (United States Laws, Vol. 15, 668).

d. 16,779 acres are embraced within the Southern Ute Indian Lands selected by the Ute Commission under the Act of Congress approved June 15, 1880.

e. Of the surveys in New Mexico, 120,349 acres were surveyed into 40-acre tracts for the Southern Ute Indians, under the Ute Commission, of which 108,534 acres had been also surveyed as public lands under the Surveyor General of New Mexico.

APPENDIX IV

NEW MEXICO LAND OFFICE CASH SALES BUSINESS
THROUGH 1891

Whenever possible, in the following tables, the original figures are used that were submitted to the General Land Office by New Mexico registers and receivers. Land Office reports are used when registers and receivers figures are not available. Figures submitted by registers and receivers frequently vary from Land Office reports (without exception in the totals) and show conclusively the inaccuracy of the Land Office in compiling figures submitted to them by registers and receivers. For details of these variations see: Victor Westphall, *The Public Domain in New Mexico, 1854-1891*, University of New Mexico, 1956, Ms. (Ph.D. dissertation). The La Mesilla land district was transferred to Las Cruces in 1883.

TABLE 1.   ORIGINAL DESERT LAND ENTRIES

Year	Santa Fe Entries	Santa Fe Acres	La Mesilla Entries	La Mesilla Acres	Folsom Entries	Folsom Acres	Roswell Entries	Roswell Acres	N.M. Total Entries	N.M. Total Acres
1877			14	5,664					14	5,664
1878	7	3,680	7	1,651					14	5,331
1879	5	1,873	12	3,800					17	5,673
1880	4	1,040	26	6,747					30	7,787
1881	1	320	22	6,200					23	6,520
1882	38	10,161	31	6,016					69	16,177
1883	26	5,918	149	40,865					175	46,783
1884	28	8,348	101	32,035					129	40,383
1885	21	6,212	135	28,045					156	34,257
1886	29	9,788	110	29,434					139	39,222
1887	44	14,751	37	7,608					81	22,359
1888	31	11,098	67	34,148					98	45,246
1889	36	12,531	86	45,911	1	400	13	5,877	136	64,719
1890	65	14,616	15	3,681	5	240	86	36,997	171	55,534
1891	22	4,664	9	1,560	2	360	63	12,964	96	19,548
Total	357	105,000	821	253,365	8	1,000	162	55,838	1,348	415,203

TABLE 2.   FINAL DESERT LAND CERTIFICATES

[Through 1894 when entries made in 1891 would normally have been completed]

Year	Santa Fe		La Mesilla		Roswell		N.M. Total	
	Entries	*Acres*	*Entries*	*Acres*	*Entries*	*Acres*	*Entries*	*Acres*
1879			1	80			1	80
1880			—	—			—	—
1881			3	1,120			3	1,120
1882			4	1,424			4	1,424
1883			4	1,103			4	1,103
1884	3	480	13	3,225			16	3,705
1885	2	320	13	3,302			15	3,622
1886	4	480	16	3,536			20	4,016
1887	1	640	10	3,108			11	3,748
1888	—	—	7	1,306			7	1,306
1889	4	1,000	32	8,547			36	9,547
1890	2	800	9	1,893	10	4,231	21	6,924
1891	1	120	9	1,880	55	28,130	65	30,130
1892	3	360	1	640	117	44,101	121	45,101
1893	15	7,658	2	1,191	32	12,580	49	21,429
1894	3	520	—	—	22	5,847	25	6,367
Total	38	12,378	124	32,355	236	94,889	398	139,622

TABLE 3.   PRE-EMPTION DECLARATORY STATEMENTS

Year	Santa Fe Entries	La Mesilla Entries	Folsom Entries	Roswell Entries	N.M. Total Entries
1861	18				18
1862	1				1
1863	2				2
1864	2				2
1865	1				1
1866	3				3
1867	—				—
1868	6				6
1869	18				18
1870	15				15
1871	18				18
1872	19				19
1873	34				34
1874	10				10
1875	13	14			27
1876	3	9			12
1877	—	41			41
1878	—	48			48
1879	288	53			341
1880	161	29			190
1881	186	59			245
1882	180	241			421
1883	231	788			1,019
1884	191	630			821
1885	85	711			796
1886	499	404			903
1887	450	272			722
1888	452	274			726
1889	305	268	38	28	639
1890	139	123	96	97	455
1891	25	25	30	20	104
Total	3,355	3,993	164	145	7,657

TABLE 4.   OTHER CASH SALES

Year	Santa Fe Entries	Santa Fe Acres	La Mesilla Entries	La Mesilla Acres	Folsom Entries	Folsom Acres	Roswell Entries	Roswell Acres	N.M. Total Entries	N.M. Total Acres
1868	3	480							3	480
1868	—	—							—	—
1870	26	2,780							26	2,780
1871	68	9,422							68	9,422
1872	49	8,393							49	8,393
1873	12	2,165							12	2,165
1874	6	395							6	395
1875	5	647	2	200					7	847
1876	2	91	5	633					7	724
1877	1	2	9	606					10	608
1878	43	5,814	6	611					49	6,425
1879	100	14,012	15	891					115	14,903
1880	132	16,995	9	858					141	17,853
1881	60	5,062	11	1,048					71	6,110
1882	113	8,683	61	7,204					174	15,887
1883	181	23,155	349	48,122					530	71,277
1884	173	22,136	316	44,039					489	66,175
1885	81	8,142	428	73,432					509	81,574
1886	68	8,433	248	31,677					316	40,110
1887	122	13,398	97	11,614					219	25,012
1888	114	12,717	108	12,063					222	24,780
1889	106	12,145	93	10,504	34	4,433			233	27,082
1890	74	8,306	59	5,983	66	11,049	48	6,855	247	32,193
1891	78	9,183	46	5,144	52	5,915	71	8,936	247	29,178
Total	1,617	192,556	1,862	254,629	152	21,397	119	15,791	3,750	484,373

TABLE 5.   TOTAL OF OTHER CASH SALES
CLASSIFIED (FROM TABLE 4)

Class of land law	Entries	Acres	Acres per entry
Pre-emption sales	2,574	369,631	143.6
Private entry sales	196	50,061	255.4
Public auction sales	112	15,671	139.9
Excess payments on homesteads, etc.	553	2,324	4.2
Homestead entries commuted to cash	315	46,686	148.2
Total	3,750	484,373	

TABLE 6. APPLICATIONS TO PURCHASE COAL LANDS

[No record was found of any applications prior to 1881, but it is obvious that there were some, since there were five coal land claims sold in 1880 (see Table 7)]

Year	Santa Fe Entries	La Mesilla Entries	Folsom Entries	Roswell Entries	N.M. Total Entries
1881	15				15
1882	—				—
1883	48	26			74
1884	40	6			46
1885	19	7			26
1886	23	16			39
1887	15	7			22
1888	27	12			39
1889	39	8			47
1890	49	5		2	56
1891	61	1	1	9	72
Total	336	88	1	11	436

TABLE 7. COAL LAND SALES

[Figures for 1880 are from the Public Lands Commission, *Final Report*, 1881, 46 Cong., 3 Sess., *H.E.D.* No. 47, 294 (1975)]

Year	Santa Fe Entries	Acres	La Mesilla Entries	Acres	N.M. Total Entries	Acres
1880	5	721			5	721
1881	—	—			—	—
1882	—	—			—	—
1883	—	—			—	—
1884	2	120			2	120
1885	—	—			—	—
1886	1	80	9	1,270	10	1,350
1887	1	80	7	716	8	796
1888	1	40	3	191	4	231
1889	3	240	1	80	4	320
1890	2	80	—	—	2	80
1891	4	571	—	—	4	571
Total	19	1,932	20	2,257	39	4,189

TABLE 8.   APPLICATIONS TO PURCHASE MINERAL LANDS

[Only totals for New Mexico are available for the years 1869 through 1880]

Year	Santa Fe Entries	La Mesilla Entries	Roswell Entries	N.M. Total Entries
1869				1
1870				—
1871				1
1872				8
1873				28
1874				4
1875				5
1876				4
1877				1
1878				7
1879				3
1880				11
1881	1	54		55
1882	4	29		33
1883	1	48		49
1884	7	89		96
1885	4	44		48
1886	6	30		36
1887	5	42		47
1888	5	87		92
1889	2	77		79
1890	8	32	5	45
1891	3	18	—	21
Total	46	550	5	674

TABLE 9. MINERAL AND MILL SITE LAND SALES

Year	Santa Fe		La Mesilla		Roswell		N.M. Total	
	Entries	*Acres*	*Entries*	*Acres*	*Entries*	*Acres*	*Entries*	*Acres*
1870	1	21					1	21
1871	—	—					—	—
1872	—	—					—	—
1873	—	—					—	—
1874	2	14					2	14
1875	1	21					1	21
1876	—	—	1	21			1	21
1877	—	—	—	—			—	—
1878	1	10	1	21			2	31
1879	—	—	1	21			1	21
1880	—	—	4	49			4	49
1881	—	—	48	983			48	983
1882	2	41	13	224			15	265
1883	3	62	60	1,126			63	1,188
1884	1	10	58	916			59	926
1885	2	21	38	582			40	603
1886	7	66	32	461			39	527
1887	3	47	42	784			45	831
1888	4	37	60	1,029			64	1,066
1889	—	—	77	1,417			77	1,417
1890	10	187	15	270	3	50	28	507
1891	3	183	19	293	5	48	27	524
Total	40	720	469	8,197	8	98	517	9,015
Adjusting figures[a]	6	97	48	721	—	—	54	818
Adjusted Total	46	817	517	8,918	8	98	571	9,833

a. These figures (not included in the total) represent sales ultimately canceled although originally approved. Land Office reports do not take this adjustment into consideration.

TABLE 10.   SIOUX HALF-BREED SCRIP ENTRIES

Year	La Mesilla		Roswell		N.M. Total	
	Entries	Acres	Entries	Acres	Entries	Acres
1881	1	80			1	80
1882	1	80			1	80
1883	—	—			—	—
1884	2	120			2	120
1885	—	—			—	—
1886	2	80			2	80
1887	—	—			—	—
1888	2	320			2	320
1889	—	—			—	—
1890	—	—			—	—
1891	—	—	8	680	8	680
Total	8	680	8	680	16	1,360

TABLE 11.   MINERAL PROTESTS, ADVERSE CLAIMS

Year	Santa Fe	La Mesilla	N.M. Total
	Entries	Entries	Entries
1881		1	1
1882		—	—
1883		6	6
1884	2	2	4
1885	3	2	5
1886	—	5	5
1887	—	7	7
1888	—	10	10
1889	—	2	2
1890	—	3	3
1891	—	1	1
Total	5	39	44

TABLE 12. MILITARY BOUNTY LAND WARRANTS

Year	Santa Fe		La Mesilla		Roswell		N.M. Total	
	Entries	Acres	Entries	Acres	Entries	Acres	Entries	Acres
1883	1	80					1	80
1884	1	160	2	160			3	320
1885	1	156	4	240			5	396
1886	6	440	8	800			14	1,240
1887	—	—	1	80			1	80
1888	1	80	—	—			1	80
1889	1	160	2	240			3	400
1890	2	320	1	120	1	80	4	520
1891	—	—	3	280	1	160	4	440
Total	13	1,396	21	1,920	2	240	36	3,556

TABLE 13. ISRAEL DODGE SCRIP ENTRIES

Year	Santa Fe		La Mesilla		Roswell		N.M. Total	
	Entries	Acres	Entries	Acres	Entries	Acres	Entries	Acres
1882	2	80					2	80
1883	—	—	1	40		·	1	40
1884	—	—	9	430			9	430
1885	—	—	4	160			4	160
1891	—	—	—	—	2	80	2	80
Total	2	80	14	630	2	80	18	790

TABLE 14. AGRICULTURAL COLLEGE SCRIP

Year	Santa Fe		N.M. Total	
	Entries	Acres	Entries	Acres
1863	4	643	4	643
1866	4	640	4	640
1871	10	1,600	10	1,600
1873	6	960	6	960
Total	24	3,843	24	3,843

OTHER CASH SALE BUSINESS

Private Land Scrip Entries: There was one entry of 640 acres in La Mesilla in 1882.

Valentine Scrip Entries: All entries were in La Mesilla with two each for 80 acres in 1882, 1885, and 1886.

Valentine Scrip Filings: All entries were in La Mesilla with two each in 1882 and 1883, and one each in 1886 and 1887.

Supreme Court Locations: There were four entries with 160 total acres in Las Cruces in 1884.

Robert Cole Scrip: There was one entry of 80 acres in Las Cruces in 1885.

Joseph S. Wilson Scrip: There were two entries with 160 total acres in La Mesilla in 1878.

APPENDIX V

NEW MEXICO LAND OFFICE LAND-LAW BUSINESS THROUGH 1891

Whenever possible, in the following tables, the original figures used are those that were submitted to the General Land Office by New Mexico registers and receivers. Land Office reports are used when registers' and receivers' figures are not available. Figures submitted by registers and receivers frequently vary from Land Office reports (without exception in the totals) and show conclusively the inaccuracy of the Land Office in compiling figures submitted to them by registers and receivers. For details of these variations see: Victor Westphall, *The Public Domain in New Mexico, 1854-1891*, University of New Mexico, 1956, Ms. (Ph.D. dissertation). The La Mesilla land district was transferred to Las Cruces in 1883.

TABLE 1. ORIGINAL HOMESTEAD ENTRIES

Year	Santa Fe		La Mesilla		Folsom		Roswell		N.M. Total	
	Entries	*Acres*	*Entries*	*Acres*	*Entries*	*Acres*	*Entries*	*Acres*	*Entries*	*Acres*
1868	5	800							5	800
1869	5	787							5	787
1870	96	14,692							96	14,692
1871	59	8,580							59	8,580
1872	10	1,400							10	1,400
1873	23	3,144							23	3,144
1874	3	400							3	400
1875	14	1,360	36	5,640					50	7,000
1876	17	2,011	10	1,360					27	3,371
1877	4	320	16	2,483					20	2,803
1878	39	6,080	14	1,880					53	7,960
1879	46	6,851	44	5,727					90	12,578
1880	159	25,236	22	3,091					181	28,327
1881	367	56,320	34	4,408					401	60,728
1882	619	110,087	163	23,567					782	133,654
1883	531	78,809	291	41,828					822	120,637
1884	182	26,027	204	28,466					386	54,493
1885	207	31,426	389	52,348					596	83,774
1886	136	19,662	173	23,413					309	43,075
1887	322	49,840	123	17,405					445	67,245
1888	785	42,924	164	22,700					949	65,624
1889	220	33,380	140	19,968	39	6,093	4	640	403	60,081
1890	178	25,740	113	15,828	87	13,798	88	13,384	466	68,750
1891	188	28,091	153	22,337	140	22,034	122	18,463	603	90,925
Total	4,215	573,967	2,089	292,449	266	41,925	214	32,487	6,784	940,828

TABLE 2.   FINAL HOMESTEAD CERTIFICATES

[Through 1896 when entries made in 1891 would normally have been completed]

Year	Santa Fe		La Mesilla		Folsom		Roswell		N.M. Total	
	Entries	*Acres*	*Entries*	*Acres*	*Entries*	*Acres*	*Entries*	*Acres*	*Entries*	*Acres*
1873	4	640							4	640
1874	1	181							1	181
1875	5	788	8	1,224					13	2,012
1876	18	2,735	17	2,521					35	5,256
1877	3	400	4	642					7	1,042
1878	2	120	5	800					7	920
1879	3	379	18	2,521					21	2,900
1880	97	15,087	1	160					98	15,247
1881	261	37,912	12	1,500					273	39,412
1882	263	37,554	43	5,377					306	42,931
1883	240	36,585	96	13,332					336	49,917
1884	110	16,214	100	12,697					210	28,911
1885	71	10,462	109	12,492					180	22,954
1886	60	8,783	75	9,513					135	18,296
1887	63	9,596	39	5,919					102	15,515
1888	101	15,158	54	6,728					155	21,886
1889	63	9,422	74	10,084	3	480			140	19,986
1890	95	14,803	72	9,819	21	3,360	23	3,475	211	31,457
1891	65	9,607	93	13,611	14	2,240	36	5,600	208	31,058
1892	156	31,024	79	11,350	53	8,331	30	4,659	318	55,364
1893	134	21,031	86	12,655	57	9,097	15	2,113	292	44,896
1894	96	14,498	47	6,360	40	5,760	32	4,756	215	31,374
1895	89	13,447	46	7,854	49	7,636	20	3,161	204	32,098
1896	79	11,717	40	5,583	76	12,123	36	5,621	231	35,044
Total	2,079	318,143	1,118	152,742	313	49,027	192	29,385	3,702	549,297

TABLE 3. ORIGINAL TIMBER-CULTURE ENTRIES

Year	Santa Fe		La Mesilla		Folsom		Roswell		N.M. Total	
	Entries	*Acres*	*Entries*	*Acres*	*Entries*	*Acres*	*Entries*	*Acres*	*Entries*	*Acres*
1875	3	480							3	480
1876	4	640							4	640
1878	2	320	1	42					3	362
1879	1	160	27	3,780					28	3,940
1880	—	—	13	1,277					13	1,277
1881	3	480	11	1,319					14	1,799
1882	24	3,493	60	7,992					84	11,485
1883	16	2,080	151	21,067					167	23,147
1884	30	4,599	77	9,933					107	14,532
1885	21	3,349	133	16,315					154	19,664
1886	35	5,028	44	5,469					79	10,497
1887	180	27,014	60	8,530					240	35,544
1888	193	29,729	73	10,441					266	40,170
1889	82	12,023	142	21,307	8	1,227	3	480	235	35,037
1890	29	4,142	15	2,028	51	7,273	93	14,682	188	28,125
1891	7	1,000	2	318	11	1,759	4	559	24	3,636
Total	630	94,537	809	109,818	70	10,259	100	15,721	1,609	230,335

TABLE 4.   FINAL TIMBER-CULTURE CERTIFICATES

[The Timber-Culture Acts were repealed in 1891 and timber-culture certificates
are carried through 1903 when the final returns were all in]

Year	Santa Fe		La Mesilla		Folsom		Roswell		N.M. Total	
	Entries	*Acres*	*Entries*	*Acres*	*Entries*	*Acres*	*Entries*	*Acres*	*Entries*	*Acres*
1887			2	167					2	167
1888			2	289					2	289
1890			—	—			2	240	2	240
1891			—	—			1	160	1	160
1892	2	200	—	—			2	240	4	440
1893	1	80	—	—			4	640	5	720
1894	1	160	—	—			1	160	2	320
1895	—	—	1	80	6	966	2	320	9	1,366
1896	3	479	—	—	5	800	—	—	8	1,279
1897	2	200	—	—	7	1,120	—	—	9	1,320
1898	5	560	2	320	7	1,120	4	520	18	2,520
1899	7	1,025	1	158	4	600	1	160	13	1,943
1900	—	—	—	—	2	317	2	311	4	628
1901	3	319	—	—	2	267	1	160	6	746
1902	1	79	—	—	—	—	2	240	3	319
1903	1	160	—	—	2	320	—	—	3	480
Total	26	3,262	8	1,014	35	5,510	22	3,151	91	12,937

TABLE 5.   DONATION NOTIFICATIONS

Year	Santa Fe		La Mesilla		N.M. Total	
	Entries	Acres	Entries	Acres	Entries	Acres
1858	1	160			1	160
1859	10	1,600			10	1,600
1860	1	160			1	160
1870	14	2,124			14	2,124
1871	1	160			1	160
1873	29	5,559			29	5,559
1874	10	1,600			10	1,600
1875	13	2,080			13	2,080
1876	31	4,800			31	4,800
1877	38	4,720			38	4,720
1878	14	2,243			14	2,243
1879	6	895			6	895
1880	172	27,438			172	27,438
1881	94	14,793	8	1,285	102	16,078
1882	23	3,681	—	—	23	3,681
Total	457	72,013	8	1,285	465	73,298

TABLE 6.   DONATION CERTIFICATES

Year	Santa Fe		N.M. Total	
	Entries	Acres	Entries	Acres
1870	7	1,120	7	1,120
1873	27	4,280	27	4,280
1876	6	960	6	960
1878	24	2,480	24	2,480
1880	162	25,856	162	25,856
1881	89	13,692	89	13,692
1882	22	3,441	22	3,441
1884	1	160	1	160
Total	338	51,989	338	51,989

TABLE 7.   SOLDIERS AND SAILORS HOMESTEAD DECLARATORY STATEMENTS

Year	Santa Fe Entries	La Mesilla Entries	Folsom Entries	N.M. Total Entries
1879		1		1
1881		2		2
1882	7	3		10
1883	3	2		5
1884	2	5		7
1885	1	5		6
1886	1	3		4
1887	1	2		3
1888	10	2		12
1889	3	2		5
1890	3	1	1	5
1891	—	1	—	1
Total	31	29	1	61

APPENDIX VI

RECAPITULATION OF APPENDIXES IV AND V

Class of land	Entries	Acres
1. Arable or grazing land deeded to individuals by land laws		
Final homestead certificates (through 1896)	3,702	549,297
Final timber-culture certificates (through 1903)	91	12,937
Donation certificates	338	51,989
Soldiers and sailors homestead declaratory statements (could be entered immediately)	61	8,461[a]
Total	4,192	622,684
2. Arable or grazing land benefiting individuals, for varying lengths of time, by virtue of applications for land under the land laws		
Original homestead entries	6,784	940,828
Original timber-culture entries	1,609	230,335
Donation notifications	465	73,298
Total	8,858	1,244,461
3. Arable or grazing land deeded to individuals by cash sales		
Final desert land certificates (through 1894)	398	139,622
Pre-emption sales	2,574	369,631
Private entry sales	196	50,061
Public auction sales	112	15,671
Excess payments on homesteads, etc.	553	2,324
Homestead entries commuted to cash	315	46,686
Total	4,148	623,995
4. Arable or grazing land benefiting individuals, for varying lengths of time, by virtue of applications to purchase with cash		
Original desert land entries	1,348	415,203
Pre-emption declaratory statements	7,657	1,099,545[b]
Total	9,005	1,514,748

a. Based on the average original homestead entry of 138.7 acres.
b. Based on the average pre-emption sale of 143.6 acres.

Class of land	Entries	Acres
5. Arable or grazing land deeded to individuals by purchase with negotiable scrip		
Private land scrip	1	640
Sioux half-breed scrip	16	1,360
Valentine scrip	6	240
Military bounty land warrants	36	3,556
Israel Dodge scrip	18	790
Supreme Court locations	4	160
Robert Cole scrip	1	80
Joseph Wilson scrip	2	160
Agricultural college scrip	24	3,843
Total	108	10,829
Total arable or grazing land deeded to individuals by land laws (see section 1)	4,192	622,684
Total arable or grazing land sold to individuals (see sections 3 and 5)	4,256	634,824
Total	8,448	1,257,508
Total arable or grazing land benefiting individuals, for varying lengths of time, by virtue of applications for land under the land laws (see section 2)	8,858	1,244,461
Total arable or grazing land benefiting individuals, for varying lengths of time, by virtue of applications to purchase with cash (see section 4)	9,005	1,514,748
Total	17,863	2,759,209
Total arable or grazing land used by individuals	26,311	4,016,717
Mineral and coal lands deeded to individuals by cash		
Mineral land sales	517	9,015
Coal land sales	39	4,189
Total	556	13,204
Mineral and coal lands benefiting individuals, for varying lengths of time, by virtue of applications to purchase with cash		
Applications to purchase mineral lands	674[c]	11,795
Applications to purchase coal lands	436[d]	46,652
Total	1,110	58,447
Total mineral and coal land used by individuals	1,666	71,651
Grand Total	27,977	4,088,368

Class of land	Entries	Acres
Arable and grazing land to individuals by land laws	4,192	622,684
Arable, grazing, mineral, and coal land sold	4,812	648,028
Arable, grazing, mineral, and coal land deeded	9,004	1,270,712
Arable, grazing, mineral, and coal land benefiting individuals for varying lengths of time	18,973	2,817,656
Grand Total	27,977	4,088,368

c. Based on the average mineral land sale of 17.5 acres.
d. Based on the average coal land sale of 107 acres.

APPENDIX VII

MILITARY RESERVATIONS

Fort	Location	Officially established	Authority	Size, acres	Initial survey	Officially abandoned	Authority	Status in 1891
Bayard	T17S, R12-13W	Apr. 19 1869	Ex. Order	8,840	Feb. 1869	(Still in use)		Military
Butler	T12-13N, R27-28-29E	Mar. 22 1861	Sec. War	76,800	Feb. 1861	July 22 1884	Act July 5, 1884	Abandoned
Cummings	T21S, R8W	Apr. 29 1870	Ex. Order	2,560	Dec. 1868	Oct. 7 1891	Act July 5, 1884	Abandoned
Craig	T7-8S, R2-3W	Sep. 23 1869	Ex. Order	24,895	June 1869	Mar. 3 1885	Act July 5, 1884	Abandoned
Marcy	T17N, R8E	Aug. 28 1868	Ex. Order	17.77	Apr. 1868	June 15 1895	Act July 5, 1884	Military
McRae	T13S, R3W	May 28 1869	Ex. Order	2,560	Apr. 1869	July 22 1884	Act July 5, 1884.	Abandoned
Selden	T21S, R1E & 1W	Nov. 28 1870	Ex. Order	9,613.74	Nov. 1870	Mar. 17 1892	Act July 5, 1884	Military
Stanton	T9-10S, R11-12-13-14-15E	May 12 1859	Ex. Order	92,160	Apr. 1870	(Still in use)		Military
Sumner	T2-3N, R26E	May 28 1869	Ex. Order	13,644.8	July 1868	Feb. 24 1871	Act Feb. 24, 1871	Abandoned

		Declaration		Acres	Date	Reverted to pub. dom.	Decision Sec'y Int.	Abandoned
Thorn	T18-19S, R3-4-5W	Never officially declared		23,040	Mar. 1857	Feb. 15 1884	Feb. 15 1884	Military
Union	T18-19N, R19-20E	Oct. 9 1868	Ex Order	66,880	Mar. 1868	Apr. 1 1894	Act July 5, 1884	Military
Wingate	T13-14-15N, R15-16-17W	Feb. 18 1870 Mar. 26 1881	Ex. Order	64,000	Nov. 1869	(Still in use)		Military
On Mora River	T18N, R20E	Nov. 28 1870 (Reserved Aug. 18, 1857)	Ex. Order	5,120		Never used by military		Abandoned

SOURCES:

L.O.R. 10/18/80, 49 Cong., 3 Sess., *H.E.D.* No. 1, 459-460 (1959).

Survey Records Section, *Field Notes and Executive Documents of Military and Indian Reservations* (B.L.M.).

Joseph S. Wilson to Spencer, 5/28/69 (N.A.).

L.O.R. 11/1/71, 42 Cong., 1 Sess., *H.E.D.* No. 1, 57 (1505).

Acting Commissioner L. L. Harrison to register and receiver at Las Cruces, 3/8/84, enclosure, Secretary of the Interior, 2/15/84 (F.R.C.).

Hendricks to Pelham, 8/29/57 (N.A.).

Sparks to Julian, 2/18/87 (N.A.).

L.O.R. 10/4/88, 50 Cong., 2 Sess., *H.E.D.* No. 1, 175-178 (2636).

Registers and receivers, *Tract Books* (B.L.M.).

Map to accompany L.O.R. 10/30/79, 46 Cong., 2 Sess., *H.E.D.* No. 1 (1910).

S.G.R. 8/25/82, 47 Cong., 2 Sess., *H.E.D.* No. 1, 526 (2099).

L.O.R. 9/23/91, 52 Cong., 1 Sess., *H.E.D.* No. 1, 145 (2933).

Stanley, *Fort Union*, 57.

APPENDIX VIII

RAILROAD MILEAGE IN 1891

[Compiled from *G.N.M.* 10/12/91, 52 Cong., 1 Sess., *H.E.D.* No. 1, 351 (2935)]

Railroad line	Mileage in New Mexico	Mileage in land grants
Atchison, Topeka, and Santa Fe		
Main line, north and south (1879-1881)	503.1	343.0
Lamy to Santa Fe (1880)	18.0	11.0
Rincon to Deming (1881)	53.0	—
Dillon to Blossburg (1881)	5.9	—
Nutt to Lake Valley (1884)	13.3	—
Socorro to Magdalena (1884)	27.1	—
Magdalena to Kelley (1885)	3.9	—
San Antonio to Carthage (1882)	9.6	—
Las Vegas to Hot Springs (1882)	6.4	6.4
Hot Springs westward (1887)	1.9	1.9
Silver City branch	48.0	—
	690.20	362.30
Atlantic and Pacific		
Main line (1881)	166.60	78.0
Sidings (188-)	22.25	11.0
San Jose Quarry spur (1888)	3.41	—
	192.26	89.00
Southern Pacific		
Rio Grande to Deming (1881)	73.46	—
Deming to Arizona line (1880)	93.76	—
	167.22	—
Denver and Rio Grande		
Colorado line to Española (1880)	85.86	15.0
Between Antonito and Durango (1880)	69.03	—
Tres Piedras lumber branch (1888)	2.15	—
Chama lumber branch (1888)	3.16	—
	160.47 [sic]	15.00
Denver, Texas and Fort Worth, in New Mexico	83.30	—
Santa Fe Southern, Española to Santa Fe	39.00	17.00
Arizona and New Mexico, Lordsburg to Arizona line, about	32.00	—
Pecos Valley Railroad, in New Mexico	35.00	—
Trinidad to Catskill, in New Mexico	27.00	27.00
Silver City and Northern, in New Mexico	19.00	—
		510.30
Total mileage in New Mexico	1,445.45	
Total mileage in grants	510.30	
Total mileage on public domain	935.15	

APPENDIX IX

ESTIMATED LAND GRANTS FOR EDUCATIONAL AND OTHER USES

[Compiled from Graham, *Know New Mexico, Acquisition of State Lands*, 2. All measurements are in acres]

School or institution	Ferguson Act (1898)	Enabling Act (1910)	Other acts (later)
Common schools	4,244,480.00	4,219,520.00	
University	111,080.00	200,000.00	
University saline	1,622.86	—	
A. and M. College	100,000.00	150,000.00	
Normal schools	100,000.00	200,000.00 a	
School of Mines	50,000.00	150,000.00	
Military Institute	50,000.00	100,000.00	
Reform School	50,000.00	—	
Blind Asylum	50,000.00	100,000.00 b	
Deaf and Dumb Asylum	50,000.00	—	
Water reservoirs	500,000.00	—	
Miners' Hospital	50,000.00	50,000.00	
Insane Asylum	50,000.00	100,000.00	
Improvement of Rio Grande	100,000.00	—	
Public buildings	32,000.00	100,000.00	
Penitentiary	50,000.00	100,000.00	
Old Palace	2.60	—	
Charitable, penal, reform	—	100,000.00	
Santa Fe and Grant counties bond payment to common schools	—	1,000,000.00	
Repayment to Santa Fe and Grant counties, etc., for payment on void bonds	—	—	250,000.00
Eastern N.M. Normal (1932)	—	—	76,000.00
Carey quitclaim	—	—	2,980.00
Total	5,589,185.46	6,569,520.00	328,980.00
	Grand Total	12,487,685.46 c	

a. Divided between Normal schools.
b. Divided between Blind Asylum and Deaf and Dumb Asylum.
c. Of this total, more than 10,000,000 acres were for educational use.

APPENDIX X

LAND FRAUD CASES IN THE UNITED STATES

[These figures, compiled from Annual Reports of Commissioners of the General Land Office, cannot be taken as an absolute index because, to some extent, they reflect concentrations of investigating agents rather than fraud. They can, however, be accepted as a reliable general indication of the extent of land fraud in various parts of the country]

State or Territory	1884	1885	1886	1887	1888	1889	1890	1891	Total
California	574	529	318	453	999	2,193	2,571	2,303	9,940
Colorado	373	451	753	1,245	579	1,389	583	479	5,852
Kansas	182	117	114	2,514	859	1,553	235	78	5,652
Dakotas	460	329	527	1,252	304	1,257	562	116	4,807
New Mexico	827	63	193	364	432	1,040	773	437	4,129
Nebraska	170	160	176	1,364	657	948	103	147	3,725
Washington	109	239	161	128	700	733	689	636	3,395
Minnesota	355	57	165	590	176	285	211	170	2,009
Wyoming	10	186	76	125	163	313	253	216	1,342
Louisiana	—	90	154	136	176	224	80	47	907
Oregon	83	37	26	137	49	172	207	195	906
Montana	24	51	97	68	203	164	75	104	786
Arizona	—	—	6	103	271	222	100	48	750
Alabama	153	12	3	82	89	113	121	134	707
Arkansas	70	44	51	66	120	142	79	47	619
Idaho	92	9	54	33	48	75	125	121	557
Utah	—	13	32	154	61	106	117	29	512
Florida	71	64	33	162	36	63	51	21	501
Mississippi	—	3	76	28	71	23	12	114	327
Wisconsin	10	67	21	90	19	35	26	44	312
Michigan	—	28	25	76	31	22	33	23	238
Missouri	—	3	12	54	4	13	16	11	113
Nevada	—	—	—	—	—	7	1	—	8
Iowa	—	—	—	—	—	3	2	1	6
Oklahoma	—	—	—	—	—	—	—	4	4
Total	3,563[a]	2,552[b]	3,073[b]	9,224[c]	6,047[c]	11,095[d]	7,025[d]	5,525[d]	48,104

a. Cases investigated including 32 cases of fencing.
b. Cases investigated exclusive of fencing.
c. Cases received during year.
d. Cases pending June 30, respective year.

APPENDIX XI

SUMMARY OF LAND FRAUD CASES IN NEW MEXICO

JUDICIAL DISTRICT	*Perjury*	*Subornation of perjury*	*Conspiracy*	*Official misconduct*	*Miscellaneous*	*Unlawful inclosure*	*Violating timber laws*	*Totals*
FIRST DISTRICT, CRIMINAL CASES, 1-1, 431								
Not guilty	61	1	4	2	–	1	7	76
Dismissed without trial	93	10	8	2	1	52	5	171
Total (presumably not guilty)	154	11	12	4	1	53	12	247
Dismissed (defendant not found)	45	–	–	–	–	–	3	48
Guilty	–	–	–	–	–	–	2	2
Total (presumably guilty)	45	–	–	–	–	–	5	50
Dimisssed, not in transcript (guilt probable)	85	1	4	1	–	–	–	91
Disposition unknown (guilt possible)	–	–	–	–	–	–	–	–
Grand Total	284	12	16	5	1	53	17	388
SECOND DISTRICT, CRIMINAL CASES, 1-894								
Not guilty	2	–	–	–	–	–	–	2
Dismissed without trial	–	–	–	–	–	–	–	–
Total (presumably not guilty)	2	–	–	–	–	–	–	2
Dismissed (defendant not found)	11	1	–	–	–	–	–	12
Guilty	5	–	2	–	–	1	1	9
Total (presumably guilty)	16	1	2	–	–	1	1	21
Dismissed, not in transcript (guilt probable)	–	–	–	–	–	–	–	–
Disposition unknown (guilt possible)	5	2	2	–	1	–	–	10
Grand Total	23	3	4	–	1	1	1	33

JUDICIAL DISTRICT	Perjury	Subornation of perjury	Conspiracy	Official misconduct	Miscellaneous	Unlawful inclosure	Violating timber laws	Totals
THIRD DISTRICT, CRIMINAL CASES, 1-933								
Not guilty	6	—	—	—	1	—	1	8
Dismissed without trial	—	—	—	—	—	—	1	1
Total (presumably not guilty)	6	—	—	—	1	—	2	9
Dismissed (defendant not found)	—	—	—	—	—	—	—	—
Guilty	4	—	—	—	—	—	—	4
Total (presumably guilty)	4	—	—	—	—	—	—	4
Dismissed, not in transcript (guilt probable)	97	6	2	—	2	1	10	118
Disposition unknown (guilt possible)	12	—	2	—	1	1	3	18
Grand Total	119	6	4	—	3	2	15	149
FOURTH DISTRICT, CRIMINAL CASES, 1-306								
Not guilty	2	—	—	—	—	5	—	7
Dismissed without trial	4	—	1	—	1	11	25	42
Total (presumably not guilty)	6	—	1	—	1	16	25	49
Dismissed (defendant not found)	10	—	—	—	—	6	6	22
Guilty	—	—	—	—	—	—	—	—
Total (presumably guilty)	10	—	—	—	—	6	6	22
Dismissed, not in transcript (guilt probable)	—	—	—	—	—	—	—	—
Disposition unknown (guilt possible)	—	—	—	—	—	—	—	—
Grand Total	16	—	1	—	1	22	31	71
FIFTH DISTRICT, CRIMINAL CASES, 1-69								
(No land fraud)								
Total criminal cases, 3,633								
Total of all Districts (presumably not guilty)	168	11	13	4	3	69	39	307
Total of all Districts (presumably guilty)	75	1	2	—	—	7	12	97
Total of all Districts, not in transcript (guilt probable)	182	7	6	1	2	1	10	209
Total of all Districts, disposition unknown (guilt possible)	17	2	4	—	1	1	3	28
Grand Total	442	21	25	5	6	78	64	641

APPENDIX XII

UNLAWFUL INCLOSURES IN THE UNITED STATES

[All measurements are in acres]

State or territory		Year	Cases reported	Cases being acted upon	Cases awaiting investigation	Total
Colorado		1885	3,115,228	—	—	
		1886	—	3,562,570	1,041,116	
		1887	—	3,273,610	526,300	
		1888	—	3,562,570	538,500	
	Total		3,115,228	10,398,750	2,105,916	15,619,894
Kansas		1885	313,540	—	—	
		1886	—	1,280,940	1,075,900	
		1887	—	1,588,340	192,000	
		1888	—	1,638,340	192,000	
	Total		313,540	4,507,620	1,459,900	6,281,060
New Mexico		1885	386,000	—	—	
		1886	—	—	803,140	
		1887	—	662,130	103,140	
		1888	—	1,381,280	103,140	
	Total		386,000	2,043,410	1,009,420	3,438,830
Nebraska		1885	418,094	—	—	
		1886	—	506,540	275,600	
		1887	—	580,780	240,600	
		1888	—	576,840	248,170	
	Total		418,094	1,664,160	764,370	2,846,624
Montana		1885	130,380	—	—	
		1886	—	168,800	17,900	
		1887	—	181,020	45,500	
		1888	—	631,500	53,410	
	Total		130,380	981,320	116,810	1,228,510
Utah		1885	137,800	—	—	
		1886	—	68,700	31,500	
		1887	—	101,420	1,500	
		1888	—	68,700	383,160	
	Total		137,800	238,820	416,160	792,780
Wyoming		1885	34,140	—	—	
		1886	—	38,060	64,640	
		1887	—	107,390	55,640	
		1888	—	253,260	57,640	
	Total		34,140	398,710	177,920	610,770

State or territory	Year	Cases reported	Cases being acted upon	Cases awaiting investigation	Total
Public Land	1886	—	—	211,000	
Strip	1887	—	—	211,000	
	1888	—	—	178,000	
Total		—	—	600,000	600,000
California	1887	—	97,440	93,440	
	1888	—	4,000	99,450	
Total		—	101,440	192,890	294,330
Nevada	1885	21,600	—	—	
	1886	—	10,000	82,780	
	1887	—	10,000	72,780	
	1888	—	10,000	72,800	
Total		21,600	30,000	228,360	279,960
Oregon	1886	—	—	67,900	
	1887	—	26,940	31,900	
	1888	—	26,940	31,900	
Total		—	53,880	131,700	185,580
Arizona	1886	—	4,000	33,080	
	1887	—	54,200	200	
	1888	—	54,750	1,400	
Total		—	112,950	34,680	147,630
Idaho	1885	8,240	—	—	
	1886	—	16,080	5,080	
	1887	—	15,380	1,280	
	1888	—	16,080	26,280	
Total		8,240	47,540	32,640	88,420
Dakota	1886	—	15,000	350	
	1887	—	15,000	553	
	1888	—	15,000	553	
Total		—	45,000	1,456	46,456
Washington	1886	—	—	11,815	
	1887	—	—	11,815	
	1888	—	—	13,275	
Total		—	—	36,905	36,905
Minnesota	1886	—	—	900	
	1887	—	—	900	
	1888	—	—	900	
Total		—	—	2,700	2,700

These figures, compiled from Annual Reports of Commissioners of the General Land Office, cannot be accepted as an absolute index because they sometimes reflect a concentration of inspectors rather than fraud. This is particularly true of Colorado. In Grant and Socorro counties in New Mexico, in 1885, over 3,000,000 acres were reported as being fenced, but evidently not on good enough authority to be tabulated. These are the only comparative figures available and can accepted as a good general indication of the extent of illegal fencing in the country.

The cattle graziers named in the above report are the following for New Mexico.

Colfax County: Lake Valley Cattle Co., Muscatine Cattle Co., F. M. Darling, J. E. Temple, Portsmouth Cattle Co., Palo Blanco Cattle Co., S. W. Dorsey, F. C. Tallman, Western Land and Cattle Co., Delano & Dwyer, Eagle Tail Cattle Co., and T. E. Owen.

Mora County: M. W. Mills, Red River Cattle Co., Dubuque Cattle Co., Lake Ranch Cattle Co., Augustine Vigil, and Akron Cattle Co.

San Miguel County: Montezuma Cattle Co., Francisco Gallegos, Fond du Lac Cattle Co., Mrs. Ellen Casey, W. A. Burnett, Cimarron Cattle Co., New England Livestock Co., A. Grysladowski, F. Huntington, Trinidad Romero, R. L. M. Ross, Tiffin Cattle Co., A. Goldsmith, R. Muejus Co., Stonewall Cattle Co., J. M. Bernard, W. H. McBroom, A. W. Rand, Y. Kohn & Co., Dutchess Cattle Co., and Juan de Dios Co.

Socorro County: Grayson & Borland, San Augustine Cattle Co., and E. E. Scates.

Lincoln County: Carrizozo Cattle Co., Coyote Valley and Red Lake Cattle Co., F. M. Goodwin, and El Capitan Cattle Co.

APPENDIX XIII

POPULATION AND LAND OFFICE BUSINESS

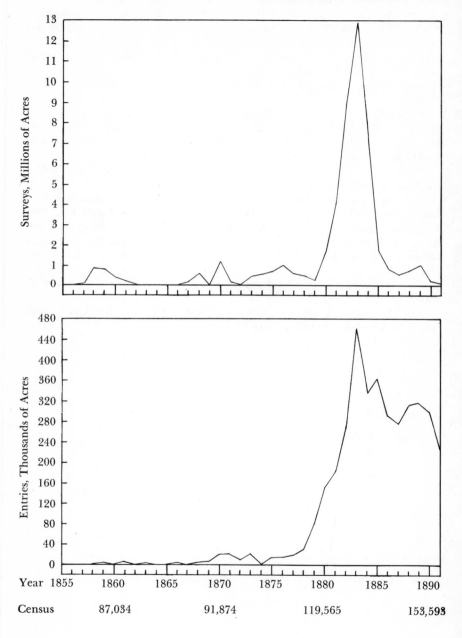

Map Explanation

1. The township and range lines are as shown on the map of climatic zones by H. J. Maker and H. E. Dregne.

2. PM = principal meridian.

   BL = base line.

   (digit) MW = (digit) guide meridian west.

       "   ME = "   "   "   east.

       "   CN = "   correction line north.

       "   CS = "   "   "   south.

   R " W = range (digit) west.

   R " E = "   "   east.

   T " N = township (digit) north.

   T " S = "   "   south.

3. A = Albuquerque; T.10N, R.3E.

   B = Santa Fe; T.17N, R.9E.

   C = Silver City; T.18S, R.14W.

   D = Clayton; T.26N, R.35E.

   E = Las Cruces; T.23S, R.2E.

   F = Roswell; T.10S, R.24E.

4. The first township in each instance (e.g., Homestead, etc.), is designated by an "X" through that township.

5. Climatic Zone 3 and better, as designated on the map of H. J. Maker and H. E. Dregne.

   Climatic Zone 4, *Ibid.*

   Irrigated areas as designated on *Map Illustrating the Progress of Irrigation Within the Arid and Semi-arid Region of the United*

States West of the 97th Degree of Longitude from Greenwich (Washington, United States Department of Agriculture, Office of Irrigation Inquiry), p. 4.

6. The rivers shown are the Rio Grande, Pecos, Hondo, Canadian, San Juan, and Gila. Their locations can be identified on any standard map of New Mexico.

7. Some public domain areas are shown in what are actually grant areas because they were unwittingly surveyed as such.

8. The following excerpts selected from Maker and Dregne's bulletin, *Climatic Zones in New Mexico,* explain the basis upon which they selected zone designations:

Climate must be considered when land is classified for agricultural purposes. It is frequently the limiting factor in plant growth. This report shows how climate can be evaluated for its influence on land capability in non-irrigated areas of New Mexico, and it correlates the zones established by evaluation of climate with land classifications used by the Soil Conservation Service.

The climatic zones established in this report should not be considered in the classification of irrigated lands, because where irrigation water is available, moisture is not a limiting factor. Even if irrigation water is inadequate in certain areas, these climatic zones would not reflect the available water supply. Therefore, the maximum land class given for each zone applies only to the non-irrigated land.

CLIMATE EVALUATION

In some non-irrigated areas of New Mexico, there is enough precipitation for relatively dependable farming without supplemental water. In others, precipitation is too slight to support crop growth. Annual precipitation alone, however, does not adequately indicate where adapted crops will grow, because of the marked differences in temperature and distribution of moisture. Wide differences in temperature are to be expected because of the extremes in elevations, which range from about 3,000 feet in the southeastern part of the state to approximately 13,300 feet at some mountain peaks. The moisture distribution pattern also differs markedly on the east side of the state from that on the west side.

The climate evaluation in this report is based on effective precipitation, which depends not only on total precipitation, but also on seasonal distribution of moisture, temperature, and evaporation.

Both favorable and unfavorable climatic conditions are considered in the evaluation of climate. If only the precipitation of the mid-thirties had been used in the evaluation of the climate of the dry farm areas of northeastern New Mexico, the areas would probably have been classified as non-arable. If the high rainfall year of 1941 had been used alone, it would have resulted in far too favorable a classification. The true condition is actually between these extremes. The data on weather used in the evaluation of climate were taken from the 1949 climatic summary of the Weather Bureau. (Climatological Data, New Mexico. Annual Summary 1949. 53(13). Weather Bureau, U. S. Department of Commerce.) Only data from those stations having at least a 10-year record of precipitation and temperature through 1949 were used.

Climatic Zone 1. Very few areas in New Mexico belong in this zone.

Climatic Zone 2. This zone has adequate precipitation for some crops. Dry years occur, but farming as a rule is rather dependable.

Climatic Zone 3. The good soils in this zone are moderately dependable cropland. The risks of drought, crop failure, and erosion, however, are high.

Climatic Zone 4. In this zone, only average or above-average precipitation is adequate for crop production. Low yields and crop failures occur more often in this zone than in Zone 3.

Climatic Zone 5. The soils in this zone are not suitable for crop production unless irrigation or supplemental water is available.

Climatic Zone 6. The land in this zone is suitable for grazing or woodland use if soils, slopes, and other factors are favorable. It is not suitable for cultivation because of limited rainfall, which also limits it somewhat for range or woodland.

Climatic Zone 7. The land in this zone is suitable for grazing when soils, slopes, and other factors are favorable. It produces less forage than similar land in Zone 6 because of the less favorable climatic conditions.

Professor Dregne, in a telephone conversation on May 30, 1955, advanced the belief that the Maker and Dregne map would be reasonably accurate for climatic conditions that prevailed in the last half of the nineteenth century. He pointed out that the map is already weighted to include all possible areas within the respective zones and that the inclusion of Zone 4 would certainly balance any slightly more favorable climatic conditions, in the nineteenth century, due to less grazing and land erosion at that time. His opinion is borne out by an examination of rainfall statistics, for past years, in various places in the state. Available statistics vary from place to place as to the length of time covered. The oldest (those for Santa Fe) date from 1850. Statistics for all areas show a reasonably uniform rainfall pattern throughout their entire history.

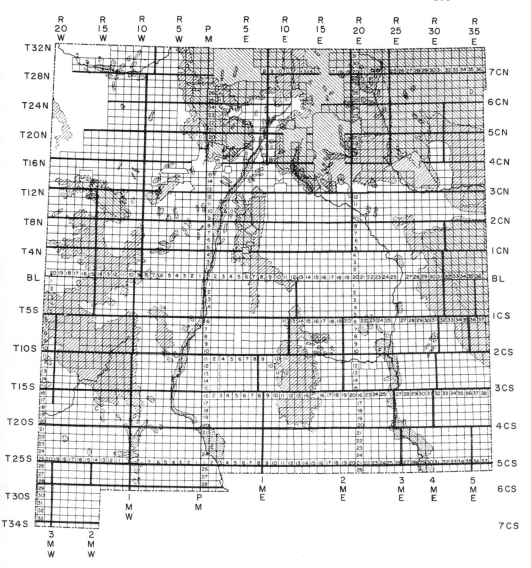

MAP 1. GUIDE MERIDIANS AND CORRECTION LINES
IN NEW MEXICO

162

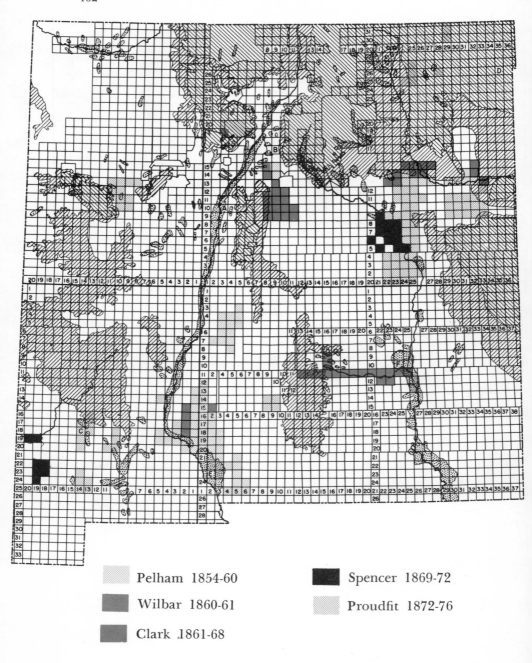

	Pelham 1854-60		Spencer 1869-72
	Wilbar 1860-61		Proudfit 1872-76
	Clark 1861-68		

MAP 2. TOWNSHIPS SUBDIVIDED UNDER VARIOUS SURVEYORS GENERAL

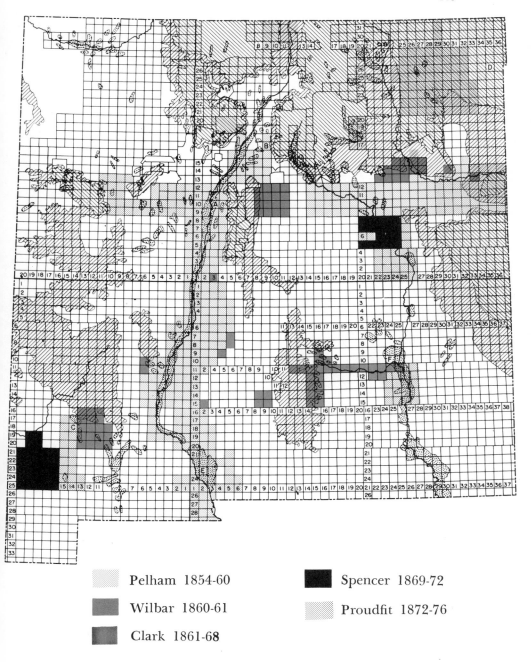

Pelham 1854-60

Wilbar 1860-61

Clark 1861-68

Spencer 1869-72

Proudfit 1872-76

MAP 3. TOWNSHIPS WITH EXTERIOR BOUNDARIES SURVEYED
UNDER VARIOUS SURVEYORS GENERAL

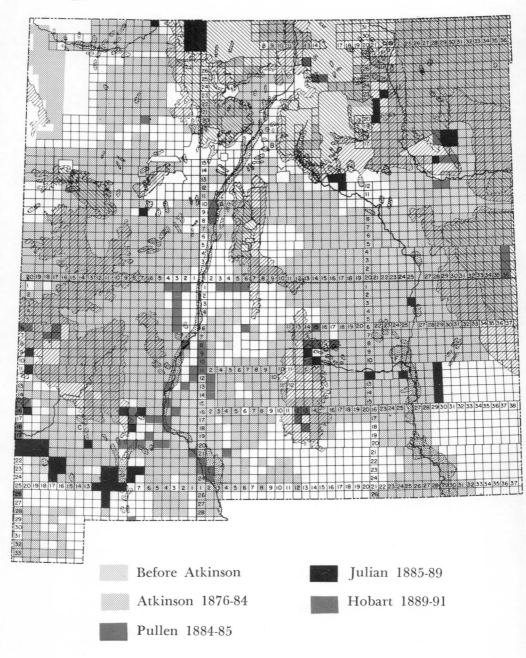

Before Atkinson
Atkinson 1876-84
Pullen 1884-85
Julian 1885-89
Hobart 1889-91

MAP 4. TOWNSHIPS SUBDIVIDED UNDER VARIOUS SURVEYORS GENERAL

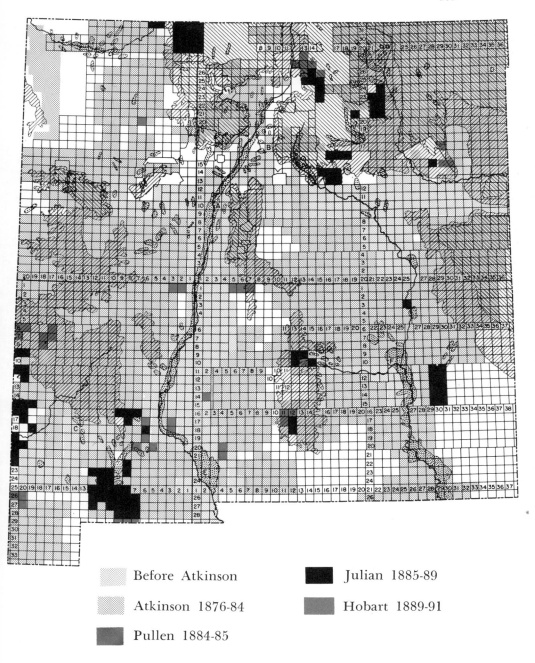

Before Atkinson

Atkinson 1876-84

Pullen 1884-85

Julian 1885-89

Hobart 1889-91

MAP 5. TOWNSHIPS WITH EXTERIOR BOUNDARIES SURVEYED
UNDER VARIOUS SURVEYORS GENERAL

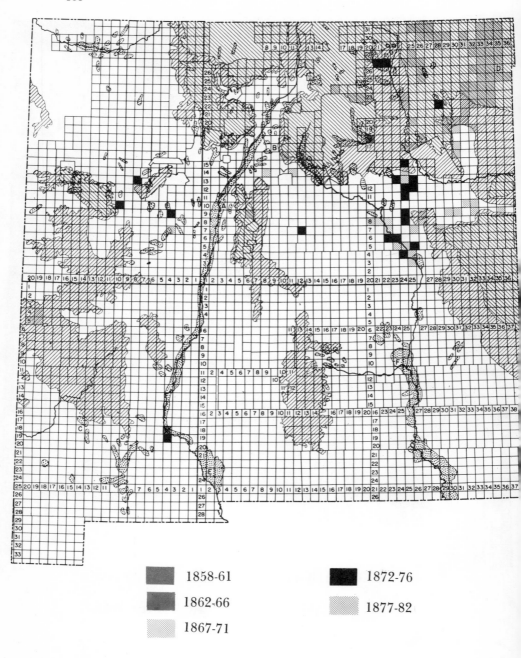

	1858-61		1872-76
	1862-66		1877-82
	1867-71		

MAP 6. TOWNSHIPS WITH DONATION NOTIFICATIONS

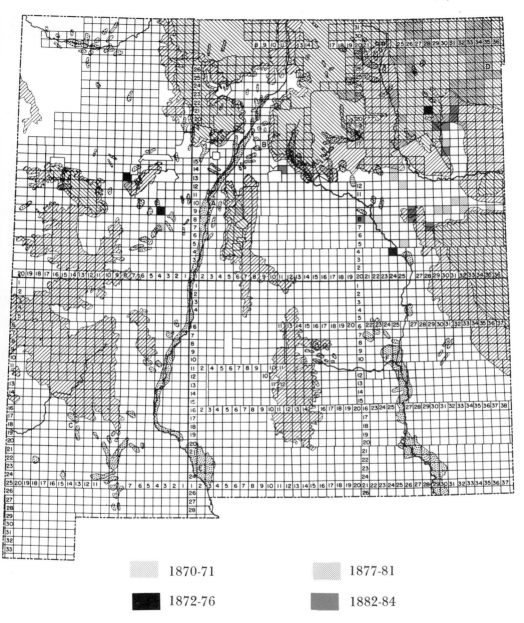

1870-71   1877-81

1872-76   1882-84

MAP 7. TOWNSHIPS WITH DONATION CERTIFICATES

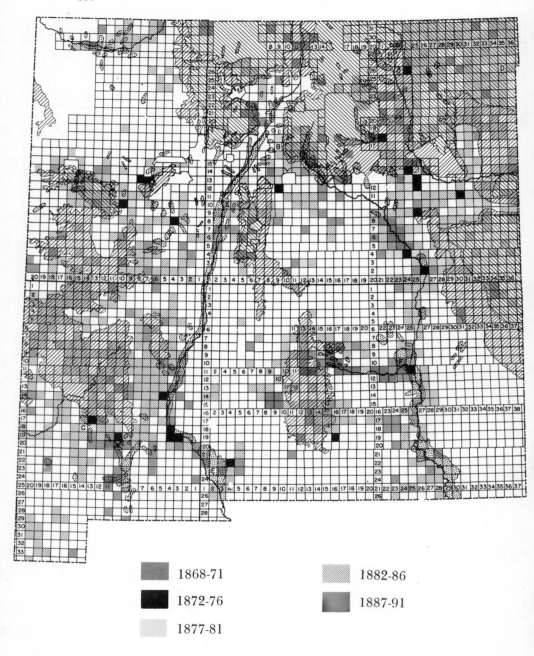

1868-71   1882-86

1872-76   1887-91

1877-81

MAP   8.   TOWNSHIPS WITH ORIGINAL HOMESTEAD ENTRIES

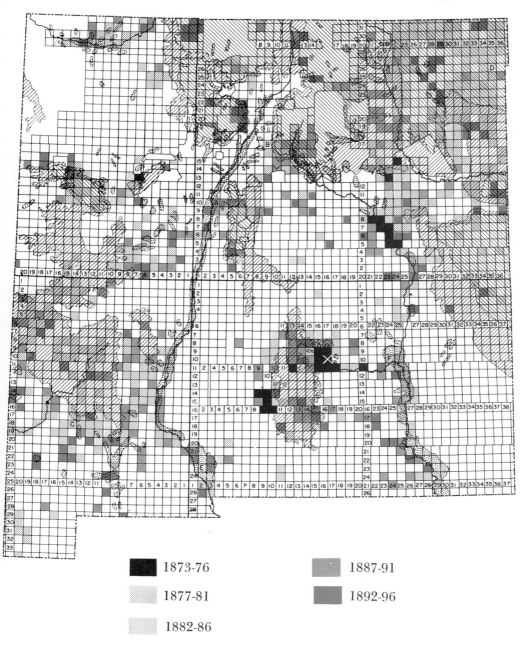

1873-76		1887-91
1877-81		1892-96
1882-86		

MAP 9. TOWNSHIPS WITH FINAL HOMESTEAD CERTIFICATES

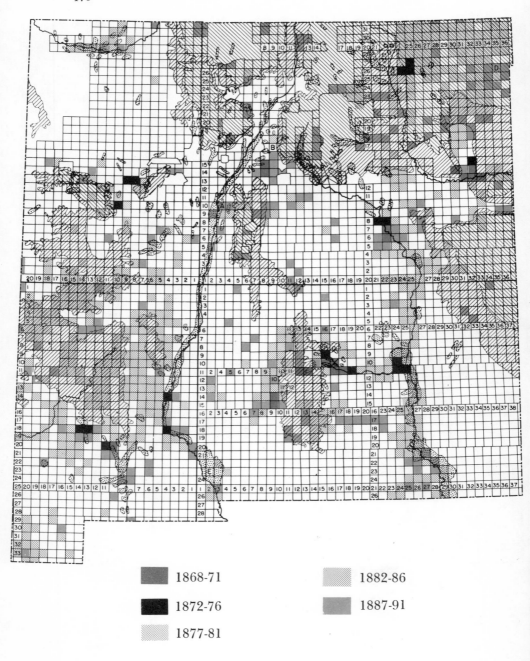

MAP 10. TOWNSHIPS WITH CASH SALES

1868-71   1882-86

1872-76   1887-91

1877-81

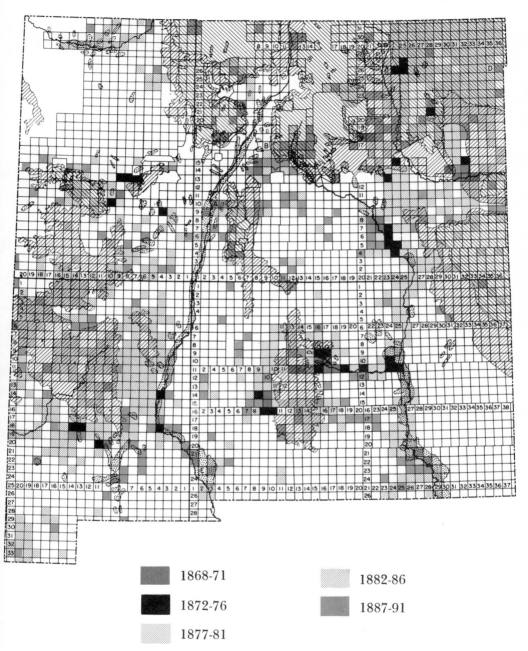

MAP 11. TOWNSHIPS WITH CASH SALES AND LAND LAW CERTIFICATES

172

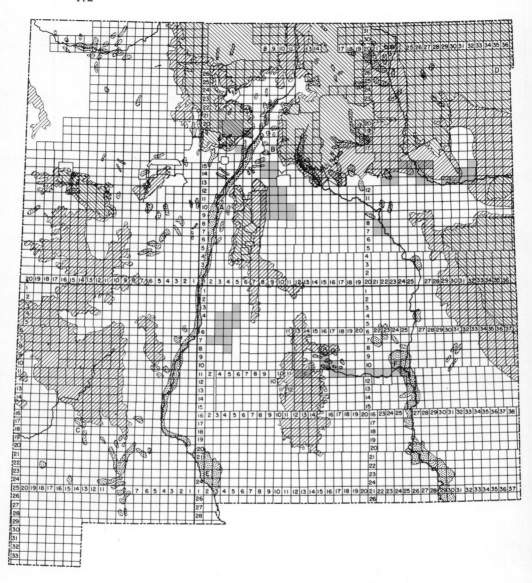

MAP 12. TOWNSHIPS INCLUDED IN THE PRESIDENTIAL
PROCLAMATION OF MAY 3, 1870

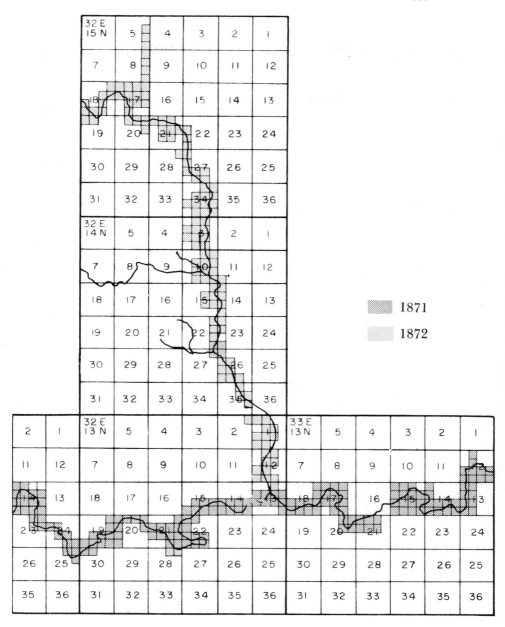

MAP 13. CASH PURCHASES OF WILSON WADDINGHAM

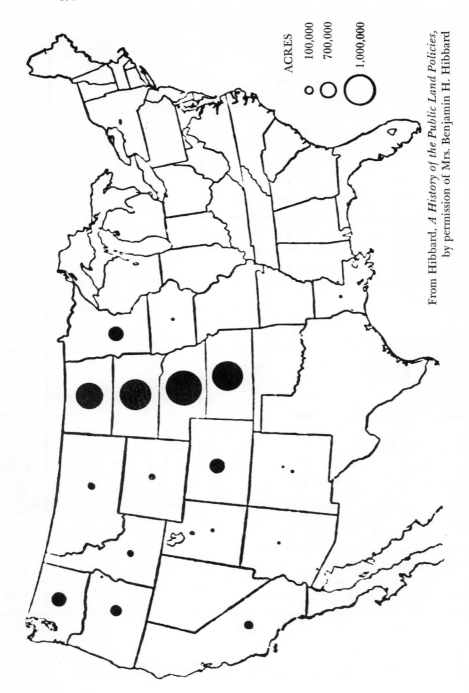

ACRES
100,000
700,000
1,000,000

From Hibbard, *A History of the Public Land Policies*,
by permission of Mrs. Benjamin H. Hibbard

MAP 14.   DISPOSALS UNDER TIMBER-CULTURE ACT

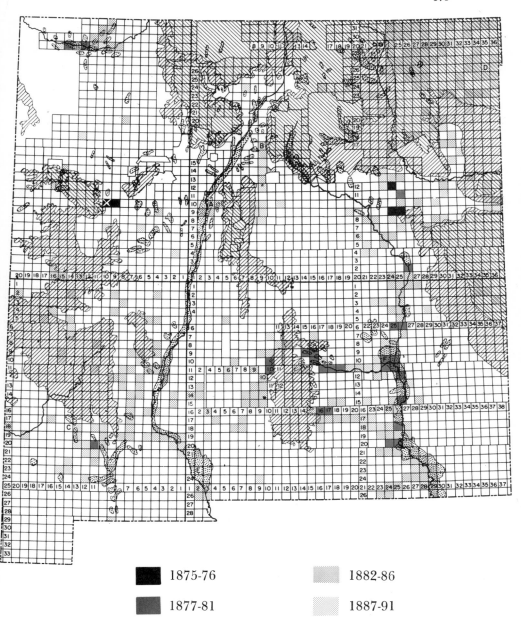

MAP 15. TOWNSHIPS WITH ORIGINAL TIMBER-CULTURE ENTRIES

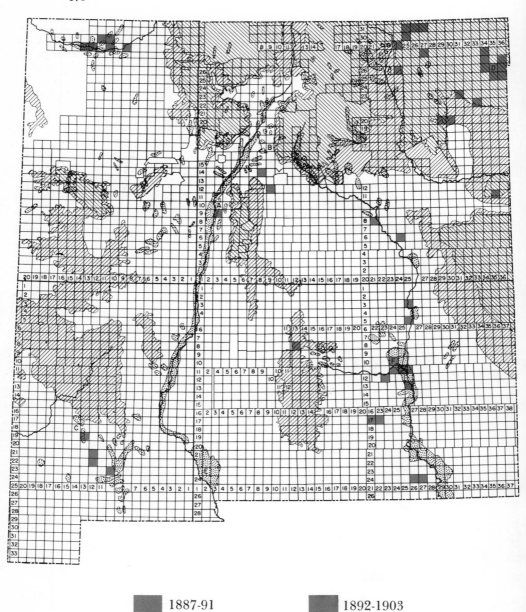

1887-91   1892-1903

MAP 16.   TOWNSHIPS WITH FINAL TIMBER-CULTURE CERTIFICATES

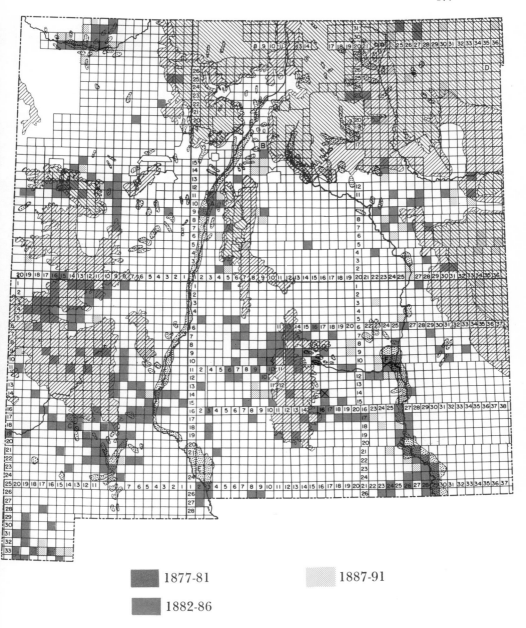

1877-81   1887-91

1882-86

MAP 17.   TOWNSHIPS WITH ORIGINAL DESERT LAND ENTRIES

178

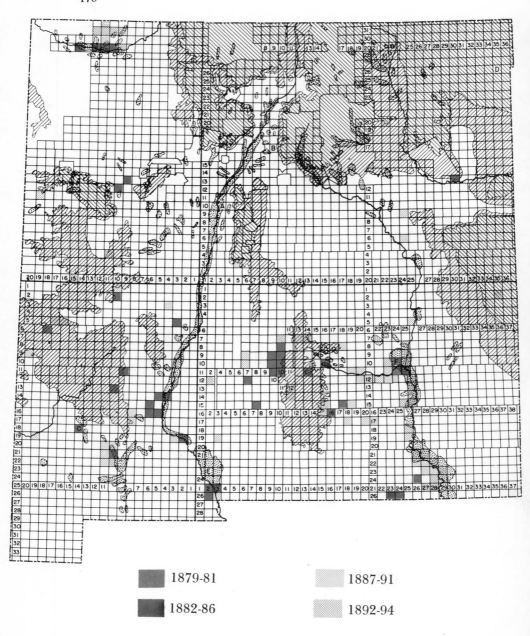

MAP 18.   TOWNSHIPS WITH FINAL DESERT LAND CERTIFICATES

1879-81   1887-91

1882-86   1892-94

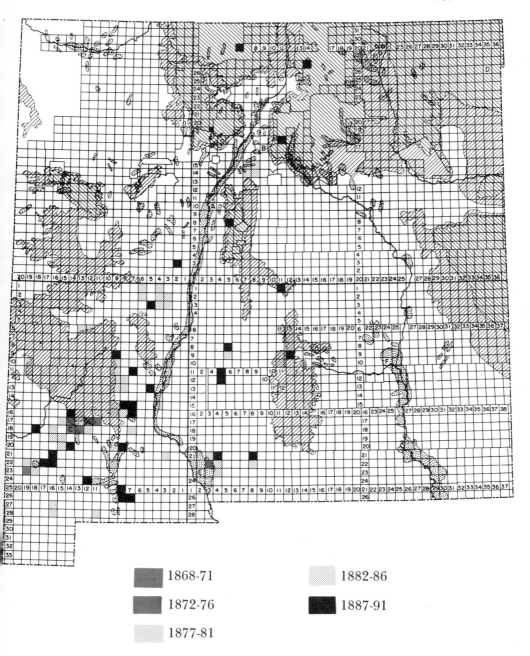

1868-71   1882-86

1872-76   1887-91

1877-81

MAP 19. TOWNSHIPS WITH MINING ENTRIES

Bibliography

1. ARCHIVES

A. The National Archives (Washington)

Commissioners of the General Land Office. *Correspondence.* To Surveyors General of New Mexico and others, 4 vols., 2,053 pp., August 5, 1854–July 29, 1891.

President of the United States. *Order for the Sale of Public Lands in the Territories of New Mexico and Colorado,* May 3, 1870 (Public Notice No. 741).

Registers and Receivers of District Land Offices in New Mexico. *Cash Entry Papers.* Receipts and certificates of purchase, and nonmineral affidavits for the purchases of Wilson Waddingham and Joseph C. Lea.

––––––. *Monthly Abstracts of Original and Final Entries under the Various Land Laws.* Santa Fe, 1861-1891, 19 vols.; La Mesilla, 1875-1891, 13 vols.; Folsom, 1889-1891, 2 vols.; Roswell, 1889-1891, 2 vols. These are the original returns sent to the General Land Office in Washington and are now preserved in bound volumes. Copies of these records were kept by the Registers and Receivers and are now preserved in the Federal Records Center at Denver, but are incomplete in some categories.

Surveyors General of New Mexico. *Surveying Contracts and Bonds,* 1854-1909.

B. Federal Records Center (Denver)

Commissioners of the General Land Office. *Correspondence.* To Registers and Receivers at Las Cruces, 1 vol., 500 pp., June 7, 1875–October 6, 1884.

Receivers of the District Land Office at Santa Fe. *Correspondence.* To Commissioners of the General Land Office and others, 1 vol., 93 pp., October 29, 1858—July 21, 1883.

Registers and Receivers of District Land Offices in New Mexico. *Monthly Abstracts of Original and Final Entries under the Various Land Laws.* These copies of records in The National Archives are incomplete in some categories.

Registers of the District Land Office at Santa Fe. *Correspondence.* To various persons, 1 vol., 385 pp., July 14,, 1860—July 17, 1873.

Surveyors General of New Mexico. *Correspondence.* To Commissioners of the General Land Office and others, 2 vols., 1,477 pp., October 31, 1887—January 3, 1895. These volumes (9-10) are a continuation of the eight volumes in the Bureau of Land Management at Santa Fe.

————. *Correspondence.* To Commissioners of the General Land Office, private individuals and surveyors, 117 vols., July 30, 1884—March 31, 1910. These are pressed copies.

————. *Correspondence.* To Registers and Receivers of the Land Offices at La Mesilla and Las Cruces, 1 vol., 280 pp., December 29, 1875—June 29, 1891.

————. *Correspondence.* To various persons concerning land grants and small holding claims, 1 vol., 640 pp., June 11, 1885—March 2, 1893.

C. *Bureau of Land Management* (Santa Fe)

Commissioners of the General Land Office and others. *Correspondence.* To Surveyors General of New Mexico and others, 1 vol., 607 pp., August 5, 1854—March 8, 1876. Letters from the Commissioner, in this volume, are duplicated in the National Archives in Washington; but there is some local correspondence here.

Deputy Surveyors in New Mexico. *Field Note Books.* Available for all the surveys ever conducted in the Territory.

Registers and Receivers of District Land Offices in New Mexico. *Tract Books.* Material here is arranged by township and range and provides information on the original disposition of land if the location is known.

Spanish and Mexican Authorities. *Records of Land Grants in New Mexico.* These records were not used for this study but will be valuable for any work on land grants.

Surveyors General of New Mexico. *Correspondence.* To Commissioners of the General Land Office and others, 8 vols., 4,187 pp., August 1, 1854–October 3, 1887. Two more volumes (9-10) are in the Federal Records Center at Denver.

—————. *Deposits for Township Surveys.* Abstracts of deposits by settlers, 3 vols., 1,192 pp., July, 1882–April, 1884.

—————. *Desert Land Claims.* Abstracts of entries, 1 vol., 237 pp., April 14, 1877–July 28, 1886.

—————. *Index to Dep't and Misc. Letters Received,* 1 vol., 510 pp., August 5, 1854–October 21, 1883.

—————. *Mining Claims Surveyed for Patent,* 1 vol., 273 pp., July 1, 1882–August 6, 1884.

—————. *Pueblo Grants.* Certified translations of the original grant papers, 1 vol., 84 pp.

—————. *Survey Plats of Mining Claims.*

—————. *Survey Plats of Townships.*

Survey Records Section. *Survey Field Notes and Executive Documents of Military and Indian Reservations,* 1 vol., 277 pp.

D. United States Court House (Santa Fe)

United States. *Territorial District Court Records.* Criminal Cases.

First Judicial District.

   Docket. No. 1, August 1, 1882–May 2, 1896.

   Index to Records. 1852-1868.

   Record. No. 1, September 3, 1860–March 6, 1871.

   —————. No. 2, July 10, 1871–February 6, 1874.

   —————. No. 3, February 7, 1874–January 8, 1883.

   —————. "A," February 5, 1883–March 6, 1888.

   —————. "B," March 7, 1888–March 29, 1893.

   Register of Actions of U. S. Attorney. Criminal and civil, 1886-1888, 2 vols.

   Transcript Record of Court Cases. Nos. 1-1431.

Second Judicial District.

   Docket. Antedating Docket "D," 1883-1891.

   Record. "A," black leather cover, June, 1861–December, 1864.

   —————. Brown leather cover, February, 1863–October, 1864.

   —————. "A"1, old letter "G," October 2, 1865–September 8, 1872.

   —————. September 30, 1872–November 20, 1878.

—————. "A" 2, leather cover, marked with dim "A," April 24,
  1883—May 19, 1887.
—————. "B," September 5, 1887—March 8, 1893.
Transcript Record of Court Cases. Nos. 1-894.

Third Judicial District.
  Docket. (Old) June, 1877—March, 1886.
  —————. Civil and criminal, September 12, 1889—October 6, 1900.
  Record. "A," May 22, 1871—November 29, 1879.
  —————. "B," March 22, 1880—October 26, 1887.
  —————. "C," October 27, 1887—February 6, 1892.
  Register of Actions of U. S. Attorney. 1886-1888.
  Transcript Record of Court Cases. Nos. 1-933.

Fourth Judicial District.
  Docket. 1, December 6, 1887—May 9, 1907.
  Record. "A," March 21, 1887—May 2, 1891.
  Transcript Record of Court Cases. Nos. 1-306.

Fifth Judicial District.
  Docket. "A," April 25, 1891—October 23, 1911.
  Record. "A," May 4, 1891—April 18, 1895.
  Transcript Record of Court Cases. Nos. 1-69.

  E. State Records Center (Santa Fe)

Governor's Papers. Edmund G. Ross. Letter from Ross to John O'Grady,
  St. Louis, March 26, 1887.

2. GOVERNMENT PUBLICATIONS

Attorney General of the United States, *Annual Reports,* 13 vols., Washington, 1891-1904.
Bureau of Land Management. *Manual of Instructions for the Survey of
  the Public Lands of the United States, 1947,* Washington, 1947.
Census Office, *Reports* (volumes on population, mining, agriculture,
  and irrigation), Washington, 1860-1900.
Commissioner of the General Land Office. *Annual Reports,* 1854-1891,
  38 vols., Washington, 1854-1891.

————. *Circulars and Regulations of the General Land Office, with Reference Tables and Index,* Washington, 1930.

————. *Circular Regarding Loyalty Oath,* January 6, 1862. To Registers, Receivers, and Surveyors General.

————. *Report upon the Survey of the United States & Texas Boundary Commission,* 1882, 47 Cong., 1 Sess., *S.E.D.* No. 70.

Commissioner of Indian Affairs. *Annual Report,* 1871, Washington, 1872.

Donaldson, Thomas. *The Public Domain,* 1884, 47 Cong., 2 Sess., *H.E.D.* No. 45, Pt. 4.

Emory, William H. *Report of William H. Emory, Major, First Cavalry and U. S. Commissioner, United States and Mexican Boundary Survey,* 1857, 34 Cong., 1 Sess., *H.E.D.* No. 135.

Governor of New Mexico. *Annual Reports,* 37 vols., Washington, 1855-1891 (called *Annual Messages* prior to 1879).

Hagerman, H. J. *Navajo Indian Reservation,* 72 Cong., 1 Sess., *S.E.D.* No. 64.

Hay, Robert. *Final Geological Reports of the Artesian and Underflow Investigation Between the Ninety-seventh Meridian of Longitude and the Foothills of the Rocky Mountains, to the Secretary of Agriculture,* 1892, 52 Cong., 1 Sess., *S.E.D.* No. 41, Pt. 3 (2899).

Hesselman, George G., Ed. *Digest of Decisions of the Department of Interior in Cases Relating to the Public Lands . . . ,* Vols. 1-40 inclusive, Washington, 1913.

Hinton, Richard J. *A Report on Irrigation and the Cultivation of the Soil Thereby, with Physical Data, Conditions, and Progress Within the United States for 1891 . . . ,* 52 Cong., 1 Sess., *S.E.D.* No. 41, Pt. 1 (2899) .

————. *Irrigation in the United States, Progress Report for 1890,* 1891, 51 Cong., 2 Sess., *S.E.D.* No. 53 (2818).

Johnson, Frank M. *Public Land System of the United States: The Rectangular System of Surveying,* Washington, 1924 (Reprint from the *Land Service Bulletin,* April, 1918).

McKinney, William M., and Peter Kemper, Jr., Compls. *The Federal Statutes Annotated Containing All the Laws of the United States of a General and Permanent Nature in Force on the First Day of January, 1903,* Vol. VI, Northport, L.I., N.Y., 1905.

Nettleton, Edwin S. *Artesian and Underflow Investigation. Final Report of the Chief Engineer, Edwin S. Nettleton, C. E., to the Secretary of Agriculture* . . . , 1892, 52 Cong., 1 Sess., *S.E.D.* No. 41, Pt. 2 (2899).

Pope, John. *Report of Exploration of a Route for the Pacific Railroad near the Thirty-second Parallel of North Latitude, from the Red River to the Rio Grande, by Brevet Captain John Pope, Corps of Topographical Engineers,* 1855, 33 Cong., 2 Sess., *S.E.D.* No. 78, Vol. II.

President of the United States. *Annual Message,* 1861, 37 Cong., 2 Sess., No. 1 (1117).

Proudfit, S. V., Ed. *Decisions of the Department of Interior and General Land Office in Cases Relating to the Public Lands from January 1, 1890 to June 30, 1890,* Vol. X, Washington, 1890.

————, Ed. *Digest of Decisions of the Department of Interior and General Land Office in Cases Relating to the Public Lands . . . ,* Vols. 1-22 inclusive, Washington, 1892.

————. *Public Land System of the United States: Historical Outline,* Washington, 1924.

Public Lands Commission. *Preliminary Report,* 1879, 46 Cong., 2 Sess., *H. E. D.* No. 46 (1923) .

————. *Final Report,* 1881, 46 Cong., 3 Sess., *H.E.D.* No. 47 (1975) .

————. *Report, with Appendix,* 1905, 58 Cong., 3 Sess., *S.E.D.* No. 189 (4766).

Richardson, James D. *A Compilation of the Messages and Papers of the Presidents, 1789-1897,* 10 vols., Washington, 1899.

Secretary of Commerce, Weather Bureau. *Climate of the States, New Mexico,* Washington, 1941 (Agricultural Yearbook Separate No. 1849).

————. *Climatological Bulletins for Albuquerque, Artesia, Carlsbad, Clayton, Hobbs, Las Vegas, Portales, Roswell, Santa Fe, Silver City, and Hidalgo County.*

Secretary of the Interior. *Annual Reports,* 38 vols., Washington, 1854-1891.

————. *Fraudulent Acquisition of Titles to Lands in New Mexico,* 1885, 48 Cong., 2 Sess., *S.E.D.* No. 106.

————. *Removal of Persons and Obstructions from the Public Domain,* 1884, 48 Cong., 1 Sess., *S.E.D.* No. 143.

————. *Unauthorized Fencing of Public Lands,* 1884, 48 Cong., 1 Sess., *S.E.D.* No. 127.

Secretary of War. *Annual Report,* 1856, 34 Cong., 3 Sess., *H.E.D.* No. 1 (894).

Surveyor General of New Mexico. *Annual Reports,* 37 vols., Washington, 1855-1891.

United States. *Public Land Statutes of the United States, A Compilation of General and Permanent Statutes of Practical Importance Relating to the Public Lands . . . ,* Washington, 1931.

————. *Revised Statutes of the United States Passed at the First Session of the Forty-third Congress, 1873-4 . . . ,* Washington, 1875.

————. *Statutes at Large,* 38 vols., Washington, 1854-1891.

————. *The Existing Laws of the United States of General and Permanent Character, and Relating to the Survey and Disposition of the Public Domain, December 1, 1880,* Washington, 1880.

3. PAMPHLETS AND PAPERS

Bureau of Immigration. *The Resources of New Mexico, Prepared for the Territorial Fair To Be Held at Albuquerque, N. M., October 3d to 8th, 1881,* Santa Fe, 1881.

Burnham, Donald R. *Climatological Data at the Northeastern Substation Tucumcari, New Mexico,* State College, N. M., 1954 (Press Bulletin No. 1088).

Cattle Sanitary Board of the Territory of New Mexico. *Second Annual Report,* Las Vegas, 1888. This item (and others marked W.R.C.I.S.) was provided by the Western Range Cattle Industry Study, State Museum, Denver.

Dorroh, J. H., Jr. *Certain Hydrologic and Climatic Characteristics of the Southwest,* Albuquerque, 1946 (University of New Mexico Publications in Engineering, No. 1).

Evans, Morris. *Precipitation and Sorghum Yields,* State College, N. M., 1952 (Press Bulletin No. 1069).

Graham, George A. *Know New Mexico, Acquisition of State Lands,* Ms. Santa Fe.

Linney, Charles E., *et al. Climate as It Affects Crops and Ranges in New Mexico,* State College, N. M., 1930 (Bulletin No. 182).

Maker, H. J., and H. E. Dregne. *Climatic Zones in New Mexico,* State College, N. M., 1951 (Press Bulletin No. 1057).

The Avarica Cattle Company (Arizona). *Prospectus,* New York, 1886 (W.R.C.I.S.).

The Carrizozo Cattle Ranch Company, Limited. *Memorandum of Association and Articles of Association,* London, 1884 (W.R.C.I.S.).

The Kansas and New Mexico Cattle and Land Company. *Memorandum and Articles of Association,* London, 1885 (W.R.C.I.S.)

The Maxwell Cattle Company. *Debenture Prospectus,* London, 1882 (W.R.C.I.S.)

The New Mexico Land and Cattle Company. *President's Report,* Boston, May 12, 1884 (W.R.C.I.S.).

The New Mexico Stock & Agricultural Association. *Prospectus,* Chicago, 1876 (W.R.C.I.S.).

The Northern New Mexico Stock Growers Association. *Brand Books, By Laws and List of Members,* Raton, 1884 (W.R.C.I.S.).

The Rio Arriba Land and Cattle Company, Limited. *Memorandum and Articles of Association,* London, 1887 (W.R.C.I.S.).

The Scottish Mortgage & Land Investment Company of New Mexico (Limited). *Memorandum and Articles of Association,* Glasgow, 1882 (W.R.C.I.S.).

The Western Philanthropic Society of New York. *Prospectus,* 1879 (W.R.C.I.S.).

University of New Mexico, Government Department, Research Division. *Symposium on the Public Lands,* Albuquerque, 1947.

Western Range Cattle Industry Study. *Bibliography of Cattle Items, 1883-1886:* Santa Fe *New Mexican,* Daily (W.R.C.I.S.).

————. *New Mexico Cattle Corporations, 1871-1900.* Summary, Ms. (W.R.C.I.S.) .

Wilson Waddingham, Red River Land and Cattle Company, La Cinta, N. M. *Bills and Invoices, 1887 through 1890.* (W.R.C.I.S.).

4. Personal Interviews

Bisbee, Wallace. Private surveying engineer, Albuquerque.

Dregne, H. E. Professor of Soils, New Mexico State University.

Dunham, Harold H. Professor of History, University of Denver.

Graham, George A. Attorney (formerly attorney for the State Land Office for 14 years).

Padilla, Celestino. Native of Quemado, N. M., born in 1873.

United Pueblos Agency. Albuquerque.

Wengerd, Sherman. Professor of Geology, University of New Mexico.

Land Office Personnel. The following interviewed persons are, or have been, connected with the United States Land Office or surveying work. Most of them prefer not to have the information they gave, or their opinions, credited to them by name.

Clement, Donald B. Assistant Cadastral Engineering Officer, Washington Office.

Delaney, James. Manager, Bureau of Land Management, Land Office, Santa Fe.

Hall, Wendell G. Office Cadastral Engineer, Bureau of Land Management, Survey Records Section, Santa Fe.

Harrington, Earl G. Cadastral Engineering Officer, Washington Office.

Harrington, Guy P. (Retired) formerly Chief of the Cadastral Engineering Office at Santa Fe.

Haste, Glenn R. Regional Chief of the Division of Cadastral Engineering, Region 5.

Kimmel, Everett H. Cadastral Engineer, Albuquerque Office.

Livermore, Marlin G. First employed by Land Office in Santa Fe in 1907, now employed part time by the Federal Abstract Co., Santa Fe.

Smith, Eastburn. State Supervisor, Bureau of Land Management, Santa Fe.

Turner, Worth O. Adjudicator, Bureau of Land Management, Land Office, Santa Fe.

Well, Geo. H. Office Cadastral Engineer, Albuquerque Office.

5. LETTERS OF INFORMATION

Gates, Paul Wallace. Chairman, Department of History, Cornell University, July 22, 1955.

Greever, Wm. S. Professor of History, University of Idaho, August 18, 1955, and January 16, 1956.

Otero, M. A., Jr. Attorney at law, Santa Fe, May 27, 1955.

Reinhold, James P. Assistant to the president, The Atchinson, Topeka, and Santa Fe Railway System, Chicago, September 16, 1955, October 13, 1955, and February 20, 1956.

Robinson, Paul W. Attorney at law, Albuquerque, March 26, 1956.

Walter, Paul A. F. Chairman of the board, The First National Bank of Santa Fe, Santa Fe, May 25, 1955.

6. MAPS AND DIAGRAMS

A Sketch of Public Buildings, Santa Fe, New Mexico, to accompany
    letter of Surveyor General John A. Clark, August 30, 1862 (Wash-
    ington, The National Archives).
Average Annual and Seasonal Precipitation, Southwest Region. From,
    J. H. Dorroh, Jr. *Certain Hydrologic and Climatic Characteristics
    of the Southwest,* Albuquerque, 1946 (University of New Mexico
    Publications in Engineering, No. 1).
Average Annual Precipitation, New Mexico, Compiled by U.S. De-
    partment of Agriculture, Soil Conservation Service, 1951 (Map No.
    2).
Climatic Zones in New Mexico, U. S. Department of Agriculture, Soil
    Conservation Service, and New Mexico Agricultural Experiment
    Station, co-operating, revised November, 1952 (prepared by H. J.
    Maker and H. E. Dregne).
*Diagram of New Mexico Showing Public Land Surveyed, Private Land
    Claims Confirmed and Surveyed under Act of Congress, also, Con-
    firmed and Surveyed under Decree of Court of P.L.C., and Indian
    Reservations, Forest Reserves and Reservoir Sites.* Drawn by Nor-
    man King in the early 1900's (Santa Fe, Bureau of Land Manage-
    ment, Survey Records Section).
Grazing Lands, Western United States. Compiled by Albert F. Potter,
    Forest Inspector, Bureau of Forestry, U.S. Department of Agricul-
    ture, 1905. From, Public Lands Commission, *Report, with Appen-
    dix,* 1905, 58 Cong., 3 Sess., *S.E.D.* No. 189 (4766).
Irrigated and Potentially Irrigable Lands. "Irrigation Agriculture in
    the West," Misc. Pub. No. 670, U.S. Department of Agriculture,
    1948.
*Map Illustrating the Progress of Irrigation within the Arid and Semi-
    arid Region of the United States West of the 97th Degree of Longi-
    tude West from Greenwich* (Washington, U.S. Department of Ag-
    riculture, Office of Irrigation Inquiry). Prepared by Frank Blais-
    dell, Civil Engineer, 1891; included in 52 Cong., 1 Sess., *S.E.D.* No.
    41, Pt. 1, 4 (2899).
Maps of New Mexico Showing Annual Surveying Progress. 1855, 1857-
    1870 (Department of Interior Library) from Reports of the Com-

missioner of the General Land Office for those years; 1856 (Library of Congress) from the Report of the Commissioner of the General Land Office for that year; 1879, 1882, 1886 (The National Archives, Cartographic Records Branch) no doubt at one time removed from Reports of the Commissioner of the General Land Office but presently mounted as isolated items; 1866 (The National Archives) was the only original map found and was in a package of letters from the Surveyor General of New Mexico to the Commissioner of the General Land Office. Other maps listed are from engravings copied from the originals.

State of New Mexico. Compiled from the official records of the General Land Office and other sources, 1936.

7. NEWSPAPERS

Albuquerque Daily Democrat. 1883.

Albuquerque Morning Journal. 1882-1886.

Albuquerque Review. 1876-1880.

Republican Review (Albuquerque). 1870-1876.

Santa Fe New Mexican. 1880-1883, 1885-1887.

Santa Fe Weekly New Mexican and Live Stock Journal. 1885-1887.

The Santa Fe Weekly Leader. 1885-1886.

Weekly New Mexican Review (Santa Fe). 1884.

8. OTHER PUBLICATIONS

A. Surveys and Settlement

Breed, Charles B., and George L. Hosmer. *The Principles and Practice of Surveying,* fifth edition, New York, 1925.

Burt, William A. *A key to the Solar Compass and the Surveyor's Companion,* New York, 1888.

Copp, Henry N. *The American Settler's Guide: A Brief Exposition of the Public Land System of the United States of America.* Washington, 1880.

De Soto, Emilio D., and Arthur R. Morrison. *Mining Rights on the Public Domain,* San Francisco, sixteenth edition, 1936.

Matthews, William B. *Matthews's Guide for Settlers upon the Public Lands, Land Attorneys, Land Agents, Clerks of Courts, Notaries, Bankers, Brokers, and All Persons . . . Having Business Before the District Land Offices, the General Land Office and the Department of the Interior . . .* , Washington, 1889.

Stewart, Lowell O. *Public Land Surveys: History, Instructions, Methods,* Ames, 1935.

B. General Land Studies

Clawson, Marion. *Uncle Sam's Acres.* New York, 1951.

Conover, Milton. *General Land Office: Its History, Activities and Organization,* Baltimore, 1923.

Du Bois, James T., and Gertrude S. Mathews. *Galusha A. Grow, Father of the Homestead Law,* Boston and New York, 1917.

Dunham, Harold H. *Government Handout: A Study in the Administration of the Public Lands, 1875-1891,* Ann Arbor, 1941.

Hibbard, Benjamin H. *A History of the Public Land Policies,* New York, 1924.

Martz, Clyde O. *Cases and Materials on the Law of Natural Resources.* St. Paul, 1951.

Peffer, E. Louis. *The Closing of the Public Domain, Disposal and Reservation Policies, 1900-1950,* Stanford, 1951.

Robbins, Roy M. *Our Landed Heritage: The Public Domain, 1776-1936,* Princeton, 1941.

Sakolski, Aaron M. *The Great American Land Bubble; The Amazing Story of Land-Grabbing, Speculations, and Booms from Colonial Days to the Present Time,* New York, 1932.

Sanborn, John Bell. *Congressional Grants of Land in Aid of Railways,* Madison, 1899.

Stephenson, George M. *Political History of the Public Lands from 1840 to 1862: from Pre-emption to Homestead,* Boston and Toronto, 1917.

Winter, Charles E. *Four Hundred Million Acres: The Public Lands and Resources,* Casper, 1932.

Zahler, Helene S. *Eastern Workingmen and National Land Policy, 1829-1862,* New York, 1941.

C. The Cattle Industry

Dale, Edward E. *Cow Country,* Norman, 1943.

—————.*The Range Cattle Industry,* Norman, 1930.

Frink, Maurice, *et al. When Grass Was King,* Boulder, 1956.

McCoy, Joseph G. *Historic Sketches of the Cattle Trade of the West and Southwest,* Kansas City, 1874. (Reprint, Columbus, 1951).

Osgood, Ernest S. *The Day of the Cattleman,* Minneapolis, 1929.

Pelzer, Louis. *The Cattlemen's Frontier, A Record of the Trans-Mississippi Cattle Industry from Oxen Trains to Pooling Companies, 1850-1890,* Glendale, 1936.

Willoughby, Roy. *The Range Cattle Industry in New Mexico,* University of New Mexico, 1933, Ms. (M.A. thesis).

D. The Railroads

Albright, George Leslie. *Official Explorations for the Pacific Railroads, 1853-1855,* Berkeley, 1921.

Bradley, Glenn D. *The Story of The Santa Fe,* Boston, 1920.

Greever, William S. *Arid Domain: The Santa Fe Railway and Its Western Land Grant,* Stanford, 1954.

Heath, Jim F. *A Study of the Influence of the Atchison, Topeka, and Santa Fe Railroad upon the Economy of New Mexico, 1878 to 1900,* University of New Mexico, 1955, Ms. (M.A. thesis).

Marshall, James. *Santa Fe, The Railroad that Built an Empire,* New York, 1945.

Riegel, Robert E. *The Story of the Western Railroads,* New York, 1926.

Waters, L. L. *Steel Trails to Santa Fe,* Lawrence, 1950.

E. General Western Background

Chittenden, Hiram Martin. *The American Fur Trade of the Far West,* 2 vols., Stanford, 1954 (Academic Reprints).

Clark, Dan Elbert. *The West in American History,* New York, third printing, 1938 (copyright 1937).

Duffus, R. I. *The Santa Fe Trail,* New York, 1930.

Dunbar, Seymour. *A History of Travel in America,* New York, eighth printing, 1937.

Inman, Henry. *The Old Santa Fe Trail,* Topeka, 1899.

Lathrop, Barnes F. *Migration into East Texas, 1835-1860,* Austin, 1949.

Mosk, Sanford A. *Land Tenure Problems in the Santa Fe Railroad Grant Area,* Berkeley and Los Angeles, 1944.

Paxson, Frederic L. *History of the American Frontier, 1763-1893,* Boston and New York, 1924.

Rister, Carl Coke. *Southern Plainsmen,* Norman, 1938.

————. *The Southwestern Frontier, 1865-1881,* Cleveland, 1928.

Turner, Frederick Jackson. *The Frontier in American History,* New York, 1945 (copyright 1920).

9. NEW MEXICO STUDIES

A. General Studies

Anderson, G. B., Compl. *History of New Mexico, Its Resources and People,* 2 vols., Los Angeles, 1907.

Bancroft, Hubert Howe. *History of Arizona and New Mexico,* San Francisco, 1889.

Bewley, Mary. *The Indians of New Mexico in the Civil War,* University of New Mexico, 1938, Ms. (M.A. thesis).

Bloom, Lansing B., ed. *New Mexico Historical Review Comprehensive Index, 1926-1940,* Albuquerque, 1941.

Brayer, Herbert O. *Pueblo Indian Land Grants of the "Rio Abajo," New Mexico,* Albuquerque, 1939.

Brevoort, Elias. *New Mexico, Her Natural Resources and Attractions,* Santa Fe, 1874.

Coan, Charles F. *A History of New Mexico,* Chicago and New York, 1925.

Fergusson, Erna. *New Mexico: A Pageant of Three Peoples,* New York, 1951.

Horgan, Paul. *Great River, The Rio Grande in North American History,* 2 vols., New York, 1954.

Keleher, William A. *Maxwell Land Grant,* Santa Fe, 1942.

————. *The Fabulous Frontier,* Albuquerque, 1962.

————. *Turmoil in New Mexico, 1846-1868,* Santa Fe, 1952.

————. *Violence in Lincoln County, 1869-1881,* Albuquerque, 1957.

Kelley, Vincent C., and Caswell Silver. *Geology of the Caballo Mountains, with Special Reference to Regional Stratigraphy and Structure and to Mineral Resources, Including Oil and Gas,* Albuquerque, 1952.

Leonard, Olen E. *The Role of the Land Grant in the Social Organization and Social Processes of a Spanish-American Village in New Mexico,* Louisiana State University and Agricultural and Mechanical College, 1943, Ms. (Ph.D. dissertation).

Nanninga, Simon Peter. *The New Mexico School System. A Textbook for Use in the Course Entitled "The Problems of Education in New Mexico,"* Albuquerque, 1942.

New Mexico: A Guide to the Colorful State. (Compiled by workers of the Writers' Program of the Work Projects Administration in the State of New Mexico, revised by Joseph Miller, edited by Henry G. Alsberg), New York, 1953.

Read, Benjamin M. *Illustrated History of New Mexico,* Santa Fe, 1912.

Reeve, Frank D., ed., *New Mexico Historical Review Comprehensive Index, 1941-1956,* Albuquerque, 1956.

Twitchell, Ralph Emerson. *Leading Facts of New Mexican History,* 5 vols., Cedar Rapids, 1912.

Waldrip, William I. *New Mexico During the Civil War,* University of New Mexico, 1950, Ms. (M.A. thesis).

B. Local Studies

Alvis, Berry Newton. *Settlement and Economic Development of Union County, New Mexico,* University of Colorado, 1934, Ms. (M.A. thesis).

Anderson, John B. *History of the Mogollon Mining District of New Mexico,* University of New Mexico, 1939, Ms. (M.A. thesis).

Duke, Robert W. *Political History of San Juan County, New Mexico, 1876-1926,* University of New Mexico, 1947, Ms. (M.A. thesis).

Foster, H. Mannie. *History of the Mormon Settlements in Mexico and New Mexico,* University of New Mexico, 1947, Ms. (M.A. thesis).

Griggs, George. *History of Mesilla Valley; or, the Gadsden Purchase, Known in Mexico as the Treaty of Mesilla,* Las Cruces, 1930.

Morgan, Henry E. *A Brief History of Roosevelt County, New Mexico,* University of New Mexico, 1938, Ms. (M.A. thesis).

Morton, Dorothy Virginia. *History of Quay County, New Mexico . . . ,* University of Colorado, 1938, Ms. (M.A. thesis).

Naegle, Conrad Keeler. *The History of Silver City, New Mexico, 1870-1886,* University of New Mexico, 1943, Ms. (M.A. thesis.)

Stanley, F. *Fort Union (New Mexico),* Denver, 1953.

Tate, Norvell Glynn. *A Brief History of Curry County, New Mexico,* University of New Mexico, 1934, Ms. (M.A. thesis).

Westphall, Victor. *History of Albuquerque, 1870-1880,* University of New Mexico, 1947, Ms. (M.A. thesis).

10. Letters, Memoirs, and Biographies

Barnes, James A. *John G. Carlisle: Financial Statesman,* New York, 1931.

Brayer, Herbert O. *William Blackmore: The Spanish-Mexican Land Grants of New Mexico and Colorado, 1863-1878,* Denver, 1949.

Brothers, Mary Hudson. *A Pecos Pioneer,* Albuquerque, 1943.

Casey, John P., Sr. *Notarized Statement,* October 15, 1892. This is an unsigned copy of the original in the possession of Clayton and Myrtle Cox, Quemado, N. M.

Coe, George W. *Frontier Fighter: The Autobiography of George W. Coe,* Albuquerque, 1951 (original edition 1934, as related to Nan Hillary Harrison).

Curry, George. *George Curry, 1861-1947: An Autobiography,* Albuquerque, 1958 (edited by H. B. Hening).

French, William. *Some Recollections of a Western Ranchman,* London, 1927.

Garrett, Pat F. *Authentic Story of Billy the Kid,* New York, 1946 (foreword by John M. Scanland).

Haley, J. Evetts. *Charles Goodnight, Cowman and Plainsman,* Boston and New York, 1936.

Harkey, Dee. *Mean as Hell,* Albuquerque, 1948.

Hefferan, Vioalle Clark. *Thomas Benton Catron,* University of New Mexico, 1940, Ms. (M.A. thesis).

Hinkle, James F. *Early Days of a Cowboy on the Pecos,* Roswell, 1937.

Julian, George W. *Political Recollections, 1840-1872,* Chicago, 1884.

Nevins, Allan. *Grover Cleveland: A Study in Courage,* New York, 1933.

Otero, Miguel Antonio. *My Life on the Frontier, 1864-1882,* New York, 1935.

————. *My Life on the Frontier, 1882-1897*, New York, 1939.

————. *My Nine Years as Governor of the Territory of New Mexico, 1897-1906*, Albuquerque, 1940.

————. *The Real Billy the Kid*, New York, 1936.

Siringo, Chas. A. *A Lone Star Cowboy*, Santa Fe, 1919.

Sonnichsen, C. L., and William V. Morrison. *Alias Billy the Kid*, Albuquerque, 1955.

Stanley, F. *Longhair Jim Courtright: Two Gun Marshall of Fort Worth*, Denver, 1957.

Stryker, Lloyd Paul. *Andrew Johnson: A Study in Courage*, New York, 1929.

Wallace, William Swilling, ed. *A Journey Through New Mexico's First Judicial District in 1864*, Los Angeles, 1956.

11. State Studies Other Than New Mexico

Dodds, J. S., *et al.*, eds. *Original Instructions Governing Public Land Surveys of Iowa: A Guide to Their Use in Resurveys of Public Lands*, Ames, 1943.

Green, Charles L. *Administration of the Public Domain in South Dakota*, Pierre, 1940.

Hoffsommer, Harold, ed. *The Social and Economic Significance of Land Tenure in the Southwestern States; A Report of the Regional Land Tenure Research Project*, Chapel Hill, 1950.

Jillson, Willard Rouse. *The Kentucky Land Grants*, Louisville, 1925.

Lokken, Roscoe L. *Iowa: Public Land Disposal*, Iowa City, 1942.

Orfield, Matthias Nordberg. *Federal Land Grants to the States with Special Reference to Minnesota*, Minneapolis, 1915.

Robinson, W. W. *Land in California: The Story of Mission Lands, Ranchos, Squatters, Mining Claims, Railroad Grants, Land Scrip, Homesteads*, Berkeley and Los Angeles, 1948.

Sheldon, Addison E. *Land Systems and Land Policies in Nebraska*, Lincoln, 1936.

Stewart, Charles Leslie. *Land Tenure in the United States with Especial Reference to Illinois*, Urbana, 1916.

Williams, Elgin. *Animating Pursuits of Speculation: Land Traffic in the Annexation of Texas*, New York, 1949.

12. PERIODICALS

A. *Surveys and Settlement*

Agnew, Dwight L. "The Government Land Surveyor as a Pioneer," *Mississippi Valley Historical Review,* 28:369-382, December, 1941.

Cordes, Frank J. "Origin of Sections, Townships and Ranges," *Lawyer and Banker,* 24:142-149, May-June, 1931.

Harrington, Earl G. "Surveys Spur Settlement," *Our Public Lands: Bureau of Land Management,* 5:7, January, 1955.

Shambaugh, Benjamin J. "Frontier Land Clubs or Claim Associations," *American Historical Association, Annual Report,* vol. 1:69-84, 1900.

B. *National and Regional*

Carter, John Denton. "Abraham Lincoln and the California Patronage," *American Historical Review,* 48:495-506, April, 1943.

"The Creation of the National Land Policy," *Chicago Historical Society Bulletin,* 3:65-67; 72-76; 82-84, February-April, 1926.

Dunham, Harold H. "Some Crucial Years in the General Land Office, 1875-1890," *Agricultural History,* 11:117-141, January, 1937.

Ganaway, Loomis Morton. "New Mexico in the Sectional Controversy, 1846-1861," *New Mexico Historical Review,* 18:113-147; 205-246; 325-348; 19:55-76; April, July, October, 1943; January, 1944.

Hart, Albert Bushnell. "The Disposition of Our Public Lands," *Quarterly Journal of Economics,* 1:174-183, January, 1887.

Hibbard, Benjamin H. "Settlement of Public Lands in the United States," *International Review of Agricultural Economics,* 61:97-117, January, 1916.

Julian, George W. "Our Land Policy," *Atlantic Monthly,* 43:325-337, March, 1879.

Paxson, Frederic L. "The Territory of Colorado," *American Historical Review,* 12:53-65, October, 1906.

Robbins, Roy M. "The Federal Land System in an Embryo State," *Pacific Historical Review,* 4:356-375, November, 1935.

Tegeder, Vincent G. "Lincoln and the Territorial Patronage: The Ascendancy of the Radicals in the West," *Mississippi Valley Historical Review,* 35:77-90, June, 1948.

Wilson, Francis C. "The Problem of the Public Domain," *Saturday Evening Post,* January 23, 1932.

C. Land Laws

Ganoe, John T. "The Desert Land Act in Operation, 1877-1891," *Agricultural History,* 11:142-157, January, 1937.
————. "The Desert Land Act Since 1891," *Agricultural History,* 11:266-277, October, 1937.
————. "The Beginnings of Irrigation in the United States," *Mississippi Valley Historical Review,* 25:59-78, June, 1938.
Gates, Paul Wallace. "The Homestead Law in an Incongrous Land System," *American Historical Review,* 41:652-681, July, 1936.
Raney, William F. "The Timber Culture Acts," *Mississippi Valley Historical Association (Proceedings),* 10:219-229, Part II, 1919-1920.
Robbins, Roy M. "Preemption—A Frontier Triumph," *Mississippi Valley Historical Review,* 18:331-349, December, 1931.
Sanborn, John Bell. "Some Political Aspects of the Homestead Legislation," *American Historical Review,* 6:19-37, October, 1900.
Shannon, Fred A. "The Homestead Act and the Labor Surplus," *American Historical Review,* 41:637-651, July, 1936.
Sioussat, St. George L. "Andrew Johnson and the Early Phases of the Homestead Bill," *Mississippi Valley Historical Review,* 5:253-287, December, 1918.

D. The Cattle Industry

Dale, Edward E. "The Cow Country in Transition," *Mississippi Valley Historical Review,* 24:3-20, June, 1937.
Hayter, Earl W. "Barbed Wire Fencing—A Prairie Invention; Its Rise and Influence in the Western States," *Agricultural History,* 13:189-207, October, 1939.
Love, Clara M. "History of the Cattle Industry in the Southwest," *Southwestern Historical Quarterly,* 19:370-399, April, 1915-16; 20:1-18, July, 1916-17.
Paxson, Frederic L. "The Cow Country," *American Historical Review,* 22:65-82, October, 1916.
Pelzer, Louis. "A Cattlemen's Commonwealth on the Western Range," *Mississippi Valley Historical Review,* 13:30-49, June, 1926.

E. The Railroads

Ellis, David Maldwyn. "The Forfeiture of Railroad Land Grants, 1867-1894," *Mississippi Valley Historical Review*, 33:27-60, June, 1946.

Greever, William S. "Railway Development in the Southwest," *New Mexico Historical Review*, 32:151-203, April, 1957.

Julian, George W. "Our Land Grant Railways in Congress," *International Review*, 14:198-212, February-March, 1883.

————. "Railway Influence in the Land Office," *North American Review*, 136:237-256, March, 1883.

Rae, John B. "Commissioner Sparks and the Railroad Land Grants," *Mississippi Valley Historical Review*, 25:211-230, September, 1938.

F. Territorial Boundaries

Baldwin, P. M. "A Historical Note on the Boundaries of New Mexico," *New Mexico Historical Review*, 5:116-137, April, 1930.

Coffey, Frederic A. "Some General Aspects of the Gadsden Treaty," *New Mexico Historical Review*, 8:145-164, July, 1933.

Donnell, F. S. "When Texas Owned New Mexico to the Rio Grande," *New Mexico Historical Review*, 8:65-75, April, 1933.

Rippey, J. Fred. "The Boundary of New Mexico and the Gadsden Treaty," *Hispanic American Historical Review*, 4:715-742, November, 1921.

Spillman, W. J. "Adjustment of the Texas Boundary in 1850," *Quarterly of the Texas State Historical Association*, 7:177-195, January, 1904.

G. New Mexico Local Studies

Alvis, Berry Newton. "History of Union County, New Mexico," *New Mexico Historical Review*, 22:247-273, July, 1947.

Baldwin, P. M. "A Short History of the Mesilla Valley," *New Mexico Historical Review*, 13:314-324, July, 1938.

Clum, John P. "Santa Fé in the '70s," *New Mexico Historical Review*, 2:380-386, October, 1927.

Wagoner, J. J. "The Gadsden Purchase Lands," *New Mexico Historical Review*, 26:18-43, January, 1951.

Westphall, Victor. "Albuquerque in the 1870's," *New Mexico Historical Review*, 23:253-268, October, 1948.

H. Indians, Defense, and Exploration

Arrott, James A. "Fort Union: Guardian of the Santa Fe Trail," *New Mexico Sun Trails,* 8:12-15, May-June, 1955.

Bender, A. B. "Frontier Defense in the Territory of New Mexico, 1853-1861," *New Mexico Historical Review,* 9:345-373, October, 1934.

————. "Government Explorations in the Territory of New Mexico, 1846-1859," *New Mexico Historical Review,* 9:1-32, January, 1934.

————. "Military Posts of the Southwest, 1848-1860," *New Mexico Historical Review,* 16:125-147, April, 1941.

————. "Military Transportation in the Southwest, 1848-1860," *New Mexico Historical Review,* 32:123-150, April, 1957.

Haile, Berard, O.F.M. "Navaho or Navajo?" *The Americas,* 6:85-90, July, 1947.

Ogle, Ralph H. "Federal Control of the Western Apaches, 1848-1886," *New Mexico Historical Review,* 14:309-345, October, 1939: 15:12-71, January, 1940; 15:188-248, April, 1940; 15:269-335, July, 1940.

Reeve, Frank D. "A Navaho Struggle for Land," *New Mexico Historical Review,* 21:1-21, January, 1946.

————. "Federal Indian Policy in New Mexico, 1858-1880," *New Mexico Historical Review,* 12:218-269, July, 1937; 13:14-62, January, 1938; 13:146-191, April, 1938; 13:261-313, July, 1938.

————. "The Government and the Navaho, 1878-1883," *New Mexico Historical Review,* 16:275-312, July, 1941.

————. "The Government and the Navaho, 1883-1888," *New Mexico Historical Review,* 18:17-51, January, 1943.

I. New Mexico General Studies

Dargan, Marion, "New Mexico's Fight for Statehood, 1895-1912," *New Mexico Historical Review,* 14:1-33; 121-142; 15: 133-187; January, April, 1939; April, 1940.

Dunham, Harold H. "New Mexico Land Grants with Special Reference to the Title Papers of the Maxwell Grant," *New Mexico Historical Review,* 30:1-22, January, 1955.

Greer, Richard A. "Origins of the Foreign-born Population in New Mexico During the Territorial Period," *New Mexico Historical Review,* 17:281-287, October, 1942.

Julian, George W. "Land-Stealing in New Mexico," *North American Review,* 145:17-31, No. 368, 1887.

Keleher, William A. "Land Law of the New Mexico Land Grant,"
    New Mexico Historical Review, 4:350-371, October, 1929.
Rasch, P. J. "The Horrell War," *New Mexico Historical Review*, 31:
    223-231, July, 1956.
Waldrip, William I. "New Mexico During the Civil War," *New Mexico
    Historical Review*, 28:163-182, July, 1953; 28:251-290, October,
    1953.

J. Letters, Memoirs, and Biographies

Anderson, Lillie Gerhardt. "A New Mexico Pioneer of the 1880's," *New
    Mexico Historical Review*, 29:245-258, October, 1954.
Bieber, Ralph P. "Letters of William Carr Lane, 1852-1854," *New
    Mexico Historical Review*, 3:179-203, April, 1928.
Espinosa, J. Manuel, ed. "Memoir of a Kentuckian in New Mexico,
    1848-1884," *New Mexico Historical Review*, 13:1-13, January, 1938.
Hinton, Harwood P., Jr. "John Simpson Chisum, 1877-84," *New Mex-
    ico Historical Review*, 31:177-205; 310-337; 32:53-65, July, October,
    1956; January, 1957.
Muir, Emma Marble. "Pioneer Ranch," *New Mexico Magazine*, 36;20,
    62-63, June, 1958.
Nolan, Frederick W. "A Sidelight on the Tunstall Murder," *New Mex-
    ico Historical Review*, 31:206-222, July, 1956.
Wadleigh, A. B. "Ranching in New Mexico, 1886-90," *New Mexico
    Historical Review*, 27:1-28, January, 1952.
Walter, Paul A. F. "New Mexico's Pioneer Bank and Bankers," *New
    Mexico Historical Review*, 21:209-225, July, 1946.
Wharton, Clarence. "Spruce McCoy Baird," *New Mexico Historical
    Review*, 27:300-314, October, 1952.

13. ESSAYS ON SOURCES

Harrison, Robert W. "Public Land Records of the Federal Govern-
    ment," *Mississippi Valley Historical Review*, 51:277-288, Septem-
    ber, 1954.
Jackson, W. Turrentine. "Materials for Western History in the Depart-
    ment of the Interior Archives," *Mississippi Valley Historical Re-
    view*, 35:61-76, June, 1948.

Index